Discipline for LIFE
Getting it Right with Children

Discipline for LIFE
Getting it Right with Children

Madelyn Swift

Childright

Fort Worth, Texas

Childright
2140 East Southlake Boulevard, PMB 640
Southlake, Texas 76092

Cover Design: Kris & Tim Swift, Sheila & Rachel Mathies
Cover Layout: Verone Travis

Printed in the United States of America
First printing: June, 1995
Second printing, First revised edition: May, 1998
Third printing, Second revised edition: October, 1999

Library of Congress Cataloging-in-Publication Data
99-096125

Swift, Madelyn
Discipline for life: getting it right with children

ISBN: 1-887069-06-2

The paper used in this publication meets the minimum
requirements of American National Standard for Information
Sciences - Permanence of Paper for Printed Library Materials,
ANZI Z39.48-1984

Childright

To the three men in my life: John, Kris, and Tim.

Acknowledgments

So many people have influenced this book that it would be impossible to mention them all. I wish first to thank Karen Hale who could "see" this book before it was there, who could always find the look I wanted, who nourished and supported me throughout its writing, and who truly gives life to the phrase, "no hill for a stepper."

Special gratitude goes to Victoria Ryland Mathies, the editor, for her professionalism, her understanding of the material, her sense of humor, her belief in the project, and her enduring friendship. And to her family, David, Sheila, Rachel, and Philip for giving her up for a time.

I wish to thank my early friends, Linda, Evelyn, Sheila, Vicky, Kathy, Nancy, Susie, Norma, and Sandra who spent countless hours discussing and practicing terrific parenting and kept me from going crazy as the mother of young children. I also want to thank my later friends, Arlene, Gerti, Diane, Colleen, Shauna, Nancy, Francie, Carole, and Jenny, who shared stories, families, food, strengths and weaknesses. And to the *amigas*, Jackie, Wendy, Jo, and Di who are ever supportive and fun, muchas gracias. And to the "Remedials" who pushed with courage and empathy into ever more difficult passages of motherhood.

I am indebted to Julie O'Keefe, who organized my professional life so well that I was able to find time to write and who brings sunshine to my personal life so I want to write. Thank you to Bob, Shannon, and Nicholas for sharing her. Thanks to Tammy Stripling who assists Julie. Appreciation also goes to Jean Illsley Clarke whose wise words so generously shared helped me improve weak concepts.

Finally, I wish to thank Kris and Tim, who taught and continue to teach me much of what I need to know and whose existence was essential to this book and to me. I owe my greatest appreciation to JDS who believed in me from the very beginning and supported me in every way.

Foreword

Many years ago, in a small town in northern Ontario, a group of mothers got together with their toddlers and preschool age children to share a warm mug of coffee, to chat, and to watch our children learn to socialize and play. For many of us just coming together that one morning a week brought us face to face with some serious challenges: How did we get two, or three, small children dressed, snow-suited, and off to a group which we knew they would enjoy, and we needed? How did we cope with the obstructiveness of a two and a half year old who was really planning upon staying in pajamas all day and coloring houses with flowers in the yard? And what did we do about those recalcitrant little ones who once in the back seat, buckled in for safety, still had arms long enough to torment the child beside them? And what did we do with our own frustrations and angers, and often our I-don't-get-enough-sleep-at-night-I'm-bone-weary spirits?

In a way the solution was in our coming together and nurturing one another. But we were lucky; we were *so* lucky. Firstly, we loved our children with an unconcealed passion and an irrepressible hopefulness. And most importantly, we had Madelyn. Madelyn, home by choice with two small boys with round eager faces, had been a school psychologist and educator, and she took our anxieties, fears and frustrations, as well as our hopes and our dreams for ourselves and our children, seriously. With Madelyn's guidance and under her leadership, our informal chats grew into hopeful, life affirming debate sessions which changed people's lives. Some of us took our first steps toward looking at the meaning and significance of our daily struggles, and others of us climbed painstakingly up the stairs towards improving our own self-esteem and challenging the careless, sloppy, and faithless way our society viewed children and child rearing.

Today, ten years later, that core group of mothers have moved on into various fields in the work force: teaching, nursing, family therapy, sculpture, retail and so on. Regardless of where our days have led us, the impact of those conversations has never left. Madelyn's wisdom and vision, and unwavering belief in our ability to solve our problems while honoring our children, have been invaluable tools for every aspect of our lives. When Madelyn and her family moved to Texas we mourned our loss, but over the years we have cheered her successes and applauded the way she has moved out into a much larger community to share her message.

I consider Madelyn to be one of those visionary mentors - not just someone who helped me cope with today, but someone who helped me build for the future. To those of you just opening this book and meeting Madelyn for the first time - breathe a sigh of relief. There is much common sense good advice here; there is much caring, love, and respect in these words. And, most importantly, there is Madelyn's wisdom and her faith in you. Believe in it. Believe in your own ability to find a vision which will help you build strong and resilient bonds with the children in your lives.

Victoria Ryland Mathies

Contents

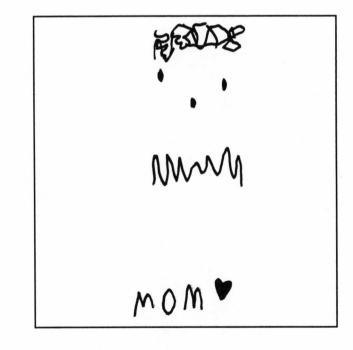

PART I - THE JOURNEY BEGINS

1:
The Journey Begins

We're all in this together ... alone. - Lily Tomlin

When my oldest son first started drawing, he drew a picture of me (see page v) as the perfect mom with blonde hair, red cheeks, a smile, a sun shining brightly, and a warm red heart - Mommy the Good. On the other side of that very same paper, he drew a second picture, a different version of me. This one had blue and white scraggly hair, a zigzag line for a mouth, no sun, and a very cold green heart. Perhaps most telling is the missing circle which would have delineated my head, which I feel represented so effectively my loss of integrity - Mommy the Bad. Never think for a moment that your children do not notice. In truth, I was both of these mommies; he, in his naivete, had captured my essence. Clearly, something needed to be done. Mommy the Bad needed to go, to be exorcized.

I started backwards. I sought skills first, but I could not judge their appropriateness with any tool other than, "Does it work?" I was missing the critical component of discipline, its root word, which means teaching and has been forgotten or overlooked for too long. I was at the mercy of the "experts" who so often disagree. I realized I was not seeking expertise; I was seeking and needing wisdom to help me guide my children to healthy, happy, responsible, humane adulthood. I failed to regain my integrity until I came to understand that every time I disciplined my son, I was not simply addressing and changing current behavior, I was also teaching him life lessons and principles he would use to guide his life both now and in the future. I needed not only to be effective in the present, but I also needed to teach healthy and helpful principles to my child.

Being a parent is far more challenging, frustrating, and sometimes discouraging than I ever thought it would or could be. And I was a school psychologist, an early childhood educator, and the wife of a teacher *before* I ever had children of my own. My close friends and I have decided that the difficulty of this challenge is one of the world's best-kept secrets. My journey into this book, the subject of which I have been speaking about and teaching for years, began with the frustration and discouragement I experienced as our first-born began toddlerhood. I had never planned to be the perfect parent; I had just expected that with all my experience with other people's children and my education (please don't laugh, I was young), I would, at least, be a good parent. Well, it wasn't necessarily so.

Early on, I recognized two factors in my poor parenting. First, and most importantly, what I *practiced* and what I *believed* were two different things. My integrity - that elusive ability to match believed principles with practiced principles - was not intact. I constantly found myself dealing with my son much more nastily and harshly than I wished (that was Mommy the Bad). Further, I found myself using practices I knew were neither right nor helpful. I did not wish to teach my children practices or ideas in which I did not truly believe, yet that is exactly what I found myself doing. I had been teaching him that I had the right to hurt him if I did not like his behavior. But, I also felt that no one was allowed to hurt me if they did not like my behavior. I had tried to buy him off and thus, I taught him that it was all right to be bought. I had also used and therefore taught him disrespect. I scared myself with the person I had become so quickly and completely. I did not like Mommy the Bad. Nothing had so baffled and beaten me as trying to rear my son, nothing (not school, not career, not even marriage) had brought forth and shown me the worst of who I was.

Secondly, I simply did not have enough skills, strategies, nor techniques to be a helpful, healthy parent. Neither did I know how to evaluate and select techniques. I needed to learn more, much more. Most jobs or positions require training; generally, the more complicated the job, the longer the training needs to be. Well, it does not get more complex than parenting. Many of us went to college for years to qualify for our occupations, and if we are honest, we admit to having needed on-the-job practice in our fields before we really became skilled. Too often, parents tackle the job of parenting with little or no training and expect themselves to be skilled from the start. This is not only unfair, but also unrealistic.

Discipline, using the term loosely here, has for years now focused heavily on behavior only. When I first started working with children, I, like most teachers and parents, believed discipline is what you do with children to get them to behave. Is this not what you have been taught? This view, however, is short-sighted, out-dated, and quite frankly, dangerous. Somewhere in our minds, we must be able to envision our child on his or her sixteenth birthday. I know where she will be - at the Department of Motor Vehicles seeking freedom in the form of a driver's license. By that time, the correct principles (of responsibility, of responsiveness, of respect, etc.) must be in place. These principles will help determine how each new driver decides to operate a car. Will she drive the speed limit only when there are police around? Will she drive fast because it is fun? Or, will she understand that *how she chooses to operate the vehicle will determine whether people live or die?* It is critical that each driver understands this last statement. The safety of each of our children and loved ones depends on it.

How we discipline a child at age two, at age five, at age nine, plays a significant role in determining how he drives at sixteen, how he handles relationships, what kind of spouse and parent he becomes, in short, how he handles his life. The future does depend on what we do in the present. In our hearts we know this. We have always recognized that the actions we take with children when they are young return to help or haunt us as they age. Thus, our discipline cannot afford to be short-sighted and look merely at how to most quickly and efficiently get a child to behave *now*. Certainly we do not want to give up immediate effectiveness; we need to be effective. But, immediate effectiveness is not enough. We need to build on this layer and move into a higher level of discipline. That next, and higher, level looks at what lesson needs to be learned and how best to teach it to a specific child. What principles are involved? Do I believe in these principles? Do I want them in my future? We all need to recognize that we will see these principles in our futures. Will they benefit ourselves and others? That, too, is part of our job description. This idea, that discipline can address more than present behavior and must also concern itself with lessons as well, needs to be our first point of agreement. We need to see that what we do in the present affects the future. We need to recognize that what we teach is critical to long-term discipline.

Also completely fundamental to this program is the principle of responsibility for actions - ownership of all behavior. Every adult needs to understand and believe and teach to each child that:

I am responsible for what I choose to do and for what happens to me and others as a result of my decisions and actions.

Teaching the ownership of behavior is one very important skill we need to impart. Accepting responsibility for our decisions and actions is essential to self-discipline, the final goal. With the rise in the "don't blame me" syndrome and the "victim" or "something or someone made me do it" defense, teaching responsibility for our actions is decidedly necessary. We need to be in complete agreement on this next issue: This responsibility for behavior and outcome, the hallmark of self-discipline, is the vision or path upon which our techniques must be based. The individual techniques and strategies we choose will vary with personality, values, child, and situation.

Yes, you can be the parent you want to be, or at least a whole lot closer to it. And yes, being a family can be mostly healthy, happy, and a benefit to you, rather than a disappointment in your life. It is critical not only for our own sanity and our children's lives, but also for our future, that we learn to guide our children through childhood and into healthy adulthood. There is so much they need to learn and know about in order to become emotionally healthy, happy, functional adults: forming healthy relationships, developing sound and helpful communication, acquiring correct principles to guide their lives, using problem solving, being responsive to others, showing respect and taking responsibility for their actions, discovering resourcefulness and negotiating skills, building self-esteem, dealing with anger. True discipline teaches all of these. It is clear we must not only be knowledgeable in these areas, but we must also know positive ways to teach them.

The task is large, but not impossible. The benefits more than offset the effort and struggle. After all, what are emotionally healthy, responsible, contributing adults worth? What is a child with high self-esteem worth? What are respectful, responsible teens worth? What is a lifelong bond with each of your children worth?

To teachers and early childhood educators:

This book is also directed to teachers and early childhood educators. Teaching, working with children, is a most noble profession. It is also mentally and emotionally taxing. Veteran teachers across North America describe changes (decreases in self-esteem, respect, self-discipline, motivation and increases in anger, emotional disturbance, aggression, apathy) which have made teaching more difficult. As is true with parenting, teaching is challenging and at times can be more frustrating and discouraging than we envisioned. Most of us began our careers wanting simply to teach and quickly discovered we needed effective disciplinary tools in order to get to the teaching.

In addition, we may not have considered the need to support and supplement the parents. This particular role has always been part of a teacher's job. From the beginning there have been orphaned, neglected, abused, and needy children. Sadly, their number is increasing at a remarkable rate. Despite the increase in this population, teachers must continue to be role models and provide discipline. Although school is not the last chance for troubled children, it is the last easy chance.

Entering and remaining in this profession is a choice; the task is large, but not impossible. One must be able to stand the heat, but if one can, the emotional benefits can be tremendous. Christa McAuliff said it beautifully, "I touch the future. I teach." Most respectfully I would add, "I touch lives; I teach." Teaching can be the profession you had hoped for, and you can be the teacher you have always wanted to be.

Let us begin by developing a guiding vision. For how can we get there if we don't know where there is?

PART II - VISION

2:
A Rope Across the River

O nly the foolhardy would start or continue a journey without knowing the destination and without having some guidelines or directions for getting there. Without question, we as parents are on an important journey. Any good book on business management and leadership stresses the need for a vision, a knowledge of where we are headed, and maps for how to get there. Both the destination and the path must be clear. As one of my friends, the mother of three young children, put it so succinctly and honestly, "It just seems like I am flying by the seat of my pants most of the time." Not unlike the pilot who reported, "I don't know where I am, but I'm making record time," we parents and educators seem at times to be sliding down a slippery slope with no control over our direction. We neither want, nor can we afford, to make record time on a path towards destruction, dysfunction, or faulty principles with our children. We need to be leaders with a very clear vision, for we are leaders into the future, whether we want to be or not.

Few in our society would question that we as parents are in a most important position of leadership. Teachers, similarly, are clearly the leaders within their classrooms. Acquiring a vision becomes not only a critical skill, but a necessity for the smooth functioning of our lives and for those for whom we are responsible.

I have never been in water so much over my head, with such a cold swift current as I was when my first child became premeditated in his behavior. Vision can be like a rope tossed across a river with a strong current, that when firmly attached to the other side, helps us arrive where we wanted, rather than where the current chose to take us. Many parents and teachers have been trying to cross the river with no rope. They inevitably end up *somewhere* down river feeling cold, wet and tired. With the rope as a guide, tied securely to a tree directly across the river, they can cross the river and *arrive where they wanted!* They may still occasionally feel cold, wet and tired, but no corrective measures will be required, for they will have arrived at their chosen destination.

Where We Are Now: The State of America's Children

> As the family goes, so goes the nation and so goes the whole world in which we live. - Pope John Paul II

It is not just individual people who are lost. Our nation is in desperate need of corrective measures. For too many years, both parents and teachers have disciplined without vision, without the necessary guidance and leadership. We have allowed ourselves to be completely engaged fighting fires. Not only have adults and children suffered, but our nation has paid a tremendous price. The United States is currently the most violent country in the industrialized world; we rather notoriously lead in the number of homicides, assaults, and rapes.[1] In 1993, it was reported that gun-related violence took the life of a child every three hours, that is 25 children - a classroom full, every three days.[2] In 1994, the Children's Defense Fund reported that a child died from gun-related violence once every two hours, or a classroom full every two days. And gun-related violence is still increasing. Further, ninety-one percent of responding teachers reported increased violence among children in their classrooms.[3] In its "The State of American Children Yearbooks 1994 and 1997," the Children's Defense Fund described One Day in the Life of American Children:

1994 Yearbook	
3	Children die from child abuse
9	Children are murdered
13	Children die from guns
30	Children are wounded by guns
202	Children are arrested for drug offenses
307	Children are arrested for crimes of violence
340	Children are arrested for drinking or drunken driving
1,234	Children run away from home
2,255	Teenagers drop out of school each day
2,781	Teenagers get pregnant
5,314	Children are arrested for all offenses
5,703	Teenagers are victims of violent crime
7,945	Children are reported abused or neglected
1,200,000	Latchkey children come home to houses in which there is a gun

1997 Yearbook

3	Children die from abuse or neglect
6	Children commit suicide
13	Children are murdered (up from 9 in 1994)
16	Children die from guns (up from 13 in 1994)
403	Children are arrested for drug offenses (up from 202 in 1994)
316	Children are arrested for violent crimes (up from 307 in 1994)
3,356	Children drop out of school (up from 2,255 in 1994)
5,702	Children are arrested (up from 5,314 in 1994)
8,523	Children are reported abused or neglected (up from 7,945 in 1994)

Every American leader, parent, and citizen personally and collectively must commit to reclaim our nation's soul and give our children back their hope, their sense of security, their belief in America's fairness, and their ability to dream about, envisage, and work toward a future that is attainable and real.
- Marian Wright Edelman, Children's Defense Fund

In order to help redirect our nation back on track, first we must become accountable; we must check our own behavior. We must determine whether we are contributing to the crisis or to the solutions. We must stop sending mixed messages to our children; we must check and improve our own integrity. "So many children are confused about what is right and wrong because so many grownups talk right and act wrong in our [sic] personal, professional, political, and public lives."[4] As Margaret Anderson states in *Raising a Family is a Pleasure*, "The struggle for moral perfection ends only at the grave."[5] Our children do not need perfect parents. They need parents who strive for integrity and moral ideals; who make mistakes but learn from them; who will share their principles, struggles and thoughts with their children; and, who put their children first, in practice not just in thought. We need to handle our lives and our children with integrity. By integrity I mean not just the ability to say what we believe but the ability to practice what we believe and the ability to do the right thing.

Secondly, we must stop viewing discipline as simply what we do to get children to behave, that is, to change their behavior right now. This viewpoint, this paradigm, is very short-sighted and dangerous. Our discipline techniques must include ideas about where we want to be in the future, what type of child-teen-adult we want, and need, in the long run. Perhaps you've heard the saying: "The cure for crime is not found in the electric chair, but in the high chair." Nothing could be more true today.

We must begin with this end in mind, or we will, as individuals and as a nation, flounder in the cold, swift-moving river of life.

Unfortunately, for many parents and teachers, there appear to be no ropes available to assist them in crossing the river of parenthood. But are there? Certainly. Correct principles are the guiding ropes. It is our correct principles which we must identify and use. It is Stephen Covey, in his book *The Seven Habits of Highly Effective People*, who provides some background ideas about principles:

> Principles are guidelines for human conduct that are proven to have enduring, permanent value. They're fundamental.... Principles are not *values*. A gang of thieves can share values, but they are in violation of the fundamental principles we're talking about. Principles are the territory. Values are maps. When we value correct principles, we have truth - a knowledge of things as they are.

Principles include *fairness, honesty, integrity, respect, responsibility, resourcefulness, responsiveness, humaneness, perseverance, and excellence.* They are like our Constitution. They are the guiding lights that help keep us focused and on track. They do not change. We all recognize their benefit. For example, whether pro-life or pro-choice, we all believe in the principle that human life has value. The disagreement begins when we interpret a principle as a value. Those who favor the *value* (interpretation of principle) of pro-choice believe strongly in the worth of a mother's life. Those who favor the *value* of pro-life believe strongly in the worth of an unborn baby's life. The point is that the fundamental principle - a strong belief in the worth of human life - is the same starting point for both groups. I have worked with thousands of parents and educators; they continue to agree on some core correct principles. Of course, they disagree frequently on values.

Some adults, many youth, and the criminal element of our population fail to value correct principles. They operate on faulty principles. These include unfairness, only working toward one's own advantage, dishonesty, lack of respect, blaming others for one's behavior and mistakes, and so forth. Neither do some of these people recognize the principle that human life is valuable. As individuals and as a nation, we continue to pay for this adherence to flawed principles. It is absolutely critical that we help children develop the correct principles to guide their lives and aid their decisions. Our children need parents who will teach them a set of correct principles and who will use and model no faulty or flawed principles.

Another way to look at principles, specifically with regard to discipline, is to ask what principles does any technique or group of techniques teach. Clearly, we want to be teaching principles we believe in, principles we want used with us as we age, and principles upon which we want our nation and future built. In other words, are we teaching correct or flawed principles? Wise or unwise principles? Beneficial or harmful principles? The Law of the Harvest - we reap what we sow - is always in effect. Our tomorrow is sown today. It is helpful then to examine the underlying principles of the four most common systems of child-rearing. In so doing, we will discover what they teach our children and, accordingly, whether or not we want to use them. We will also see how the way we have managed children in the past has contributed to our present.

3:
What Do I Want to Teach?

We must believe the things we teach our children. - Woodrow Wilson

Control - Power

The first system we will explore is a system based on control. By control I mean that thumbs-pressed-down-on-them, autocratic, brute force (either by physical or verbal superiority) way of dealing with children. In a word - Power. Clarity is important here. Power can be very beneficial; nutritive, integrative power is beneficial and emotionally healthy. (For more information on types of power see Rollo May's *Power and Innocence: A Search for the Sources of Violence*.) Here, however, I mean exploitive or manipulative power used not in a child's best interest but for the best interest of the one who is wielding the power. Those of us who have an audio-tape playing in our heads which tells us "good parents control their children" or "good teachers control their classrooms" qualify. During the holidays, at the Thanksgiving dinner table with your parents and relatives present, can you hear this recording? Or as a teacher, do you hear this tape when the principal walks by your classroom? Are you a bottom-line, get things done efficiently, productive person? Do you prefer to have situations under control? These personality types and values are not wrong or bad; however, we need to consider where this principle of Power may lead us and what it teaches children.

CONTROL - POWER		
Belief		Question or Statement by Child
Good parents control their children. Good teachers control their classrooms.	⇨	"Who will make me?"
Good kids always behave.	⇨	"Make me!"

Two problems occur when we consistently use power to get our way with children. First, children determine that in families, in classrooms, in life, it is fair and right to use power to get one's way. We, the older generation, can be very short-sighted; for inevitably, the balance of power will shift from us and return to haunt us. I do not wish to be removed from my home against my will by my children. If I teach power as a way of operating, as an acceptable method of dealing with people, I am foolish not to expect power to be used against me (remember the Law of the Harvest). Second, many children learn from our modeling exactly how to wield power. They become tyrants in their own right. As these children enter adolescence, they rebel harshly. Some of us live with two-year-olds who understand and love power (NO!). But as tyrants age, they can and do make family life extremely difficult and unpleasant. They seem to bring out the worst in all of us. They also frequently grow up to become autocratic heads of a new family and pass on this dysfunctional style of interaction.

My favorite demonstration of power is to approach a participant with my hands raised towards her with palms facing forward, fingers up, and hands flat. I ask this helper to raise her hands in exactly the same manner so that our palms can touch. As long as I do not push, everything goes nicely, but when I push, each participant pushes back. No matter how much force I exert, she will exert at least equal force. When we push, they push. Anyone with any self-respect will do the same. The use of power breeds the use of power. The use of negative power teaches exploitation and manipulation. And I have never met the child for whom the issue (whatever issue, cookies, the car, homework) was not at least as important as it was to the parent. The use of exploitive power spawns resistance.

Be aware, many children by personality or inclination seem to thrive on power from an early age. Two's, five's and thirteen's are in developmental stages which include separation and finding one's own identity. These stages typically include the wielding of power, yet they are necessary parts of growing up. Wielding power against these children aggravates an already present proclivity or personality.

Some children learn a different lesson from being controlled. They learn the opposite end of control - submission. In order for one person to dominate, another must become submissive. Do you want submissive children? (I know, it sounds lovely in theory, and some of you are thinking a little submission would be nice.) Submission is, as we have learned of late, a very dangerous lesson to learn. There are many men and women who have learned this lesson well. However, it is women who have been the focus of concern most recently. It is clear from the need for Women's Shelters all over our country that too many women learned the lesson of submission. If they married emotionally healthy spouses, they only have trouble saying no to volunteer work or to their children. If, however, they married emotionally unhealthy spouses, they are being abused physically and emotionally as you read this. Children and adults tend either to believe that they are victims and things happen to them, or tend to believe that they are in charge of their lives and have control over the direction their lives take. Do you want to risk your child? In the section on Building Self-Esteem, we will discuss more thoroughly the loss of self-esteem linked to submission, learned helplessness, and victimization.

It is important to consider what a child schooled in power and control asks himself or you when he is deciding how to behave. This question represents the principle by which he is deciding to guide his life. "Who's going to make me?" is typical. My younger son was stronger than me when he was eleven. Had we taught power as a principle of operation, I would have been in trouble this early in his life. Consider this potential scenario: I tell him it is his turn to empty the dishwasher. He replies, "Who's going to make me?" and I have to answer, "Your dad when he gets home." Not my idea of fine discipline! As he gets older and stronger still, he turns the question into a statement, "Make me." Dad, who of course, has gotten older and slower becomes less able to make him. Who, then, is left to make him? Well, the police force maybe, when they can catch him. And, the police making our children behave is not the goal toward which any of us wishes to head.

When the drug dealer approaches this type of child and offers drugs, the child's question becomes, "Who's going to stop me?" Parents will likely not be present during this offer, nor will there be a teacher or police officer around. Successful drug dealers avoid the latter with skill. *There is not going to be anyone to stop her.* And the chain of substance abuse is started. Another significant question to ask is how does this child drive? Very, very well - when she sees a police car. As she pleases (and frequently in rebellion), when she sees that the policeman has pulled someone else over and that the odds are slim to none that there is another officer on this same street. There is *no one around to make her* drive the right speed through your school zone. Does the phrase "no cop, no stop" ring a bell?

And what happens when the youth, whose parents have managed to control her all through high school, goes away to college? What are her chances of success? This young adult is constantly asking herself, "Who will make me study?" and "Who will make me go to class?" and "Who will keep me from partying yet again tonight?" Because this student is so accustomed to outside control, she fails to come to grips with an all important concept, "So if no one else is going to make me, maybe I better make myself (a demonstration of self-discipline)." The lesson that each of us is in control of our behavior and that we own our behavior, indeed we own all that we do, comes too late and often comes very expensively.

So what do we know? *Power*, for many of us, is seductively tempting. Who doesn't like things his way? But a system of child management based on control teaches dangerous lessons and is based on the flawed principle of exploitive power. Is this the legacy you want to leave - "My way or the highway!" Or do you want something more for your child(ren)? And, since it is sometimes difficult to tell who will seize the idea of power and run with it and who will learn submission, do you want to teach lessons which may prove very harmful and unhealthy for your child? Healthy families are not built on the foundation of control by power.

Yes, there is a time for control. Life-threatening situations may call for a powerful response. Situations where emotional health is involved also call for immediate action. A parent can and should place a child in drug rehabilitation or residential treatment when needed, or physically remove a child from danger. But please keep in mind, picking up the toys or taking out the garbage is not a life-threatening situation.

Remember, that although we are not in control of their behavior, nor are we in control of everything that happens. We are in charge: we must be in charge. Children are not capable of being in charge. We make the decisions, set the limits, enforce the rules, and carry out the discipline. In short, we carry authority, and we can and must be effective. Too many parents and educators confuse control with authority and believe that because they cannot be in control that they also cannot, or do not have to be, in charge. This is not so. The section on Authority gives more detail.

What price has our nation paid? The use of "power without discipline" is increasing dramatically. There was a time when attainment of power - political, financial, physical, or influential - was accompanied by the development of self-discipline. Money accrued through hard work. The martial arts take years and years to master. Wise, respected, respectable leaders mature through years of experience.

Not so any more. Money is stolen. Political office can be bought. Physical power over others is just one handgun away. The procuring of power without the development of self-discipline is not only possible, it is too easy.

The price exacted is reflected by our number one ranking in violence in the industrialized world. Violence and aggression are forms of abuse of power. The increase in the use of handguns to get or to take what is desired (not earned or deserved) represents an abuse of power. So does driving while under the influence of alcohol or drugs. Families run by power suffer and children who believe others must make them behave make classroom discipline very difficult. Sexual harassment is also a form of use of power without discipline. Abuse of power riddles both private enterprise and the public sector. When we add physical, emotional, and sexual abuse, the toll is staggering. How many people continue to believe that if someone else (a parent, teacher, boss, or other authority figure) cannot or simply does not make them behave appropriately, they do not have to; they are free to do what they want without regard for others or the consequences to others. They can do whatever damage they choose.

Each of us must decide what principles we choose to use and teach. We must decide whether short-term or long-term gain is more important. And we must each foresee that we will reap what we have sown.

Rewards & Bribes: Behavior Modification

When I was in graduate school, B.F. Skinner, the author of operant conditioning and thus, reward systems, was considered a giant in the field of psychology. During my college career, I took a graduate-level course focused solely on reinforcement theory and practice, and as a result set up numerous reinforcement programs for school children. Now, despite its founder's concerns and new understanding in the past decade, this system continues to be found in many books and schools. As we look at reward systems, the appeal will become clear, as will the dangers. Two facts must be remembered. First, Dr. Skinner was a brilliant man who made major contributions to our body of knowledge. Second, the laws regarding rewards and punishment (operant learning theory) which he discovered and described are true and operate regardless of whether or not we are aware of them. And we need to be aware of them.

REWARDS & BRIBES	
Belief	Question or Statement by Child
Rewarded behavior repeats itself.	⇨ "What will I get?"
	⇨ "What's in it for me?"

Many parents and teachers continue to believe that giving a child a reward is innocent, even nice. After all, it can feel good to both parties involved. The audio tape we play to ourselves here is, "What can I use to get this kid to behave?"

What if it is phrased another way, as "How can I buy him off?" Ouch, that one does not sound so good does it? Do we want to teach our children to be bought? Rewards buy children's behavior. In other words, children sell or trade their behavior for the reward. This is a fundamental concern about rewards. The now nine year old daughter of my friend and associate Julie is one of my favorite kids. She, like her mother, is bright and alive. Shannon is also exceedingly tuned in to human dynamics, what is really going on during human interactions. Shannon's third grade teacher used a reward system for good behavior. At the end of each day, she called students up to her desk to receive a ticket for good behavior; the tickets were saved and used to purchase small objects at the end of each week. During the first week of class (honeymoon time in most elementary classes), Shannon, like the rest of her classmates, received a ticket at the end of each day. However, by the third week the honeymoon had ended and Shannon's outgoing personality was beginning to surface. Lo and behold, one afternoon she was not called up for the coveted ticket. On the surface, nothing seemed to have gone wrong. Shannon was not visibly upset by this. However, at the end of the next day, her mother received a phone call from the teacher who reported that Shannon was called up to get a ticket this next day and refused to move. What did this mean? It meant Shannon had figured out two important dynamics. First, if I am not good enough for the teacher every day, then I am not good enough, period. Either like me all of the time, or not at all. I have value to you all of the time or never mind; this was truly a self-esteem issue. Secondly, Shannon sent a strong message that says she can't be bought. Neither she nor her behavior are for sale. Imagine what would happen to classroom reward systems if more children decided not to be the kind of person who can be bought. Wouldn't it be nice if more children and adults could not be bought? Wouldn't that change the tenor of the nation, the way businesses are run, the way laws are made, the way people deal with each other? Yet, we continue to start rewarding or buying our children at early ages, when they are far too young to have developed moral character and the necessary strength of resistance.

If we look with a more thoughtful eye, we can see how other underlying principles help us to decide what is appropriate and helpful. Most of us, especially those in education, have been taught that the purpose of rewarding behavior is to increase the probability of that behavior's return - to get a child to do something favorable again (use the toilet, not talk in class). Rewards work in theory and practice with both animals and people. Usually, when we reward a child's behavior, the child does repeat the behavior again. This can be accomplished quickly with little effort, thought, or struggle. This, in turn, *rewards us* and makes us believe we are being effective. Two of us have been rewarded, the child and the adult. The adult is most likely to repeat this behavior of rewarding children. This behavior management system is the most difficult to give up because it reinforces the teacher's or parent's behavior as well.

What we also overlook is that we have to continue to reward more and more frequently as children become dependent on reinforcement. Eventually, they begin to believe that the world owes them, and they expect to be rewarded for any and all good behavior. One mother reported that she was tired of her children being ugly to each other. So she set up a small reward system for nice behavior. When one of her children was good to another one (said something nice, did something for another, or shared), she would reward him. Very quickly, her children were asking a question before determining what they would do for each other. The question was, of course, "Will you give me something if I share this crayon with my brother, if I get the milk for my sister, or if I do anything nice?" This mother realized that her children were now being nice only if they got paid in some way. "What have I done?" she asked. "My kids are nicer to each other but only if there is something in it for them. There are no more pure and simply kind acts in my house." We do, indeed, reap what we sow. We also quickly discover that what was once motivating to the child is no longer working. Children begin to operate on the faulty principle of greed. They require more and more and bigger and bigger rewards. If we look down the road this is what we see: we view the high school student who gets paid for grades or gets a car for a year of good grades. We find a fourteen year old who says he is not going to take out the trash because he already has enough money to go to the movies on Saturday. We have adolescents searching for the now-elusive kick one receives with a great reward and finding it in drugs, alcohol, promiscuity, and sadly, even violence.

Were you paid to fix dinner or to do the dishes last night? If not (and none of us was), we need to ask ourselves if we want our children to operate under a different system and set of principles than we operate from; often we do, indeed, pay children to do household chores. This comprises a different system. Please see the section on Chores in the Life Lessons chapter for additional information on chores and allowances. It must be clear in our minds why we did the dishes for no pay; we must recognize the principles upon which we base our lives. We chose to do dishes for no pay because everyone over the age of two needs to contribute to the family unit; no one has the right to be a parasite. No matter what group we belong to (family, classroom, church, organization, business, or nation), we must help maintain or improve it. Groups cannot stay alive without this principle. It is part of belonging. Too many parasites and the group surely falters and may not survive.

What else do rewards teach? Rewards teach external motivation at the expense of internal motivation. Rewards teach that it is *our* job to motivate them, rather than *their* job to motivate themselves. When we place a carrot in front of a child, she focuses on the carrot rather than on the important internal motivators such as feeling good with a job well done, learning something, or accomplishing something. These internal motivators are far more powerful and longer-lasting. Teachers, especially secondary teachers, often ask me, "How can we motivate these students who have become so dependent on rewards and external motivation?" This question takes us in the wrong direction; it keeps us searching for outside motivators. The more helpful question is, "How can we increase intrinsic motivation? How can we help them motivate themselves?" (The answers to these questions lie in making things challenging, interesting, purposeful and in helping them understand and feel that accomplishment, a job well done or having learned something feels good.) Rewards, as a form of external motivation, prevent or destroy internal motivation. It is very difficult to even consider why something makes us feel good inside when there is always a carrot out in front of us demanding our attention. We give them class work to do and they ask, "What will I get?" We fail to answer with the truth, "Smarter, that is why your parents send you to school!"

Internal motivators are the true building blocks for self-esteem. Repeatedly we have been told we need to reward children to build self-esteem. This is not so. In fact, rewards and praise (verbal reinforcement) frequently do more damage to self-esteem than good. They focus on only one area of self-esteem and do harm to the other two areas. Please see Over-Emphasis on Accomplishment and Praise in the section on Self-Esteem for a more thorough discussion of praise.

This leads us to a related concern. Reinforcement or rewards also prevent children from developing a good sense of evaluation. Adults are in charge of determining what is good enough, what deserves a reward. Do you know someone who will not select an outfit without another's aid and approval? Evaluating issues and candidates is an important skill for voters. Democracies require adults who can evaluate; so do businesses, schools, and families. Children who do not practice evaluating for themselves have difficulty developing this vital skill. Even as adults, they are unable to say to themselves, "I did well - I was great!" without confirmation from someone else. Clearly, being unable to say "well-done!" to yourself limits self-esteem. Do we want to teach children to look for a pat on the back or is it more helpful to teach them to pat themselves on the back? Please see the section on Self-Esteem for changing praise to descriptive appreciation and teaching children to pat themselves on the back.

In addition, rewards teach immediate gratification - "I want what I want *now*." Do you know anyone in trouble with credit cards because he had to have something right now despite the checkbook balance? Deferred or delayed gratification is indeed a virtue and a sign of maturity. Deferred gratification helps us wait with grace.

For years we have overlooked a hidden factor in reward systems. They are by nature manipulative. Webster's Seventh New Collegiate Dictionary defines *manipulate* as "to control or play upon by artful, unfair, or insidious means especially to one's own advantage." When we determine what behaviors we want, when we shape behavior and mold children without their consent or knowledge to our own advantage, we are, by definition, manipulating. The words we use to describe these concepts are generally quite revealing and accurate. Consider *behavior management* and *behavior modification.* Do you want your behavior managed or modified, without your understanding of what is being done to you? Do you want to teach manipulation as a skill you would like your children to use? Research and experience repeatedly inform us that our modeling - our actions, what we do - is the best, most powerful teaching tool. Use manipulation, teach manipulation, and expect to be manipulated in return. This is the Law of the Harvest, once again. One of the most common complaints I hear about reward systems is that children frequently manipulate them to their advantage. Quick learners!

We must consider our own aging and the increasing vulnerability which will accompany it. News accounts of senior citizens being manipulated and swindled are all too common. The trend of elderly parents being left to fend for themselves or any form of elder abuse is distressing, and we are witnessing increasing amounts of it.

Do you like to be manipulated by others? Not likely. The next question to ask yourself is do you believe in the Golden Rule: "Do unto others as you would have them do unto you." If you answered no to the first question and yes to the second, then your integrity is jeopardized by using reward systems. Another way to phrase the Golden Rule is: do you choose to treat others in ways you do not wish to be treated? For our own integrity, we must treat children as we wish to be treated.

Lastly, what question do reward systems teach children to ask when they are deciding how to behave? "What will I get?" or the more sophisticated version, "What's in it for me?" This is harmful to individual children, as well as to our nation. First, the drug dealer has a response to "What's in it for me?" It is, "You're going to feel wonderful - better than you've ever felt before (this could be a temporary replacement of real self-esteem); it's going to happen right away (they will get immediate gratification). Trust me (don't use your evaluation skills). And, if I decide I like you (this is manipulation), you can make more money (the world owes us) in one night with me than both your parents do in two months (greed)." All of this sounds mighty good to this child. And, again, we lose another child down the path of illicit drug use and addiction.

Our nation has paid a huge price for the use of these faulty principles, and not just in terms of increased drug use and related crimes. B. F. Skinner reportedly spent the last years of his life explaining to people that if we continue to treat children like rats (use manipulation), they will indeed become rats. And, that if we continue to use rewards as a major form of child management, our nation will reduce its ability to function as a democracy. Some citizens lack the ability to evaluate candidates, issues, and policies. Increasing numbers of people can be bought; fewer are refusing to sell themselves and living by principles and morals and with integrity. The "what's in it for me" attitude is identifiable. Too often individual interest prevails over community interest. Too many allow themselves to be driven by the question, "What's in it for me?" They fail to ask the more important questions such as, "Is this good for the family? For the community? For the future?" or "Is someone else in greater need?"

A democratic government cannot survive too many special interests without sacrificing what's in the best interest for all.

Healthy individuals do not develop from rewards and the harmful principles that they teach. Families, classrooms, and democratic nations require healthy individuals who think for themselves. Rewards are dangerously and seductively short-sighted. Again, each of us must determine what we choose to teach.

Punishment

No more tears now; I will think upon revenge. - Mary Stuart, Queen of Scotland

Punishment is not truly a separate system; it operates under the same learning principles as behavior management. However, punishment is an ancient system. It is helpful to look at punishment separately, as an entity itself. "This child is going to pay" is the audio tape those of us who lean toward punishment hear in our minds.

PUNISHMENT		
Belief		Question or Statement by Child
"There's nothing wrong with this child that a good spanking wouldn't fix."	⇨	"Is it worth it?" "Who's looking?"
"This child is going to pay."	⇨	"You can't get to me."

We cannot ignore inappropriate behavior; certainly a lesson must be taught. But there is a difference between hurting emotionally or physically to try to teach a lesson and simply teaching a lesson. *Punishment is different from discipline.* Punishment, by definition, is doing something ugly or hurtful to another because we do not like what he did. Discipline is teaching - period. Punishment is, by contrast, based on revenge and hurting to make a point. It is a faulty perception: the more I hurt you, the better you will listen to me. Punishment includes: 1) social pain - taking away unrelated privileges, objects, and freedoms, 2) emotional pain - verbal assaults, name-calling, belittling, attacks on self-esteem and value, and 3) physical pain - slapping, shaking, pushing, spanking, and so forth.

A first concern about punishment involves the lessons it teaches. We teach children that when they do not do what we want, we have the right to hurt them either physically, socially, or emotionally. My husband is not allowed to hurt me or hit me if he doesn't like what I do. He is supposed to have the skills to work things out, to find another way to solve the problem. He does not get to punish me for poor behavior choices, a bad incident or day. A pediatrician may not like it when a parent does not ensure that his child finishes her antibiotics (harmful to child and public health), but it is considered unprofessional and illegal for her to strike a patient or to refuse treatment because she does not like his actions. It is interesting that our culture still allows us to strike one group only, the population who is most vulnerable, most innocent, most uncivilized, most likely to make mistakes, and most in need of teaching - our children.

As stated earlier, our nation is currently ranked first among industrialized nations in violence. Too many people believe they have the right to hurt another because they do not like what someone else does or looks like or has. And yes, we want to teach children what is appropriate and what is not, or that a digression is quite serious or must never be repeated. *There are many excellent discipline tools which not only accomplish these lessons without needing punishment, but also teach them more effectively.*

Second, punishment is something negative we do to children, such as taking away an *unrelated* privilege, or hurting them physically or emotionally to improve behavior. It need not be fair or just. Punishment creates resentment. Resentment results in people working *against* one another. A significant component of healthy families is their ability and desire to work *with* one another, to trust that the others will operate with every member's best interests at heart. Punishment works in contradiction to this important method of operating. No form of child management works well or easily when a child consistently chooses to work against us. Creating resentment makes our job far more difficult.

Here is a common scene. A mother is standing in line at the checkout counter in the grocery store late one afternoon. She has four children with her. Her ten year old daughter is bugging her mother to buy her something from the candy rack so handily placed. Mom says no repeatedly and is beginning to get annoyed. The daughter continues to push and badger. The baby is whining, the toddler running away, and mom reaches her limit. In frustration or from her past experience, the stressed mother reaches over and slaps her daughter and tells her to be quiet. The daughter, who has tears welling in her eyes from having her cheek slapped, looks her mother straight in the eyes and says what all punished children eventually say, "Didn't hurt." What this child's words truly mean are, "You can't get to me!" This is the last thing you want to hear from your children, because they mean it. You and your words no longer count with them. How could we think that hurting them would make them listen better? If you hurt me, I will not respect you more, nor will I listen to what you have to say. Your credibility with me is destroyed. If your child rides his bicycle into the street and you tell him that as a result he cannot now watch his video tonight, some children, generally the younger ones, will dissolve into tears. But sooner or later, each changes to "I didn't want to watch it anyway." That is simply another form of "You can't get to me." Other forms are "I hate you!" and "I don't care" and "I didn't want it anyhow." If you punish, expect this response; it is coming. It signals the time you have lost virtually all of your child's respect and regard for your authority. It signals the time their revenge and desire to hurt you have entered your relationship. Any type of discipline or punishment now has a reduced probability of working.

Some final words of wisdom come from a young, easy-going, cooperative child whose mother had managed not to spank her until she was five. After this first encounter with spanking, Elyse looked up at her mom and asked her, "Mommy, if you love me, why would you want to hurt me?" This simple question stopped her mother, Suzanne, cold. The question was, and is to this day, valid. Why would we want to *purposely* hurt someone we love? The answer "for their own good" simply is not true. There are always other ways to teach a necessary lesson without hurting; these involve true discipline. It is our job to discover these so we have them on hand when we need them. Children are going to misbehave; it is their job to show us what they need to learn. Our job is to teach without the need of being cruel, unfair, ugly, or mean. We need to teach without destroying the child's self-esteem or our bond with the child. This is in the child's best interest. This is what love is. We can be good for children without being ugly to them; of course, we would have to be skilled to do so. I have not said they will enjoy discipline; often they will not. The difference is that punishment uses pain as a means to the end; discipline does not. The end does not justify the means, especially when there are so many other means available. Those who defend spanking often hold two false beliefs. First, they believe that there are no strategies between reasoning (which, of course, does not work with very young children) and spanking. Second, they often believe that spanking and hitting are different. To spank, by definition, means *to strike* especially on the buttocks with the open hand.

Research and experience show us that punishment is not effective. Results are temporary, short-term. Parents have to continuously punish. This is *spend discipline* at its worst, and in complete contrast to *investment discipline*. As a parent, I want to do less and less discipline as my children get older (investment discipline). Teachers, as well, want to do less, not more and more (spend discipline) as the school year progresses. As children age, we want to see fewer incidents requiring us to discipline them and ever increasing incidents where they discipline themselves (self-discipline). If spanking really worked, all of our children would be self-disciplined and well-behaved. Everyone knows how to spank, and besides, it is quick and easy. We would not have missed such a wonderful tool. But spanking does not work long term. Please remember that not only do we require children to own *their* behavior, we adults must also accept responsibility and ownership for *our* behavior. No one, not any expert, pastor, doctor, or anyone else can give you permission to spank. You will own every single hit.

In addition, a punishment that once worked soon fails, and something harsher and nastier must replace it. In order for punishment to work, we need to be increasingly cruel and hurtful until we have done enough damage to hurt self-esteem and to create victims. It is easy to see how parents can be tricked into believing that hitting works. A slight, innocuous tap on a three year old often produces desired results quickly; the child improves his behavior. As a result, this parent is reinforced or rewarded for striking her child. The parent, at wit's end, believes she has finally found something that works. The parent's belief that hitting works is strongly reinforced. But teenagers do not respond to a small tap; they require a much more severe blow to get results. It is also easy to understand how with no other skills to fall back on this parent has trapped herself into leveling a blow to the head to get a fifteen year old to behave. Thus we perceive how a parent who unknowingly or unwittingly began to change her young child's behavior with a very small tap is, over the years, lulled and seduced into hitting harder and harder. Bear in mind, calling a three year old naughty may help improve his behavior, but much stronger and uglier words will be needed for an older child or adolescent. Damage to self-esteem occurs from the first put-down. Sooner or later, the small belittling grows to verbal and emotional abuse. Again, parents travel down a steadily steeper path into harm. No one knows exactly when crossing the line into physical and emotional abuse occurs, only that it does. Far too often.

The questions that frequently punished children ask themselves when they choose how to behave are, "Who's looking?" "Will I get caught?" and "Is it worth it?" Frequently, the answers are respectively, "No one," "Probably not," and "Probably." These children need *constant* monitoring. They do not own their behavior; they just *pay* for it - occasionally. When the drug dealer approaches these children, they look around to see if there is a police officer nearby. If not, they feel free to go ahead. After all, "I'll never get caught" is a common belief system of adolescents. (A friend of mine tells me that teenagers believe in the 3 I's: they believe they are Immune, Immortal, and Infertile!!) Let us imagine this child driving through your child's school zone. As he enters, he ponders, "Who's looking?" (probably no one who can arrest him), "Will I get caught?" (probably not), and "Is it worth it?" (probably, it's only a ticket). "So why not?" Using these faulty principles and reasoning, there is no reason to slow down.

The other message noted earlier that this type of child sends is "You can't get to me." Not only do we lose our effectiveness with these children, they may become lost to us emotionally or physically. Families become divided and filled with resentment. These families can become "holiday" families who only see each other on special holidays because they have to. They become families who really don't like each other and that is very sad.

Lastly, let us address the common question, "Shouldn't people pay for what they have done?" It depends on what is meant by pay. Live with fair consequences, make amends, learn the lesson involved - these are forms of helpful discipline. If these are your idea of pay, then the answer is yes. But if by pay you mean suffer violence, be hurt emotionally, feel vengeful, then the answer is no. Mean, evil, wicked people can pay - be punished - despite the fact that sociologists have long recognized that even severe punishment is seldom a deterrent. Murderers, rapists, perpetrators of heinous crimes can pay for their evil deeds. But children who misbehave (for example, do not pick up their toys) are neither criminals nor evil people. Children need to *learn*. Our job as parents is not to wound or damage them, but to guide them to health. Criminals pay; children learn, so that our children will never need to pay for crimes as adults or as children.

> ☞   When a child does cross over into severely maladaptive or malicious behavior, the child and his family are in need of immediate psychological help and intervention. Seek professional diagnosis if you are unsure.

Since our society has used punishment for some time, what price has our nation paid? There are increasing, almost unbelievable numbers of abused children today. The Children's Defense Fund's "The State of America's Children Yearbook 1997" listed 3,111,000 children reported abused or neglected. Which is worse - emotional or physical abuse? I do not know. They both destroy - one the soul, the other the body. In America, a child is gunned down and killed every 90 minutes.[6] As a nation, we must stop teaching children that violence and aggression are acceptable; we must stop teaching that one person has the right to hurt another because he does not like what he does; and we must stop teaching that violence and hurting others is an acceptable way to solve problems. We are finally beginning to accept that men and women do not have the right to strike or physically or psychologically abuse one another. When will we extend this protection to children? We can neither condone nor continue the violence done to our children. It is this generation's responsibility, *our* responsibility to stop passing on pain, abuse, and violence. We must become transition figures, someone who stops the transmission of negative tendencies from one generation to the next.

How else do we pay for our continuing punishment strategies? More people solving problems with aggression means fewer having and using good problem-solving skills. Many families are emotionally or physically wounded because of long-held resentment, and grandparents rarely or never see their grandchildren, let alone their own children. This lack of connectedness between people, and lowered emotional health, are the prices exacted.

Discipline - The Road Less Traveled

Two roads diverged in a wood, and I -
I took the one less traveled by,
and that has made all the difference.
    - Robert Frost, "The Road Not Taken"

What type of discipline system can accomplish what we and our children need? What is our vision, our path? It is discipline in its original meaning. The root word of discipline is *disciplina*, meaning teaching or learning. Disciple (learner) stems from the same word. Discipline at first meant the teaching or guidance we give to children. Discipline involved lessons: life skills lessons, lessons in correct moral principles, lessons in respectful communication, and lessons in healthy relationships. It did not mean make them behave so we look good. It did not mean pay them to be good. It did not mean make them pay. *It recognized that children arrive in this world uncivilized and require substantial instruction.* What is the most fundamental principle we need to teach?

You are responsible for what you choose to do and for what happens to you and others as a result of your decisions and actions.

DISCIPLINE	
Belief	Question or Statement by Child
Self-discipline is the goal. ⇨	"Is this a right or good thing for me to do?"
You are responsible for what you choose to do and for what happens as a result. ⇨	"What could happen if I choose to do this?"

To be a man is to be responsible. - Antoine de Saint-Exupéry

Self-discipline is what we seek to encourage in our children, the ability to discipline themselves, to own their actions, to make good decisions and then take the right action. Sooner or later, we will not be around to discipline them, and they must pick up this critical task themselves.

A child who has been brought up with this type of system learns to ask himself, "Is this a right or good thing for me to do? What could possibly happen if I choose to do this?" These questions can guide children to think ahead to consequences and effects rather than just immediate behavior. As well, they help place ownership of actions squarely where they belong - with the individual, in this case, the child.

When a drug dealer approaches a child who asks himself these questions, the answers (prison, loss of everyone and everything valued, death) completely foil the drug dealer. The drug dealer does not stand a chance, but our children and our nation do. When this type of teen is driving through a school zone, she can and does choose to slow down to minimize her risk of hurting a child; no visible police car is necessary for this responsible behavior to take place. These young adults choose not to drink and drive; they know how to designate a driver for their own good, and ours I might add. In short, they make good behavioral choices, good for themselves, good for us, and good for others. As well, children growing up with true discipline have learned excellent problem-solving skills, respectful communication, responsiveness to others, and responsibility. We need people like this.

A true DISCIPLINE (using the term strictly from here on) system leads to self-discipline, is based on correct principles, is investment discipline, and constitutes **DISCIPLINE FOR LIFE**. It also changes and improves present behavior as well. This system teaches each child what he or she needs to learn to function as an emotionally healthy, humane, responsible adult.

Fortunately, each child arrives with some life lessons already or nearly learned. Some children will never be helpless victims. They look after themselves and their needs without being taught. They seem intuitively to know that they can think and do for themselves. The other side of the coin is that these children frequently need to learn sensitivity and awareness of others. Another group is much more vulnerable to helplessness. Still others seem innately to recognize and consider other people's feelings and needs. We do not need to teach them responsiveness or empathy. Still others seem to more easily accept ownership of actions; their counterparts fight it tooth and nail. Why do children arrive in this world in so many different guises? I believe it is one of life's little jokes on us. Any parent of more than one child and every teacher recognizes these two truths (or jokes on us) about children. First, *no two children are alike*. Some are easy; some more difficult. Some are like us; some are very different. Each has a different personality, different skills, and different strengths and weaknesses. In short, each child has different life lessons to learn. Secondly, each learns differently. Thus life's second joke is that *what works with one child does not necessarily work with another*. We need many, many skills, and we must be adept with each. We must be extremely skilled to accommodate any given child, let alone a number of them. Understanding the features of a true DISCIPLINE system will help us.

ONE GOAL FOR DISCIPLINE

1 Goal for Discipline	Lead to SELF-DISCIPLINE • by providing opportunities for learning • by allowing the child to be and feel responsible for his behavior "What lesson needs to be learned here; how can I best teach it to this child?"

The goal for discipline then is to teach children and to lead them increasingly toward self-discipline. We do this by regarding misbehavior as opportunities for our teaching and their learning. Furthermore, we not only allow but actively encourage a child to be responsible, and to feel responsible, for his behavior. Discipline first and foremost asks the questions:

What lesson needs to be learned here? How can I best teach it to this child?

Notice that I am not suggesting the more common question, "How can I get this child to behave?" This is the mistake many of us have made for far too long. We have focused only on changing behavior. We have judged our success only by how quickly negative behavior changed. We forgot about teaching lifelong lessons. We forgot about teaching correct principles. And we forgot about the future.

TWO INGREDIENTS OF DISCIPLINE

2 Ingredients of Discipline	Maintain the DIGNITY - of both parties • by using the Golden Rule and Respectful Language Require AUTHORITY - • "Don't start what you can't finish!" • Say what you mean; Mean what you say; Take action stated

Two essential components of discipline are: maintaining respect and carrying authority. Treating children with respect is another way of describing what I mean by maintaining dignity. It is critical that we safeguard dignity, both our own and the child's, when we discipline a child. Otherwise, we tend to create resistance rather than cooperation. Consider the last time someone treated you disrespectfully or violated your dignity. What was your response? Did you like them less, cooperate less? Perhaps you even chose to work against them - enjoyed working against them? Further, did your self-esteem suffer? To destroy a child's self-esteem is never the goal of discipline. When we add the ingredient of respect to our dealings with our children, we are acting upon the principle of the Golden Rule: "Do unto others as you would have them do unto you." We all want to be treated respectfully. Not only do we experience more cooperation, we model a correct principle for all of their life's relationships. One of my favorite definitions of respect is by Bernard Malamud:

"Respect is what you have to have in order to get it."

We will have to *give* respect before we can expect to *receive* respect. The next section, Gaining Cooperation Without Losing Your Mind, addresses using the Golden Rule and Respect as a Second Language.

Please notice that I did not say the ingredient we need is being nice. Although being nice belongs in our relationships with our children and with others (I, personally, like nice people), it tends to get in the way of discipline. We become so passive, so gentle, so nice, that we make requests when direction would be more helpful; in short, we are wishy-washy and namby-pamby, weak when we need to be strong. Or we try to be nice, be nice, be nice again, and then we let them have it because nice hasn't worked. We go literally from zero to ninety in twelve seconds. Respect covers the tools and lessons we need.

"We are permissive until we can't stand our kids, then autocratic until we can't stand ourselves." - Unknown

The second ingredient of discipline is our ability to establish and carry authority, authority based on expertise or position, not power or fear. There is a difference between the unhealthy fear of being hurt emotionally or physically and the healthy fear of what someone you respect will think or feel, or fear of hurting others or oneself.

Authority, however, is necessary for effectiveness. In other words, discipline without authority is ineffective. We cannot afford to be nice but ineffective. "Don't start what you can't finish!" is an important factor in maintaining authority. To be effective in discipline, it is critical that we are able to consistently follow through with the three steps to maintaining authority:

Say what you mean - respectfully
Mean what you say - remember what you started
Take action stated when necessary

Whenever we do not follow through and finish discipline we have started, we teach children to test us. This is neither good nor fun for us. Since children don't know whether or not we might follow through on what we have said, they would be foolish not to try to get away with something. Earlier it was mentioned that we need to be aware of Skinner's operant conditioning principles functioning in our lives. Here is a prime example from research:

When pigeons were rewarded with food for pecking a certain spot, they learned to peck at the right place when they were hungry. Then the researchers tried to get rid of or extinguish this behavior. The pigeons who had been reinforced at consistent or fixed intervals (every peck, or every 3 pecks, or every 20 pecks) soon gave up. They learned when it was futile to keep trying. However, the researchers found that it was extremely difficult to extinguish pecking behavior with the pigeons who had been intermittently reinforced (food at random intervals - sometimes at 1 peck, sometimes after 13 pecks, sometimes after 5 pecks). These pigeons never knew when the food would come and thus had no way of learning when it was time to quit or when it was foolish to continue trying. The pigeons had learned to be persistent, stubborn even, in their behavior.

Gambling is another excellent example of an intermittently reinforced behavior which can be subsequently difficult to eliminate. When we sometimes follow through and sometimes do not, we place our children in an intermittent reinforcement situation. After all, getting away with something is usually rewarding. The resultant "testing and pushing to the limit" behavior is inordinately difficult to extinguish. We would benefit by following through each time we discipline and finishing what we start. Testing becomes a pointless and, therefore, foolish thing to do.

Please note that never was it stated that it is necessary to discipline every incident - only that we must follow through with what we started. Choose your battles wisely. But, once we have chosen to start discipline but have not followed through, we have not done what we said we would. We overlook that we have virtually lied to the child and lost their trust. Our word is not good; we cannot be trusted. This can be damaging to any relationship. Distrust is toxic to relationships and returns to haunt us when our children believe it is not necessary for them to be trustworthy.

I talk with more and more parents who have difficulty following through. They start out saying, "no, you can't stay up any later," and end up allowing the child another hour or two. They say, "no cookie, no cookie, no cookie - okay, but just two." Indulging children because we are too weak or too weary to follow through is very unhelpful to our children and threatens both our relationship and our ability to be effective; in short, our authority is diminished. Please see the section on Being Told No and Indulgence in Life Lessons.

Discipline requires both components: discipline without respect generates resistance, disrespect, and emotional ill health; discipline without authority is rarely effective.

THREE CRITICAL LIFE BELIEFS

3 Critical Life Beliefs	I like myself I can think and do for myself I can solve problems

Two of the critical life beliefs and a revised version of the third belief Barbara Coloroso describes in her seminar are woven throughout this discipline system. Liking ourselves is, of course, critical and colors perceptions, feelings, and deeds. Being and feeling capable are also key ingredients to our perception of ourselves and others. We all, children and adults, need to learn that we can solve problems, that we can seek and receive help from others, and offer and give help to others. Later, when we look at building self-esteem, we will again see the importance of helping children develop these beliefs about themselves. These form the foundation for self-esteem. When discipline is grounded in these beliefs, we build rather than destroy self-esteem with our discipline. None of us had children or chose to work with them to make them feel bad about themselves. How we discipline will be a significant factor affecting self-esteem, for it is during discipline that we are frequently at our worst.

FOUR STEPS TO DISCIPLINE

4 Steps to Disciplinary Action	Determine the lesson Identify the problem respectfully Take action when necessary Evaluate: lessons learned, feelings generated, outcome

1. Determine the lesson.

This is the step that advances discipline beyond the "change behavior now" level and moves it into a higher, more beneficial, long-term level. The single most important task adults do during discipline is to ask themselves the questions:

What lesson needs to be learned here? How can I best teach it to this child?

Asking these questions sets us on the correct path and helps us stay there. We move into investment discipline and DISCIPLINE FOR LIFE. Determining the lesson is absolutely essential.

Asking ourselves what we are about to teach keeps us in the realm of DISCIPLINE FOR LIFE, or true discipline. It is always important to ask this relevant question, or one of its various forms: "What lesson needs to be learned?" or "What life lesson is this child missing here?" or "What flawed principle is this child operating from?" or "What correct principle does this child need to learn?" The answer to any of these questions directs or guides discipline and helps us head in a helpful direction.

2. Identify the problem respectfully and with authority.

It is here where we are most likely to create resistance rather than desired cooperation. It is of utmost importance that we think before we speak. We must decide what we want to say (what is the real problem) and how we want to say it (respectfully and directly).

3. Take the action stated when necessary.
This is where we become effective without being nasty. It is also the step we seem to begrudge, despite the fact that we chose to learn much of what we know the hard way, through experience. We did not always listen to our parents and teachers either. (You, of course, immediately stopped seeing a friend or romantic interest the moment your parents disapproved. I don't think so!) Children also choose to learn this way.

4. Finally, don't forget to evaluate:
- The lessons and principles learned - Did the child learn what was important?
- Feelings generated - How do we both feel?
- Outcome - Was it effective? If it did not work, it does not count for much no matter how good it sounded in theory.

Experts: The Ideas are Theirs; the Decisions are Yours!

When my children were young, my husband could always tell when I had read another book on child rearing because I would have visibly changed my tactics. I had forgotten that it is my responsibility not just to seek out information, but also to evaluate it. *Each of us is ultimately responsible for how we choose to discipline our children - no one else is or can be.*

I have a very clear memory of a parent in a workshop who was distraught with her teenager whom she could not handle. She was begrudging the fact that spanking no longer worked. In frustration, she said, "But my minister told me to spank; he said it was okay to spank." No one can give you permission; no one else owns this important decision. Only you can give yourself permission. Each of us owns our choices. So let us set ourselves free from the experts forever; let us remove ourselves from any "You should," "You should never," and "Oh, by the way, we're not doing that anymore." We will continue to use the experts for ideas, thoughts, and more rapid understanding - but never for permission or ultimate ownership. The buck, indeed, stops with you.

It is absolutely essential that we are able to judge any system of child rearing and any technique or tip. By slightly altering the question in the first step of discipline, we can accomplish this feat. We need to ask ourselves the following questions: What principle is this system or technique based on? Is this a principle I believe in? Is it a principle that is correct and healthy? Is it a principle I want my child to base his life on? Is this a principle I want to see used in my future? What lessons or life lessons will be learned? If the answers are positive, you can be comfortable and confident in proceeding. If the answers are negative, it is time to look for other solutions.

These questions are helpful in determining which of the experts' ideas and books you value and which you do not find helpful. What we seek is wisdom, not expertise. With these questions, we can find and identify wisdom.

4:
How Do I Decide What Lesson Needs to be Learned?

Determining what lesson is needed is more difficult than it would seem. Time and time again in parent groups, I have listened as parents struggle with what lesson is suggested by a child's behavior. And what is the most important, the deepest level lesson which needs to be taught? Almost always at least one aspect of the lesson necessary is the ownership of behavior and its consequences. Sometimes that is the most important lesson; sometimes it is only the constant, ever-present smaller aspect. Sometimes the lesson changes right during discipline; a child walks away from us or shows us with a disrespectful gesture or phrase that she does not have to listen to us. As long as a child believes you have nothing of import to say, you will have no effect whatsoever, regardless of how wonderful your words are. The lesson has changed from the issue at hand to yes, I do have important things to teach you. Parents must learn to identify not just the original problem but also when the problem changes.

Remember, our job is to teach the lesson; it is the child's job to learn it. As Jean Clarke[7] phrases it, "Parents are responsible for the process. Children are responsible for the outcome." Each child learns at his own pace. It is my experience that each child has a number of lessons she learns fairly easily and quickly, and then there are the 1,000 time lessons which haunt every child and vary from child to child. This is the oft repeated lesson where we feel as though we are beating our heads against the wall, where we question the child's intelligence or ability to learn ("She can't be this stupid, I know it") and where our frustration is sorely tested. And remember, too, that each child arrives in this world with a few lessons already known. It is not uncommon for a first born child to know from the start how to look after herself, yet have no idea that other children may have feelings, desires, and needs too. The first is a given lesson or piece of information, the other will require a 1,000 time lesson. Another child may from the beginning feel other's pain and have empathy without ever being taught. Yet this same child may not protect himself, will let others take advantage of him over and over and never react. There is no predicting what you will get.

I have a theory that babies-to-be are categorized and stored somewhere up above in bins according to their personality and the lessons needed. The first child we get is simply the next bin due, but after that they use computers to track us and send us babies from a different bin each time. That is why no one ever gets two of the same kind of child. And the keepers have strange senses of humor. I envision them up there saying, "Ooh, look it's Mrs. Smith again. She did so well with that Bin 7 baby we sent her. Let's see how she does with a Bin 13!" Or "Let's send her one just like herself, or one totally different, or better still, one like her husband or mother. Won't this be fun to watch?" Perhaps they have perverse senses of humor. This is only a theory, of course.

To help sort out various behaviors and their lessons, let us look at some common lessons which children need and various ways we can teach them. This is a new way of thinking; it takes some practice and some guidance.

Common Situations and Accompanying Lessons

A CHILD REFUSES TO PICK UP TOYS

A very young child often only needs the lesson that this is expected behavior. Everyone who plays picks up. And I don't care whether you played with it last or not; I am too smart to go there. Encouraging positive habits, such as picking up after you have played, prevents discipline problems and is a wonderful investment of time and energy. Good habits make life more pleasant and easier; they smooth the way. Parents are frequently amazed at what children will do without argument when they know it is expected behavior. I have watched guests be impressed with my own children clearing not only their own dishes, but also those of the guests after a meal. It is a simple habit, established early. As Anderson says, "Make an ally of habit" for your children and yourself. Be vigilant in preventing bad habits from developing. Bad habits are difficult to break. Remember, habits are simply repeated patterns of behavior which will help or plague you.

An older child may need the lesson which says it is your job or responsibility to pick up after yourself, to put back what you have messed up, or perhaps not to expect others to take care of your business. Please see the sections regarding Disciplinary Consequences or Remedy and Amends. Too often parents will themselves pick up in frustration and because it is easier and quicker for them to do so. They teach an unhelpful lesson which will return to haunt them. That is, if I don't take care of business, someone else (more responsible) will take care of it for me. In business or in any workplace, and in marriages, this attitude is exceedingly irritating to those of us who are responsible. It is also an unhealthy way to operate one's life.

A CHILD HAS BEEN TOLD NO

It cannot be over-emphasized that parents must tell children no for their safety, for our sanity, and for the child's own good. Constantly giving in to a child teaches the child that life will and should always go her way. It is the quickest route to classically spoiling (an interesting and apt description) a child. This is a path I see increasing numbers of parents traveling. What contributes to this? Many parents feel guilty for working or being away so much, they lack confidence, and they indulge because "I love him so much." Any of these issues influencing your life must be addressed before you can be a helpful and emotionally healthy parent. If you feel guilty about not spending enough time with your child, adjust your schedule, be it work or outside activities, to allow as much time as possible with your children. If you feel guilty, look hard at the reasons. Change what can be changed (this may take effort, sacrifice, and honest appraisal) and learn to accept the rest.

A parent who lacks confidence in his ability to parent may also overindulge children and fail to say no at appropriate times because she is afraid or too weak to refuse her child something. This parent may also fail to take appropriate action because she does not know what it is. Learning helpful skills and techniques is critical. These skills help build confidence in parenting. Very often, I see many parents who simply do not feel comfortable telling a child no. The child fusses or becomes unhappy. We act because, after all, isn't it the parent's job to bend around the child? Only sometimes. Children must learn that life is not always going to go their way; they need to develop coping skills for the inevitable frustrations life brings and develop their ability to handle frustration without blowing up or dissolving into tears. These are critical life lessons that hold them in good stead later in their lives. As a child ages, it is important to learn how to handle disappointment and adversity with grace. (For many of us, this is a lifelong lesson.) No child should ever be without this lesson. Parents who cannot tell a child no must relearn what true love is. Love is putting someone else's best interest first; it is not giving them any and all things they desire.

We must learn to do what is right and best for our children in the long run, not the short run.

There is a definite difference between being good *to* and good *for* a child. The parent who loves his child chooses good *for* over good *to* every time. Being good to a child is easy and fun; everyone enjoys this. Difficulties arise when good *to* conflicts with good *for*. For example, if a child asks for a cookie right before dinner is served, the parent who can only choose good *to* will give him a cookie and disrupt the child's nutrition and dinner habits. The parent who chooses to be good *for* the child, tells her no and sticks to her guns. This parent has taught that rules ("Cookies are for after dinner") are important and need to be followed; this is the precursor of the lesson that laws are important and apply to each of us. This parent provides much needed structure; rules stay the same for long lengths of time so that you can count on them. As well, this parent teaches her child that his word is good, that he can be trusted (no waffling), and that he is confident he knows about this and other issues. This parent's knowledge and wisdom can be counted upon for guidance. When a parent starts out saying one thing ("no cookie") and ends up doing another ("cookie now"), he teaches a child his word is not good, he cannot be trusted; this is undermining to healthy relationships. Another potential consequence of this is that the child also learns to push and test (becomes a demander), to cry (a whiner), or to manipulate (a con artist) to get his way. These are not helpful lessons or life skills. Please remember what a disservice it is to give in to a child for the wrong reasons.

Too often over-indulgence of children leads to a family which is child-driven. Families need to be parent-driven, especially when children are quite young. This is not to say that no decision may be the child's. Early on, we want to help them learn to think, to make decisions and choices, but always these choices must be age appropriate. A young child may choose which pajamas he will wear to bed, but not whether or when he will go to bed. He may decide which book to have read, but not how many or for how long. Parents often abdicate their decision-making role too much and too often and to the detriment of the child, themselves, and the family as a whole. I watched a mother and father struggle with a 2½ year old one day while I was trying to answer their questions concerning this toddler. Mother, quite appropriately, did not want to speak about the child in front of the child. The child, however, would not stay put to watch his video and kept returning to his mother (of course). So Father intervened and tried to distract him, all to no avail, as long as "number one" (mom) was in eyesight. This child interrupted repeatedly. Each time Mother picked him up, loved him, and then gave him back to Dad who then cajoled or enticed him to do something else for a time. Both parents knew it would be best to take the child outside so that Mom could talk with me freely and without stress. What can be worse than having to discipline your child in front of a parenting expert? And they asked the child a number of times if he would like to go outside and see various things. Each time the toddler said no. This would not have been an option for me; I would never have asked. I simply would have taken him outside, protests or not. This toddler was in control of the entire situation. He was also the only one in the room who had no clue why Mom needed time alone with me, how important that was. These parents were allowing him to make a decision for which he was in no way qualified. The only information with which he had to make this decision was that he loves to be with mommy. Giving in, in this situation, is bending over backwards foolishly for a child and giving the child authority where it is not appropriate. This child is learning that he should (because he does) control the family (and others), and that his decisions need only be based on his immediate needs and desires alone, and that neither of his parent's needs are important. Again, these are unhelpful lessons.

Parents give in to a child's demands, crying, or tantrums and set the child up to believe that whatever he wants is what he should and will get. Giving in to the child may stop the tears of the present, but it also certainly contributes to the tears of the future. Give a child what you had planned, what is appropriate and his due; do not give more because his behavior turned ugly or cute and appealing (crass manipulation). If a child learns to be a whiner, a princess, or a demander, the world will shun her and disappoint her; her life, though fine, will seem empty and unfulfilling. How will she learn that other people's interests are important, as important as her own when decisions are being made. What type of student, worker, spouse, friend, and parent will this child become? Sometimes we must fight our own personality leanings to become a better parent. We may become a better person in the process. We teach our children, but our children teach us much as well, generally some of our hardest lessons of all. See the sections on Disciplinary Consequences and Maintaining Authority.

BEDTIME
The keys to getting children to go to bed and stay in bed include habits, rituals, and schedules. I don't mean going to sleep; you can lead a child to bed, but you can't make them sleep. Whenever possible it is helpful to keep children on a predictable, regular, daily schedule. Establishing a clear routine is perhaps most important with regard to bedtime. The lesson children learn is that all of these, the habits, rituals, and schedule,

help keep things in the household, and the family, running smoothly. Knowing what is going to happen is very comforting for children and grown-ups. Children also learn to count on this structure to be there and to work. Dependability is important.

Remember, the goal is to keep them in bed, not to make them sleep. However, helping them to relax is important so they can fall asleep when they are tired. First, ensure that your child gets enough exercise during the day. Remember, watching television or playing video games is not exercise. Second, teach your children that although their minds know no limits, their bodies do. A parent may read to a child to help calm him down; he will often take time to listen to the day's worries, accomplishments, interests, and stories in order to connect with the child and show value for him. The child, having had time, interest, and affection lavished on him, needs now to occupy himself. Talking books, tapes both of stories or familiar songs, stuffed animals, and pretend games are all appropriate activities in bed before falling asleep. And the child needs to know that should he get up he will, without fail, be returned to bed. He needs to understand that at bedtime he belongs in bed, quiet and preparing to sleep. Please see Disciplinary Consequences and Outsmart Them.

CHORES

Doing chores is a very important part of growing up and being a member of a family. Even very young toddlers can do small chores such as carrying napkins to the table or picking up toys. As children age, the number of chores required of them should increase. Children learn three very important lessons from doing chores. First, they learn what their job description as members of a family group is: to contribute freely (voluntarily and with no pay) to the group's maintenance and progress. Every true family member must do so. Please see the section on Encourage Each to Contribute. Thus you first learn to take care of your own dishes; later you learn to clear or wash all of the dishes.

Second, a child learns that "work is a blessing."[8] This currently seems to have become a novel concept, a forgotten precept in our society. Work is essential to physical and emotional development. It is also essential to life. Someone has to work and produce; you can't depend upon someone else to take care of you. Attitudes towards work develop early. Life is so much easier when we realize that work is a necessary and important component of everyone's life, something to be embraced not shunned. Woe to the mother who always says, "You go play. Mother will do the work." Why should anyone be exempt from work? What message does that send to a child? Please see the section on Disciplinary Consequences and Anger Without Destruction for strategies to get children to do their chores.[9]

Third, our children need to learn how to do chores, all chores. How else can one run a household? All of our children must learn self-sufficiency. One of my finer moments as a mother came the day we visited the dorm where my older son would live in his freshman year of college. As we toured, the guide took us into the laundry room, and pointed out not only the washers and dryers, but also the large, bold instructions for running each. She turned to Kris and said, "Here are the instructions - in case your mom didn't teach you to do laundry." Without missing a beat, Kristopher responded, "Oh, she taught me alright." Of course I did, repeatedly. Who wants to send a child off to college or work needing to call home to find out why his underwear is pink? Or more importantly, missing the self-esteem and confidence that come from knowing how to do basic tasks?

We owe it to our children to provide them with the knowledge of how to perform, and take care of, all household chores. Their autonomy depends on it. They cannot expect their future spouses to do it all. Please remember that teaching each chore requires patience, repetition, encouragement, and well-earned appreciation for a job well done or effort given. Please see the section on Take Time to Teach.

Most children love to help. They build self-esteem, confidence, and competence through their efforts. Mastering new skills or helping others simply feels good. Do not deny your children this experience.

ALLOWANCE

Questions about allowances are some of the most frequently asked in my parent education seminars. The first question is whether or not children should receive one. The answer is definitely yes. The reason for this is that children need to have money of their own so that they can learn to mismanage it. After they learn how to blow it, and they will, believe me, they can begin to learn how to spend, budget, and save it wisely. In short, they will discover how to handle money. Children are bombarded with commercial messages to buy products, to buy them now, to buy them to have eternal happiness; they must find their way through this morass of commercialism and greed and instant gratification. Most children handle money very badly in the beginning. They will give in to the pressure of desire and spend it like drunken sailors only to discover shortly that they *need* something else and now have no money. How disappointing - and how enlightening. Impulse buying gives way to smart shopping, saving, and better decision-making.

Giving children an allowance sets up a wonderful disciplinary tool as well. Whenever a child asks for something while you are out, you can always respond, "Of course, you may have that; you have money." Very quickly my children discovered that what they would spend my money on and their money on were very different things.

The second question asked is whether or not allowance should be linked to chores. Absolutely not. Children need to do chores for the family as members of the family. First, as discussed earlier, so that they feel they belong. Second, if you link chores and allowance, you will one day face a teenager whose turn it is to take out the trash. He will reach into his pockets, find enough money to go to the movies and have popcorn, and tell you he doesn't need to take out the trash because he doesn't need the money. You can take it out. Not a pretty picture, but illustrative of how we set things up to teach lessons we never meant to teach. This teen is right; he does not need to take out the trash according to this system. Let me be very clear. My children are going to do chores period. And I am never going to pay a child for removing trash, making his bed, helping with dinner, learning to do laundry, etc.

I am sometimes asked if this is giving a child money for nothing. Yes, it is. And you do it all the time. You were going to buy your child some toys, some discretionary items. Instead of your making and handling all of the money decisions, let your child practice some decision-making by giving him the money up front. I also advocate teaching children about free enterprise and work for pay. There are tasks at our house that I would pay anyone, including my children, to do: washing windows or cleaning my car, for example. They can earn money starting at home. But the vast majority of income sources need to come from outside. And yes, you do get paid for your job. Shouldn't we pay children for their "job" - going to school, for doing well, for getting good grades? No. First of all, school is their work not their job. Second, at your job, you provide a service or product and get paid for it. At school, teachers get paid; they provide a service. Your children receive a service, an education. When I go to the doctor, she gets paid. Even if I am a good patient and take all my medicine, I still don't get paid because I was the one who received the service and performed expected behavior which, by the way, benefitted me. I get well sooner. If our children work hard in school, they get smarter. What a great deal!

The final question involves how much allowance and when. I would not start an allowance until children show an interest in and understanding of money, usually around five or six years of age. Amount depends on: 1) your income, what you can afford and 2) what the child will be responsible for buying. At first, start with fun items only. But as they age, they need to learn how to shop for clothes (you were going to buy some anyway) and other necessary items. As they become teens, this allows you to tell them that they have so much money for clothes; they can buy one pair of designer jeans or three pairs of plain ones - their choice. By the time they start work or go to university, they will be ready to handle the demands (budgeting and record-keeping) of a checking account. Err on the side of too little money, not too much. It helps them find jobs and helps them to think twice about items like cigarettes and drugs. It also helps them learn the important lesson that money really doesn't grow on trees.

QUARRELING

Quarreling between children offers us the opportunity to teach a number of important lessons. The first is that it is each child's job to get along. Period. Their removal from the group is one the easiest and most productive methods of discipline for this digression. It demonstrates to a child that being with others is a privilege which is earned and maintained by getting along. Getting along does not mean we must give in to everyone else; it means we must learn how to disagree with ideas or actions without getting contentious or belligerent. Of course, this means parents must also model this behavior with spouses, children, friends, coworkers, etc. It is especially important that at least one parent remains calm in any situation where the other has become disturbed. The section on Respect as a Second Language provides many suggestions and examples of ways to speak directly without becoming disrespectful or ugly.

Another lesson which may need to be learned is how to get along when problems arise. It is unfair to expect young children, or children unexposed to good problem-solving skills, to know how to do this. Sitting down with two or more children who are having difficulty sorting things out and walking them through problem solving not only teaches children that they must learn to solve their own problems (because you do not solve these for them), but also teaches them helpful problem-solving and negotiating skills they will need later in life. The sections on Problem Solving and Problem? Think! offer methods for teaching problem-solving skills. It is important for children to flex and strengthen their child-size problem-solving skills on child-size problems. It is also critical that a parent guide and teach these skills so that brute force, verbal coercion, and manipulation do not take place.

Another lesson quarrelsome children may require is another part of their sibling job description; it is your job as a sibling (or friend) to treat others only in ways which maintain or increase their self-esteem. Put-downs, belittling, sarcasm, name-calling are all off limits because they are hurtful and reduce good feelings. The section on Remedy and Amends discusses one method of teaching and handling this lesson. This lesson clearly includes the lesson of the Golden Rule, treat others only as you yourself wish to be treated. It is that simple - in theory; actually practicing the concept is far more difficult.

HITTING, HURTING, AND REAL FIGHTING

Let's face it, children fight. Occasionally, we let them spend too much time with each other, or some seem to have a natural proclivity for it. Some do not know how to handle frustration, and others just want what they want and have found uncivilized ways to get it. First and foremost we must teach children that hurting of any kind (physical, verbal, emotional, social) is wrong. This means we must model this principle. We must teach them that they do not have the right to hurt others. The sections on Rules, Policies, and Rights, Anger Without Destruction, and Disciplinary Consequences, all address strategies for teaching this important lesson.

Many children have no idea how to handle their own frustration and disappointment when things or people do not go their way. They must learn to recognize their own frustration and how to express it appropriately. Next they must learn to tolerate frustration and not go ballistic over every little thing. As well, they must master alternative methods for dealing with people and things that do not do what they want them to do. We call these social skills. Every child must spend time with other children to learn how to handle peers, and must spend time with younger and older children as well as adults (who are hopefully modeling excellent social, getting-along, and courtesy skills) to learn "dealing with people" skills. In addition, one cannot simply tell a child not to hit; we must teach her that there are other skills to negotiate life's pitfalls; otherwise, she is most likely to revert to hitting which may get her her way but causes a host of other problems. Again, we must teach and coach these skills using life's never ending opportunities. The sections on Outsmart Them, Give Alternatives, Disciplinary Consequences, Use Humor, and Determine What Child Needs offer various techniques.

HOMEWORK, MOTIVATION, GRADES, AND SCHOOL CONCERNS

Everyone seems to have one child, or at least know one child, who from Grade One was able to responsibly handle getting homework done and back to school on time. And then there are the rest of the kids. Some even get it right through elementary school and then seem to lose the skill during middle school or high school. Others never seem to have it. What do all of these children need to learn? Every teacher knows. Every child must learn that he owns his homework (the doing and the getting back to school on time). His mother does not; his teacher does not. To paraphrase an age-old adage, "You can lead a child to the desk, but you can't make him think!" And, you can't make him work. We are not helpless, however, and we do have a role to play. The "lead them to the desk" suggests the parent's role. We must supply support: "It's 5 o'clock," or "Yes, I will take you to the library." We must demonstrate problem solving: "How can you find time to get your school work done and go to baseball practice? Will you have to give up watching television?" or "How can you help yourself stay on task? Would a timer help?" We assist organization: there are supplies, a desk, and good lighting. And, we maintain and enforce structure: "When your homework is done, you may do what you like or go to practice, etc." The children supply the work and the motivation. The earlier a child learns this and begins to own his homework, and this includes asking for help when needed, the easier it is for everyone. As long as homework is more important to the parent than to the child, the child need not acquire any motivation of his own. Techniques can be found in the sections on Disciplinary Consequences, Problem Solving and Learned Helplessness.

Motivation is an internal product. We can create challenge, interest and purpose, but not the push to actually do it. That must come from inside the child. The child's level of self-esteem, their early teaching, and their participation in discussions and modeling of the importance of education and school, all affect real (internal) motivation. When parents demand, cajole, and try to force work, they adversely affect motivation. Please see the Building Self-esteem section, especially Descriptive Appreciation, Mistakes, and Descriptive Criticism, for additional information. Children motivate themselves. Don't you? The lesson children must learn is that motivation comes from inside themselves, not from any place else. External incentives (read bribes here) also prevent children from developing internal motivation. One father described to me that he was giving his first grade son an "incentive," one dollar for getting 100% on his weekly spelling test. He was somewhat disconcerted when I asked him what he thought this would cost him in fifth grade, let alone in high school. Please see the section on Rewards. Learning *is* important; what you know alters your life and life's opportunities. One can waste a life or use it. They were right: a mind is a terrible thing to waste. Teach your children this fact. And teach them only they can waste or use their own mind.

Most children will grapple with parental values about grades during their school career. Many, fortunately, choose middle school to do this. This is fortunate because no one (no employer and no college) ever asks you what your marks were in junior high school. These grades do not truly count towards anything later in life; poor junior high marks rarely come at long-term expense, and are a relatively cheap experiment. It is a good time to let the child see what it feels like not to do as well as he can. Usually, it does not feel very good, and this is an important life lesson. It is an excellent time to teach how to set goals at appropriate levels, how it feels to make or miss goals, and how to discover what hindered or helped you.

The most important thing a parent does when a report card comes home is allow the child to speak first. Bite your tongue. Let your child tell you how he feels about each grade, what caused it to be high or low, how she will handle the subject next time - less procrastination, actually do homework, get tutorial help, spend more time studying for tests, ask you to check homework before it is turned in. Please remember that your child simply saying, "I'll do better" is not a plan of action, and they need a definite plan with easy to follow steps. Please see the section on Teach Problem-Solving Skills in Learned Helplessness for additional information.

Most school concerns are best solved with a problem-solving conference which involves the teacher(s), parent(s), and student. Trying to solve a problem without the key figure, the child, is foolhardy. Generally, teachers and parents provide ideas, encouragement, and supportive actions; the student will actually be the person who takes the key action(s) to solve the problem. Try to use a perspective which looks after the child's best interests and which also must include the class' best interests. Regarding the parties involved as a team is most helpful. Don't allow yourself, as a team member, to be dragged into blaming and attacking. Too often I see parents and teachers become defensive, fail to understand the whole picture, and as a result, work against rather than with each other.

STEALING

Most children try stealing at least once. After all, stealing, getting something for nothing, is very tempting. The life lesson a child who steals needs to learn is that stealing is completely unacceptable; indeed, it is wrong. You do not have the right to take things which belong to another. No matter the inconvenience, ill-gotten goods must always be returned to their original owner with a heart-felt apology and promise never to steal again. No child does this easily; facing the music is very difficult and requires considerable courage. However, frequently one trial learning takes place. Under no circumstances can a child be allowed to keep the item; this would teach that at least sometimes one can get away with stealing. In this scenario, it would be foolish not to try again. This is a very risky and destructive lesson. Return the goods and, if impossible (the candy is already eaten), the child must replace them.

At age five, my son Kris swore he hadn't stolen a little Smurf figure, he had "found" it on the store floor. Since it was not in the box with the other Smurfs, he rationalized that he had not stolen, but found. As his four year old cousin Jenny and his three year old brother Tim and I walked down the hill, I discovered his stolen Smurf. After Kris' explanation, I calmly asked him if we had paid for it. Well, no, we had not, but ... but nothing. Throughout his insistence that he found the Smurf, I persisted in telling him that anything not paid for in a store is stolen goods. As we proceeded back up the hill to return the item to the store owner, Kristopher tearfully begged me not to make him talk to the owner and promised me he would never steal again. He has never been so heart-wrenching. We asked for the store owner. Tearfully, Kris confessed to her that he had taken the Smurf. Luckily for him, he happened to be dealing with a very respectful and understanding mother as well as store owner. She told him she did not like stealing and that if he was going to steal she did not want him in her store again - ever. However, if he could promise her he would never steal again, she would allow him in her store. She was firm, but kind. Kris promised he would not steal again. To this day, not only has he not stolen, as far as I know, his cousin and brother have not either. Vicarious learning also took place. One cannot always count on such an excellent reaction from a store owner. (This one is a great lady who later became my sister-in-law and Kristopher's aunt.) Regardless, it is still critical to have the child return the stolen goods.

Responsibility and Freedom

CHILDREN NEED TO LEARN TO HANDLE LIFE WITH EVER INCREASING RESPONSIBILITY

The lesson teens need to have learned before they are allowed to drive alone is that they do not have the right to risk lives, their own or others' lives. A teen who is caught or ticketed for speeding or driving carelessly loses the privilege of using the car - period. He has demonstrated irresponsibility which leads to restricted freedom. All children can begin to learn this important life lesson, even at very young ages. Handle your life (vehicles, physical actions, words, tools, toys, etc.) responsibly and continue to earn increasing freedom and privilege. Handle it irresponsibly and lose that freedom and privilege. Please see the story about Frankie in the section on Disciplinary Consequences.

This brings us to an explanation of how the whole system works, information which is helpful to every child. The good news is that each of them will give us an opportunity to share this with them. When our youngest son was twelve, he looked at me one day and in total frustration said, "I just want you off my case and out of my life." Sound familiar? Somehow, I found the truth and grace (rare for me) I needed. I looked him straight in the eyes and replied, "Tim, you do not seem to understand; we both want the same thing. I want off your case and out of your life." (First, I could be doing something else besides disciplining you, and second, the goal here is self-discipline which by definition includes me out of your life and off your case.) "I want these so much I am going to tell you how to get them. All you have to do is handle your life responsibly and I back out of it a step. Handle it again responsibly and I back out farther. You could choose to handle your life responsibly from this moment on and have me out of it. However (and the "however" was necessary because at twelve, we all know he could not pull this off), should you handle your life irresponsibly, you will have sent me an engraved invitation back into your life. And because I am your mother, I will accept it and I will be there. And despite the fact that I will do my best never to violate your dignity, you will question whether you ever want to invite me back in the same way ever again." This is my job, and I take it seriously. Can you hear the authority these words carry? And their truth? Bringing up children (from our perspective) and attaining freedom and autonomy (their perspective) can be as simple as this.

This brings us to the three most important life lessons we teach children. They underpin every single disciplinary action we take and every other lesson we teach. In short, our effectiveness as disciplinarians depends on these three lessons.

The Three Most Important Life Lessons a Child Needs to Learn

Each of these affects any disciplinary action you take:

1. LYING OR BREAKING TRUST

Most children try lying at least once; a number of them must revisit this lesson many times. In many ways, it would be foolish not to, for if you get away with the lie, you win - or seem to win. You at least seem to get away with what you have done. Children lie for the same reasons adults do: the punishment is too great for the crime or too huge to pay (they will not be allowed to go to a specific place); no one listens to their viewpoint so there is no reason to even try to make a point (think of marijuana use); dishonesty has worked in the past; they do not wish to own a specific misbehavior and/or be perceived as what they are (perhaps they failed a test); or, they do not understand the real consequences of lying and breaking trust with others. It is important that we as parents or teachers do not set children up to lie. Asking a child, with juice dripping all over her face and shirt, if she has gotten into the juice is our mistake. Telling her you see juice all over her shirt gives her an opportunity to confess. Never ask a child anything you already know. Let them know you know, without blaming. See Descriptive Language.

How can we reduce or eliminate lying? Always apply discipline, not punishment. Teach your child that the original misbehavior is never as bad as the lie; the lie is never worth it. Avoid over-exaggerated statements such as "I'll never believe you again," or "You always lie," and overly severe actions like grounding for a month or spanking. Try to discover why the child felt the need to lie and solve the problem.

Listening to children, and helping them understand that their viewpoint is important and worth taking time for, are very important. Please see Take Time to Listen. If a child knows you are willing to listen, she will talk to you. Taking time and energy to listen to your children during times of crisis as well as times of calm is an excellent investment which will repay you many times.

If a child lies and you know it, always address it. Do not pass over lying and do not let it work and become a viable technique. Every child must learn that he owns all of his behavior, whether anyone else knows about it or not, or whether he lies about it or not. And you are how you behave, not how you say you behave. Liars lie, thieves steal - by definition. Teach your child that everyone makes mistakes and that these become some of our best lessons in life, if we are willing to first own them. Only by owning the mistake and learning from it can we move on with our lives in an emotionally healthy manner.

Finally, the most important lesson concerning lying is that lying breaks trust. Relationships depend on trust. Lying shatters a relationship. And as my child, you are one person with whom I must have a relationship; you are entirely too important. The child's job becomes rebuilding trust. He does this by telling the truth repeatedly and without exception, and by doing what he says he will do. As the child rebuilds trust, the parent can begin to give back freedom. Freedom is also dependent upon trust. If I cannot trust you to do what you said you would, how can I possibly let you out of my sight? Breaking trust, shattering the parent-child relationship should be taught as a most destructive situation, and one to be avoided. Telling the truth is always better, no matter the original violation.

2. NOT WANTING TO OWN BEHAVIOR

Each of us would like to *act* like a jerk at times; interestingly, none of us wants to *be* a jerk though. Yet, these are inextricable; they go together. If you act like a jerk, you are one - at least for that time. (Please see Separate Deed from Doer for more information.) It should not then surprise us that children will find excuses, or try to distract us, and give reasons for why they shouldn't own their behavior. For example, a child throws a pair of scissors at another and counters with, "I didn't hit him though." Or a child responds with, "But Maria told me to do it," or "I didn't mean to." Each of these is an effort to not own behavior. Each time a child tries to get out of owning behavior, it is important to teach the lesson which underpins all of true discipline, *You are responsible for what you choose to do and for what happens to you and others as a result of your decisions and actions.* If you tell me, you didn't mean to, I will tell you that you needed to mean not to do it. Drunk drivers never set out to kill others; they just do. And like it or not, they own this action.

When a child who has been taught she owns her behavior falls back on this type of flawed thinking, I abandon the issue at hand and move to the more fundamental issue: you always own what you do. Without this underlying, fundamental principle in place, discipline is difficult or impossible. Encouraging the development of this principle also requires a great deal of authority. Please see Descriptive Language and Anger without Destruction for examples of exactly how to handle this issue.

3. CHOOSING NOT TO LISTEN OR LETTING YOU KNOW THAT THEY DO NOT HAVE TO LISTEN TO YOU

Your effectiveness in disciplining your children hinges on their listening to what you say. In order for them to believe that what you have to say is important, *you* will have to believe it first. You will also have to be willing to address their dismissal of you with authority and respect, something which is frequently very hard to do. Nothing seems to rile us so much as being told with words ("Whatever!" or "You have no idea what you're talking about," or "Who cares?" or "Big deal!") or actions (walking away, or rolling eyes and turning away, or shaking head) that a child is not listening. It is perhaps the most important and opportune time to increase rather than lose authority. Letting a child walk, roll eyes, or simply say "whatever" disrespectfully teaches a very large lesson. That lesson is that they really do not have to listen to you. You are lost to them and they are lost to you. Do not let this happen. Address it immediately always. Our words must change from the time they are young (Descriptive Language) to when they become teens (Anger without Destruction). But our necessity to address these situations immediately never diminishes. This lesson, "Yes, you do need to listen to me because I know what I am talking about," is essential and indispensable to discipline and your effectiveness with children.

Now, how do we do it?

With a thorough understanding of what discipline is and is not, we have a clearer idea of what we want to achieve with our discipline. Adding a feel for types of life lessons also helps. We are now ready to discover how to actually accomplish discipline and to learn specific strategies that both teach our principles and are effective.

1	Goal for Discipline	Lead to SELF-DISCIPLINE • by providing opportunities for learning • by allowing the child to be and feel responsible for his behavior "What lesson needs to be learned here; how can I best teach it to this child?"
2	Ingredients of Discipline	Maintain the DIGNITY - of both parties • by using the Golden Rule and Respectful Language Require AUTHORITY - • "Don't start what you can't finish!" • Say what you mean; Mean what you say; Take action stated
3	Critical Life Beliefs	I like myself I can think and do for myself I can solve problems
4	Steps to Disciplinary Action	Determine the lesson Identify the problem respectfully Take action when necessary Evaluate: lessons learned, feelings generated, outcome

PART III - GAINING COOPERATION WITHOUT LOSING YOUR MIND!

5:
Barriers to Cooperation

In the first section we looked at the first step of discipline: asking the questions, "What lesson needs to be learned?" and "How can I best teach it?"

Now we examine the second step: the parent or teacher must identify the problem respectfully. We also begin to determine the difference between generating resistance or encouraging cooperation. Frequently, at this early stage of discipline, we inadvertently create resistance. Have you ever noticed that after having said just a few words to a child, you are suddenly in the midst of a power struggle - and all you wanted was for this child to pick up his toys or find a pencil.

Blaming & Accusing	Put-Downs & Belittling	Threats & Intimidation	Commands & Orders	Lecturing & Moralizing
Barriers to Cooperation				
Reminding & Nagging	Guilt	Labeling & Name-Calling	Comparisons	Sarcasm

First, let's look at how we so frequently provoke resistance and defiance. There are many barriers to cooperation; we will identify ten. In the process, we will discover how large a part respect plays in cooperation. We will also determine how many of the ways we have learned to address adults and children hinder more than help us.

Examples throughout this text appear in the following order and next to the symbols indicated:		
🏠 Parent	🧍 Early Childhood	🍎 School

As you read through these unhelpful approaches, try to recognize those you say most frequently. After you have discovered which of these you do use, listen for them in your dealings with children. Then observe how much resistance they cause.

Blaming and Accusing[10]

🏠 "You knocked your sister's blocks down."
"You left the car with no gas again; it's always you."

🧍 "You pushed him down again, didn't you?"
"You pulled her hair and made her cry."

🍎 "You didn't do your homework, *did* you?"
"You're cheating."

When do we accuse a child of a misdeed? Only when we are absolutely certain that she has done the deed. When we see the child with fresh purple stains on his face, hands, shirt, and pants, we accuse him of having spilled the juice. When there is only one child in the room, we blame that one, of course, for the broken lamp. Yet, if we take a look at what most frequently occurs when *we* are blamed for something, we can more readily see why an accusation creates resistance. If I tell you, "There was entirely too much fat in your dinner last night," you are most likely to answer, "No, there wasn't!" (without even thinking about what you ate). Do you sense resistance in this response? Suddenly, we are in a "prove-it" situation. When we are certain, our job is not to prove it; our job is to deal with it. Another common type of response to this accusation is "So!" or "I enjoyed it immensely." These constitute the "what's-it-to-you" defense. We would not have brought up the situation if it were not important. Suddenly, we are defending why the issue is important rather than dealing with the actual issue. Again, we have come up against resistance. Yet, the older the child, the more likely the prove-it defense, and the more sophisticated. In short, accusing someone is the quickest route to an argument over proof or justification.

An accusation feels like a push; it makes us uncomfortable. We push back or we build a defense. Our first thought is not cooperation. Nor is a child's first response cooperation. Certainly we need to address what has taken place. The point made here is that accusing is not a helpful way to bring up a problem because it most often creates an argument - in other words, resistance.

Put-Downs and Belittling

🏠 "Your shoelaces are a disaster. Will you ever learn how to tie your shoes?"
"You call that a clean room?"

🚶 "I've never seen anyone dressed like that!"
"Big girls can use the toilet; they don't need diapers."

🍎 "Anyone have a better answer?"
"This homework is terrible. I can't even read it."

We are all aware that belittling a child is harmful; it clearly lowers self-esteem. Yet, I have not met a parent or a teacher who has not put down a child - when frustrated, fatigued, or stressed. Put-downs and belittling are well named; we make children feel smaller and less valuable. Trying to regain this lost stature or value, generally and unfortunately at the expense of another, is why we so frequently see a series of put-downs run through the family or a classroom. A child is put down by someone; as soon as possible, this first child tends to belittle a less powerful child, who in turn puts down an even weaker child. This child may have to kick the family dog or find a younger child on the playground in order to pass off the belittling. The belittling has a life of its own and cycles through the family or school.

We overlook Abraham Lincoln's wisdom that, "You cannot help small men by tearing down big men." Making someone feel or look like less than me only seems to make me look better because everything seems relative. We must take time to teach that having or making someone lower than me does not make me any higher or better. In fact, making someone else feel lower actually reduces me. That's where Booker T. Washington would say, "You can't hold a man down without staying down with him."

Belittling hurts. When someone hurts me, I am less, not more, likely to cooperate. As well, the bond between us is weakened.

> ☞ Put-downs are easily accomplished without the use of nasty words. A tone can imply disapproval; tone can change respectful words into a put-down. A look alone or accompanied by a gesture easily gives away our feeling. Be very careful; body language, though silent, speaks loudly.

Threats and Intimidation

🏠 "If you touch it again, you're going to be in big trouble."
"If you don't stop it, I'm going to send you to your room."
"Drink and drive one more time, and I won't ever let you use the car."

🧍 "If you don't pick up your crayons, I'm going to take them away."
"If you touch that again...."

🍎 "If you don't start turning in your homework, I'm going to fail you."
"Forget your book one more time, and I'll give you a zero for the day."
"You're one of my finest art students, maybe the best, but if you don't change your behavior in my class, there is absolutely no way I'll even consider you for the award for best artist."

Threats are some of my own personal favorites. Each of us has used a threat with a child especially when we feel our backs are up against the wall, when we have tried numerous other strategies which have not worked, or when we finally really mean business.

Some of us have managed to make threats work on occasion. And they can work, especially if we have a big enough menace or punishment at the end and if the child believes we will follow through. However, we must be able to see that what we threaten to do must always continue to grow to be effective. What we can threaten a four year old with will not work with an eleven year old. The threats must get more and more hurtful, *sometimes to the point of physical or emotional harm.* This is not where we are headed legally or morally.

Threats fail to work on many occasions. Some children love to rise to the challenge in a threat; they love to live dangerously as it were. Let us uncover a synonym for threat. When we tell a child, "If you touch that knob one more time, you're going to get it," we can count on almost any child to touch the knob - no matter who she is and even if she had not considered touching the knob again. Generally, if she has any self-respect, she will feel a strong need to touch the knob just one more time - merely to test us. Our threat, our last-ditch effort to stop a behavior, becomes an *invitation* to do exactly what we do not want. A synonym for threat might be invitation.

The threats we have issued previously are not entirely wasted; we can find out about our children's personalities when we threaten them. The aggressive-aggressive child is the one who will look you straight in the eye and touch the knob right away. His actions tell you two things. First, let the games begin and thank you for starting this game because things were boring here for the moment. Second, it is your move. The passive-aggressive child smiles acquiescence and then waits for you to get distracted or busy - which, by the way, takes hardly any time at all. Then she quietly touches the knob and hums some form of "nanny nanny boo boo" and is comforted by the knowledge that she got around you once again. The child who can find the loophole in any situation will touch the knob with her stuffed dog and sweetly tell you that you did not say anything about Rover touching the knob. And a very bright child will touch it as he asks, "Do you mean this one?"

As you can see, what we have determined is that threats easily become invitations to the very behavior we least want. As well, we know that to continually back up our threats, we move more and more closely to harm. In terms of gaining cooperation, threats more often gain us exactly what we did not want.

Threats are often confused with disciplinary consequences where, for example, we tell a child that to continue a behavior (riding a bicycle into the street) will result in a specific consequence (not riding the bike for a day). A threat may be based on the same concept as the disciplinary consequence - that choosing to behave in a certain way (riding the bike into the street) will result in a certain outcome (not riding the bicycle for a time). However, threats are different. To be effective the tone and intent of a threat require power and intimidation. Threats are based in power (if you..., I will....) and punishment (you are going to pay).

In contrast, a consequence seeks to *inform* a child of the disciplinary outcome should the child choose a specific behavior. A consequence does not depend on power, intimidation, or punishment to be effective. *A true disciplinary consequence relies on informed choice.* It is very easy to hear ourselves as offering disciplinary choices and consequences when in fact we are issuing threats. To be sure, 1) check your heart and your intent (to get what you want - control or to make the child pay - punishment), 2) check the child's response (thoughtfulness or continued resistance), and 3) invite another to listen and tell you honestly what she hears. The chapter on Discipline Strategies describes disciplinary consequences more fully.

Commands and Orders

🏠 "Get off there NOW!"
   "Stop that!"

🧍 "Don't throw another one."
   "Give it back to him."

🍎 "Put your feet under your desk."
   "Keep your hands to yourself."
   "Hurry up!"

A command, in some ways, seems to be the most direct form of communication: you tell me what to do, and I do it. Pretty simple. Let's just turn it around. I tell *you* what to do and *you* do it. There is the snag. We each want to be the speaker not the doer. Whenever I issue a command such as, "Stand up!" in a workshop, I obtain various responses. Some participants continue to sit and look at me like I am crazy, an aggressive-aggressive response. One woman dropped a pencil and said, "Just a minute," a passive-aggressive response. Another participant asked, "Do you mean me?" (bright, very bright). Fortunately, only rarely does someone stand up. I continue to be concerned by this response which allowed me to violate dignity. What I have learned is that each one felt uncomfortable with the directive. The rest of the audience empathizes and agrees that they, too, would have been ill at ease. Seldom does a group understand why they are so uneasy with this directive. Perhaps because our dignity is violated more and more often, or perhaps because we try to ignore it when it happens, many of us have lost touch with violation of dignity. For when anyone orders us to do something, our dignity is violated. Not only does self-esteem diminish, but also a sense of defiance develops. We do not like complying with anyone who orders us around. At best, if we are intimidated (perhaps our job depends on this person), we give the letter of the law, not the spirit, in cooperation. And given an opening, we work against this person at every opportunity - maybe even enjoy working against him. *Our children feel the same way.*

No discipline works well or for long when a child chooses to get back at us and work against us. This is an extremely detrimental dynamic and outcome. Families and classrooms deteriorate as a result of this type of toxic relationship. The best analogy for this is the master-slave relationship. Two outcomes are possible: the slaves accept their position and lose dignity and self-respect, or the slaves can choose to rebel and gain back their rightful status and respect. Our children respond exactly the same way. They may accept domination and reduce their own self-worth, or they may rebel and let us know their dignity and self-respect need to be preserved. Unfortunately for us, this important lesson usually sounds like this: "NO!" or "I can't!" or "You can't make me!" or "There's no #*&@ way you can make me!" (the most sophisticated version). It is still a valid and vital message and lesson to us.

In healthy families and in healthy classrooms, indeed, in any type of healthy relationship, people generally choose to work *with* each other, not *against* each other. It is critical that we learn how to talk to one another and to create this healthy dynamic, not the unhealthy abuse of power and "make me" dynamic. Sooner or later, the abuse of power will return to haunt us. Many of us, including those who do not intend to use power, will be amazed when we listen to ourselves and hear how frequently and easily we issue a quick command.

☞ There is, however, a time for commands; dangerous situations require commands. If a child is leaning out of a third floor window, a command is in order. Be sure to direct toward what you want. "Get back in!" is much more helpful and less precarious than "Don't jump!" At important times like these, a command is much more likely to work if they have not been previously overused.

Lecturing

🏠 "If I've told you once, I've told you a thousand times: You are supposed to do unto others as you would have them do unto you. If you are nice to others, they will be nice to you."

🧍 "How many times do I have to tell you, if you just drop your things on the floor and don't put your jacket and lunch box in your cubby where they belong, others may trip on them and get hurt. Then what would we do?"

🍎 "You can't get good grades without studying and doing your homework. Good grades are important. You're going to need good grades to get into college. And if you don't go to college, you'll never have a good job that pays well."

Both parents and teachers have told me that they lecture because they do not know what else to do and because it feels good. Except for very young children who need brief explanations of why something is important, most of our children already know the why - we have told them - innumerable times. Children, like adults, stop listening when they already know. Have you ever seen a child's eyes glaze over while you were lecturing to her? Do you remember "teacher talk" or "parent talk" - grown-ups talking at you not to you?

The common mistaken belief is that if we tell them just one more time, they will understand *it* or remember *it* this time. In reality, they already know, understand, and remember *it*; in fact, they can usually give us the lecture quite well. The real problem is that understanding has not altered their behavior. *Telling them again does not increase their understanding and does not change their behavior.* We need to find other techniques to change attitude and behavior; we do not need to increase understanding. Yet another lecture will not net us the cooperation we seek.

☞   Brief explanations for young children and of new situations can be helpful discipline tools. Helpful explanations yield that recognizable light-bulb-turned-on look. Lectures produce a bored, blank, I've-heard-this-before look.

Reminding and Nagging

⌂   "Remember, you need to take your baseball hat and glove to practice."

🚶   "Don't forget your shoes."

🍎   "Have you started your book report? They're due on Friday."

Some of you are thinking that without your reminders nothing would get done. For young children, reminders are helpful and necessary as youngsters learn routines and necessary elements. However, we want to remind less and less as a child gets older or as the school year progresses. As well, we only want to be reminding children about things *we are still willing to own.* As one four year old, whose mother had complained of his memory lapses, explained to me, "I don't need to remember my shoes; my mommy always tells me to put them on." Out of the mouths of babes sometimes comes wisdom.

Most children need to be taught how to remember. Remembering is an acquired skill.

Notes, timers, placement of items at the back door, in the car, or under a desk, are some of the ways we can teach remembering. As well, forgetting something important can be helpful in learning to remember; let them learn this lesson young. Allowing a child to forget an important-to-her, but non-essential item or activity may at first seem cruel. It is not. Forgetting while you are young so that you see and feel the need to learn how to remember is a gift. It is also a good investment.

72 DISCIPLINE FOR LIFE: GETTING IT RIGHT WITH CHILDREN

Assignments, test dates, and project deadlines written on a specific corner of the blackboard can greatly ease the need for reminders. A student always has access to important information simply by taking the initiative to look. Asking ourselves, "Whose job is it?" often helps alleviate reminding.

Guilt

⌂ "You know how it bothers me when you two fight with each other like this."
"When your grandparents get here, you are going to *have* to behave."
"Eat your beans for Daddy."

🚶 "Only a baby would do that."
"Pleeease be quiet."

🍎 "You *have* to be on your best behavior today. The evaluator will be here."
"Don't do this to me."
"Don't you care about the other students? They need to learn."

By guilt, here I mean that paralyzing, no matter what I do I will be wrong feeling, rather than the activating and healthy I did something I wish I hadn't and need to make amends or take corrective action feeling called accountability. The person who taught us guilt is usually one of the easiest to recognize or recall. We still hear his voice even after he has left us, moved, or even died. Guilt for heinous crimes we commit may be healthy; but for daily decisions we make, guilt is not helpful. Guilt tends to prevent us from taking corrective actions. Guilt puts a child, or anyone for that matter, in a lose-lose position. For example, you decide to spend Thanksgiving dinner with your new in-laws rather than your own family. When you try to tell your mother, she replies, "You're going where for Thanksgiving? The whole family will be here. No one has ever missed a Thanksgiving. You know how important it is to me!" You lose if you go to your mother-in-law's because you will feel guilty. You also lose if you change your plans and go to your mother's because you will feel manipulated. No matter what course of action you choose, you lose. Not a comfortable feeling. The result is that we begin to distance ourselves both physically and emotionally from those who make us feel guilty and tense. When we do cooperate, it is begrudgingly. Again, this is not our goal.

Labeling and Name-Calling

🏠 "You are so clumsy."

👤 "You really do have trouble remembering things."

🐞 "I haven't seen such poor work in years. You have terrible work habits."

Each of us has been taught, "Thou shalt not label children." Labeling is harmful to self-esteem because children believe what we adults tell them. The well-known danger is that the child begins to believe and to become the label - the self-fulfilling prophecy. Let a child know she is clumsy often enough, and she will become clumsy or clumsier, not less clumsy - which is what we were trying to accomplish.

It is frightening to realize that we can quite effectively give a negative label to a child without words - with only a look. Each of us recognizes these looks: the "you dummy" look, the "you're doing it again" look, the "I'm losing my patience, I really don't like you" look, and the "you'll never get it right" look. Sadly, we fail to recognize these on our own faces. Nor do we realize, as a general rule, the power of these forms of non-verbal communication.

There is even danger in over-doing positive labels which require living up to and maintaining. Ironically, when we tell a child how very honest he is, often within a few hours, he may lie to us. Sometimes children let us know dramatically how hard it is to live up to an image. Too often they hurt themselves physically or emotionally or learn to suppress personality and emotion in order to keep the image alive. Neither is healthy.

Comparisons

🏠 "Your brother never pulled this stuff."
   "Just look at Kelly's room; isn't it nice and clean!"

👤 "Your sister never bit anyone."
   "I like the way Jeremy is paying attention."

🍎 "Your sister was such a great student."

"I wish all my classes were more like my third period class."

Anyone who was compared negatively to a sibling or friend can feel their blood begin to boil with the resentment to this day. Intriguingly, even those of us who were the recipients of positive comparisons (the good one, the smart one, the pretty one, the athletic one) remain uncomfortable. We fear falling off the pedestal, and we hate the resulting rivalry, bitterness, and alienation. None of us likes to be compared to someone else.

Some of you may have experienced proximity praise - "I like the way Jeremy is paying attention." This is a form of comparison which alienates children from one another and sets up competition, not cooperation. In both a family or classroom situation, competition increasingly is viewed and documented as destructive. Please see the discussion on praise and proximity praise in the section on Self-Esteem for additional information.

A more positive side to labeling and comparing involves their usefulness in problem solving. Both, especially used together, can be most helpful in discovering how to deal with a specific child. For example, if you have a very determined child, it is helpful to mentally recognize or label this trait. Comparing how you dealt successfully or unsuccessfully with others who are very determined can help you quickly find the most effective way of dealing with this particular child. For example, pushing them did not work, but convincing them or appealing to their best interests did. Similarly, in the classroom setting, a child who is an auditory learner benefits from a teacher who recognizes his learning strengths and weaknesses (labeling). This teacher can then draw from her previous experience with other auditory learners in order to make learning easier for the current student.

When we use labels and comparisons *and keep them to ourselves* to help us be more effective with a child, each of us benefits. The danger occurs when we share (either purposely or unintentionally) the label or comparison with the child. Always strive for the positive label: determined rather than stubborn, curious rather than nosy, imaginative rather than day dreamer, tired rather than cranky, high energy rather than overactive.

Sarcasm

🏠 "You are an accident looking for a place to happen."

🧍 "You'd forget your head if it weren't glued on."

🍎 "Of course, you can't turn it in if you don't do it."

Sarcasm is like a knife. We throw it; it cuts and does damage. Most of our children have learned some self-defense; they pull out the knife and throw it back with intent to hurt. If we did not learn sarcasm at home, we learned it from our peers during middle school or high school just to survive. Sarcasm is sometimes confused with wit, since both tend to include humor. Sarcasm is humor at the expense of someone else; wit is simply humor with words, no damage and no pain involved for anyone. Our tone, even more than our words, is always an indicator of sarcastic intent. Sarcasm is a wonderful example of the adage, "what goes around, comes around." With sarcasm, it is pain.

In conclusion, the purpose of describing the above ten disrespectful barriers to cooperation is two-fold. First, it should be clear that these methods of addressing people do not work and instead create resistance, defiance, antagonism, and rebellion. Second, it is hoped that you have identified the barriers to cooperation which you use. You may want to take a moment and think about which you use the most. Then begin to catch yourself using it. From there, you can begin to eliminate the barriers from your language - the real goal.

What then, do we want to say? How do we gain cooperation? The answer is evident. If violating dignity and being disrespectful create resistance, it is likely that maintaining dignity and being respectful will result in cooperation. Well, at least a much higher probability of cooperation. After all, we are talking about children and the real world.

The second ingredient of discipline, Authority, must be present. We need to be able to generate and maintain authority to be effective, to carry influence. The need for respect at a high level is constant; the requirement for authority varies in degree.

Some situations and children require a small amount of authority. At other times or with different children, a high level of authority is necessary in order to get a response. An old Chinese proverb which has some relevance here is:

Do not use a hatchet to remove a fly from your friend's forehead.

Thus, the examples that follow always remain respectful but vary in intensity of authority. Here are five phrases, in increasing degrees of authority, which you can use and even alter to make sound more like you. We are now entering the second step of discipline: Identify the problem respectfully.

6:
Respectful Language

The following are five respectful and effective ways to identify the problem and improve the odds of gaining cooperation and reduce the probability of creating resistance. It may be helpful to keep in mind that no phrase is effective in all scenarios and that each phrase may need some fine-tuning to sound right to you, to become the way you feel comfortable speaking.

Guide Toward Helpfulness

How does it feel to help someone? Wonderful? At the very least, it feels good. Being able to be helpful is good for the helper; it is easy to recognize the sense of worth and accomplishment generated by helping others. Self-esteem increases as does emotional health. Offer someone an opportunity to be helpful and most will rise to the occasion. Four types of people will not: those who do not like you, in which case, you have told them exactly what not to do; those who are extremely tired, because this group is about to fall asleep and is just too tired to do anything; those whose self-esteem is so terribly low that they do not even recognize this opportunity to rebuild it; and finally, the fourth group, children who love what they are doing and strongly want to continue doing it. Otherwise, most everyone enjoys a chance to contribute to another's life. Children, especially, like the feeling of importance and "bigness"which accompanies helping.

🏠 "IT WOULD BE HELPFUL IF you brought your dishes to the dishwasher."
"IT WOULD BE HELPFUL IF you took out the trash now."
Instead of:
"You'd forget your head if it weren't glued on." (Sarcasm)
"Take out the trash!" (Command)

  ♣ "IT WOULD BE HELPFUL IF you kept your hands in your pockets."
Instead of:
"Get your hands off him!" (Command)

  🍎 "IT WOULD BE HELPFUL IF you put your feet under your desk."
Instead of:
"How many times do I have to tell you to keep your feet underneath your desk.
Someone could get hurt!" (Lecture)

To be more direct and immediate, you may add: "Will you do that now?"

Obviously, there is no suggestion here that should you discover two children pummeling each other you say, "It would be helpful if you stopped hitting each other." "IT WOULD BE HELPFUL" does not carry nearly enough authority for such a situation. This phrasing is most useful in easy, non-threatening situations. We will discuss phrases carrying more authority later. However, both parents and teachers frequently tell me how amazed they were to discover how well this phrase works. Giving an opportunity to be helpful, rather than giving an order changes a situation dramatically. Only complying with the first opportunity is easy on our self-esteem and self-respect. Do not underestimate the capacity and potential of this phrase.

This phrase is an excellent replacement for "please." Please is a wonderful word and belongs in our communication with children. However, please does not belong in discipline because it implies a request and the option to disagree. We frequently turn ugly at this juncture. At other times, please may sound like begging, which also has no place in discipline.

Life Lessons

This phrasing teaches helpfulness and thoughtfulness and helps children feel the benefits of being helpful. Self-esteem is always higher when we choose to be helpful and contribute.

Comfort with cooperation and responsiveness to others is also learned.

Life Messages

Bonds are strengthened when we treat children gently and considerately. Children view themselves as positive, helpful, cooperative individuals.

Children learn that they are capable.

Those who contribute to the group (family or classroom or organization) feel more welcome and attached to the group. They begin to become true members of the group. Members behave differently than non-members do. The message "I belong" is very important.

As we will discuss more in the section on Self-Esteem, this sense of belonging is a very important component of behavior, attitude, and values. Too many of our children do not feel they *belong* anywhere.

Descriptive Language

This very broad method of communicating is useful in many different types of situations. By simply reminding myself to *be descriptive*, I have often managed to avoid my most common barriers to cooperation. What we are trying to accomplish is remaining purely descriptive without tossing in any accusation, guilt, command, evaluation, or threat. We simply describe the problem, the situation, or the solution. By describing what needs to be done rather than what has gone wrong, we can avoid accusations and negative comments. Some examples help make the concept clear.

🏠 For the child who arrives home and walks out of her shoes and leaves them on the kitchen floor or in the doorway.
"Shoes belong in the closet."
"You need to put your shoes in the closet."
Instead of:
"You forgot your shoes, again." (Blame, Put-down)

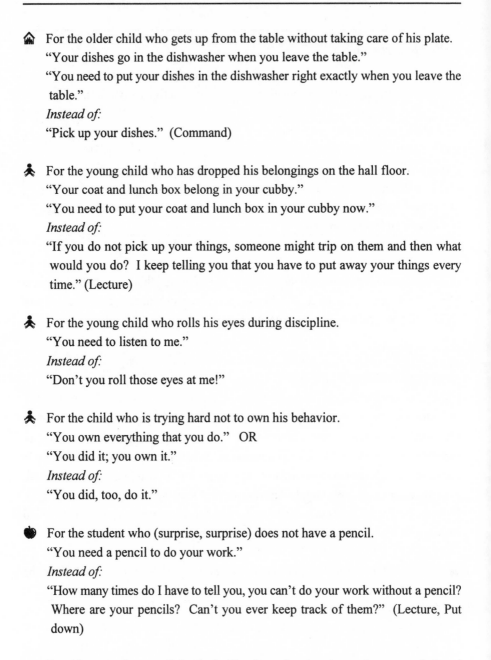

For the older child who gets up from the table without taking care of his plate.
"Your dishes go in the dishwasher when you leave the table."
"You need to put your dishes in the dishwasher right exactly when you leave the table."
Instead of:
"Pick up your dishes." (Command)

For the young child who has dropped his belongings on the hall floor.
"Your coat and lunch box belong in your cubby."
"You need to put your coat and lunch box in your cubby now."
Instead of:
"If you do not pick up your things, someone might trip on them and then what would you do? I keep telling you that you have to put away your things every time." (Lecture)

For the young child who rolls his eyes during discipline.
"You need to listen to me."
Instead of:
"Don't you roll those eyes at me!"

For the child who is trying hard not to own his behavior.
"You own everything that you do."   OR
"You did it; you own it."
Instead of:
"You did, too, do it."

For the student who (surprise, surprise) does not have a pencil.
"You need a pencil to do your work."
Instead of:
"How many times do I have to tell you, you can't do your work without a pencil? Where are your pencils? Can't you ever keep track of them?" (Lecture, Put down)

In each example, we tell the truth, illuminate the situation or lesson needed, and avoid barriers to cooperation with a description. We also avoid irritation and rancor.

There is debate about descriptive language and the amount of directness most helpful for individual children. For example, "You need to put your shoes in the closet" is more direct than "Shoes belong in the closet." Many experts, among them Virginia Satir in her book *Peoplemaking* and Jean Clarke in *Self-Esteem: A Family Affair*, stress the importance of direct versus indirect communication. They note that the more clear and direct, and the less ambiguous and indirect communication is, the healthier it is. There is less room for doubt, miscommunication, and mixed messages.

Jean Clarke suggests another problem with the less direct descriptive phrases such as "Shoes belong in the closet." She points out that many children will answer, "So!" Ms. Clarke prefers the "You need to put your shoes in the closet" to "Shoes belong in the closet" because the first is more direct and clearly sets up ownership of the responsibility for the shoes. A child is less likely to respond, "So!" to this type of phrasing. A good argument. On the other hand, some children are inclined to respond, "You do it!" or "NO!" to this more direct type of phrasing. These children react defensively or defiantly to the more intrusive quality of direct communication.

Because of this type of response, Faber and Mazlish emphasize, in their book, *How to Talk So Kids Will Listen & Listen So Kids Will Talk*, a desire to do as little pushing or intervening with a child as necessary to reduce this probability of defiance and obstinance. They prefer the less direct and less intervening "Shoes belong in the closet" for this reason. This, too, is good reasoning. Clearly, much depends on the child involved. Many of us recognize both types of children - those prone to replying with "So!" and those more likely to answer "No!"

Confused? Both types of descriptive language can be helpful. One, "You need to put your shoes in the closet," is more direct and healthier communication, but also more intervening and hence may cause defiance. The second, "Shoes belong in the closet," is less intervening and more likely to be responded to positively but also less direct and therefore less healthy and less honest. Generally, the choice of which to use or, in other words, how direct to be is determined by an individual child's response to them. If a child is likely to say "So!", it is more helpful to be more direct and tell her, "You need to put your shoes in the closet," or even "You need to put your shoes in the closet now." If, however, a child tends to look for a fight and power struggle, you may find that "Shoes belong in the closet" creates less resistance and is more helpful.

Both sets of authors make good points. You will need to choose whichever phrasing best suits you, or the phrasing which is more effective with each of your children or students.

Descriptive language, describing what a child needs to do, is an effective communication tool and is useful in most situations requiring a middle range of authority. It does require thought; there is no blanket statement involved. However, with practice, describing becomes a more easily accessible format for identifying problems.

Life Lesson

Descriptive language teaches ownership of problems or mistakes and responsibility for correcting them.

Give Alternatives

Limiting inappropriate behavior and redirecting it to similar but appropriate behaviors which also meet the child's need are suggested here. In addition, if we first acknowledge the child's intent, need or desire, we not only convey acceptance and understanding of the child, we also tend to reduce the potential for strong emotion, backlash, and resistance. Children who feel understood are less likely to resist alternatives. Our empathy is especially helpful when children are angry.

Providing our children with alternatives is helpful when a child is about to choose (or has chosen) an appropriate activity in an inappropriate manner or place, such as writing on a wall. The act of drawing is not inappropriate: the place selected is. When we only tell the child not to do something, "Don't write on that wall," she asks herself one of two questions. She may ask, "Will I quit what I want to do?" and respond, "Nah, it's fun; that's why I was doing it." Or she may ask, "Shall I do what he said or not?" and respond, "I want to do what I want to do." Most children who perceive the situation this way decide to continue doing what they want. If we add positive alternatives, we accomplish two things at once. First, we help the child focus on something other than the unwanted behavior. Second, the child still ends up with a decision to make, but a much more constructive, helpful decision: "Shall I do the first alternative or the second?" prompting "Well, which one do I like the best?" Frequently with this type of phrasing, a child passes over those first questions: "Will I quit what I want to do or continue doing it because I want to?" or "Shall I do what he said or not?" and addresses only the question, "Which of the acceptable alternatives do I want to do most?" We have bypassed a major struggle entirely. This is good. Here, the child's decision becomes which type of paper does she like most today? Either decision is acceptable. The child is happy because she got to make a decision, and she is still able to draw. We are happy because, at least for the moment, our walls are safe from budding artists.

It is always more helpful and responsive to tell children what to do, rather than what not to do. However, in a panic, we often start with "Don't"; should this happen to you, try to add the reason. Altering our phrasing to include descriptions and reasons helps us circumvent a quick, negative command.

⌂   "You really feel like drawing. YOU MAY NOT draw on the walls;
     WOULD YOU RATHER draw on the plain paper
     OR on the colored paper?"
     Instead of:
     "DON'T write on the wall."

⌂   "You are ready to ride your bike. YOU MAY NOT ride your bike on the busy
     street
     BECAUSE it's dangerous;
     WOULD YOU RATHER ride it on the driveway
     OR on the back porch?"
     Alternatively:
     "You love to ride your bike. Streets are for cars; (or Streets are dangerous for
     children and bikes; or You may not ride your bike on the street;)
     WOULD YOU LIKE TO ride your tricycle on the driveway
     OR on the sidewalk?"

⚑   "You are ready to get busy and play. Lunches don't belong on the floor;
     you may put it in your cubby
     OR in your backpack."

⚑   "You didn't like it when Beau took your crayon. Use your words not your hands;
     say, 'I don't like that!' or 'That hurts.'"

🍎 "Failing a test is disappointing. I am uncomfortable with rudeness.
Rephrase and speak respectfully
OR take a moment and calm down and then talk to me."

Alternatively:
"You were hoping for a better grade on your paper. What you said was disrespectful; disrespect will not work (or disrespect is absolutely unacceptable;) DO YOU WANT TO start again respectfully,
OR WOULD YOU RATHER take some time to calm down before you talk to me?"

🍎 "Sometimes homework can seem overwhelming. It's important to turn in all of your homework.
You can turn in your Social Studies page 12 assignment by 3:00 tomorrow or go to ZAP (Zeroes Aren't Permitted program) on Wednesday or Thursday morning."

There is one drawback to this phrasing; there can be an element of manipulation. What we have done is create a forced choice. Some salespeople use it to manipulate and trap us. Before we have said we are going to buy an item, a salesperson asks us ever so cleverly, "Do you want it in the blue or the red?" And we answer, "Well, the blue is nice." We just omitted the first decision - are we really going to buy it. We have been manipulated. On the positive side, we set up an excellent preventive dynamic by moving the area of decision-making to one that is appropriate for the child. It is important to check your intent. Are you truly offering positive alternatives or trying to slip one past a child?

Life Lesson

Alternatives teach children that they make some decisions; and that they still need help with others. The range of decisions increases with maturity and responsibility.

Demonstrating understanding a child's motivation or desire creates good will and more cooperation.

Rules, Policies, and Rights

Authority calls for brevity. Only the weak explain themselves. - Haim
Ginott

A child's perception of the rules develops with age writes Becky Bailey.[11] Three
year old children seem only to recognize that they are not supposed to do some things,
like hitting or grabbing. By age four and five, children put rules in the context of what
one has to do and that one "gets into trouble" when a rule is broken. The rules and
consequences which exist both at home and at school flow together and become mixed.
By age six, children have a much better understanding of rules; rules prevent people
from getting hurt, and getting into trouble can mean a variety of disciplinary outcomes.
Until age six or seven, children really do not have a good concept of rules or their
purpose, and more or less pretend to follow them. Young children, therefore, require
a limit-setting environment, not a rule governed one. Since young children are still in
the process of discovering cause and effect, they are not likely to be able to use rules
to govern their behavior.   In an early childhood setting, rules may hinder the
development of problem-solving skills because too often teachers put into motion
"consequences" for misbehavior and fail to work first through problem solving with
the children. For example, rather than working through the problem of one child
grabbing a toy from another, the grabber is simply isolated or placed in time-out. No
new skills for handling similar situations are learned when this happens. Such a waste
of good conflict!

Young children need limits to understand first that they are not unlimited
creatures. As well, limits set the boundaries which allow children to feel safe, cared
for, and free to explore what is allowable.[12] Becky Bailey very aptly describes the
difference between rule-governed and limit-setting environments:

> Rules say, *You may not break the rule, do not even try, or something will
> happen to you.* Limits say, *I am here to keep you safe, you may test the
> limits, and I will redirect you so you may learn that the territory outside the
> boundaries lacks the protection that lies within the boundaries.* Limits help
> children develop self-discipline based on safety and accountability; children
> learn skills to deal with various common conflict situations which arise.

Clearly, young children require limit setting rather than rules. However, as children enter grade one, rules can begin to become helpful. Rules are the precursors or forerunners to laws, and we must teach important lessons about their necessity. A quick warning: rules are easily abused and overused.

Often, routine can replace rules, especially for young children. Rather than making putting your lunch box in your cubby *before* playing a rule, make it a part of the morning routine, a habit. Develop a song about putting things in the cubby before playing, practice doing so with small groups of children, draw pictures of the morning routine and post them where they will be seen, or have puppets remind them by acting out the routine.

It was catching myself explaining to my seven year old, for the thousandth time, why he had to brush his teeth that gave the phrase "Only the weak explain themselves" a new, inspired meaning for me. One helpful answer to a child's ever-present question "Why?" is, "You tell me." Children rarely bother, and they stop asking. Most of our children know the "whys"; we have spent years explaining to them. When it comes to discipline situations, there are several quick phrases which carry authority and are brief. Here are four in increasing order of authority.

🏠 "THE POLICY IS everyone makes her bed in the morning."

🧍 "THE POLICY IS everyone who brought a jacket wears it outside to play."

🍎 "THE POLICY IS no food in the classroom except during celebrations and special projects."

Policies tend to be broader and more flexible than rules.

🏠 "THE RULE IS he who makes the mess, cleans it up."

🧍 "THE RULE IS if you play, you help pick up."

🍎 "THE RULE IS raise your hand and be called on before speaking during class discussions."

The good news about rules (and policies) is that you cannot argue with a rule, unlike a person. Thus, if it is the rule, rather than the adult, which prevents a child from doing something, there tends to be much less argument, especially with young children.

Rules and policies are most helpful when they smooth out operation rather than try to control behavior.

Notice that the rules and polices above address what needs to be done and help homes or classrooms run more peacefully and efficiently. Rules which address only "Don'ts" often prove ineffective. Rules are best stated positively as what to do, rather than negatively as what not to do. Further, negatively stated rules cannot ever cover every situation. There is always one child willing and able to think of something you have not thought about - spitting, washing with paint, etc. Rules can be like swords: live by them and die by them. There is danger in becoming rule-governed rather than self-disciplined. Rules are most helpful with young children where they quickly help provide structure. The reasoning behind rules needs to be explained to help children understand why a rule is in place. Our goal is not simple obedience, but understanding, agreement, and support.

In addition, a child who has helped develop and determine rules is much more likely to follow them. Changing and negotiating rules takes place at family meetings, family dinners, class meetings, or other specified times, not when the rule is about to be enforced. But don't forget, it is important that rules be enforced consistently; this is one of their most important lessons. Rules are rules - for everyone (you, too) and for always (not just when convenient or when we feel like it). We either choose to teach children that rules and laws apply to them always (that means the stop signs and the speed limit signs are for them, too) or we teach them that rules and laws only apply to them when it is convenient (no cop, no stop; or "I was in a hurry"). Very important lifelong lessons are involved with rules.

Rules for Rules

☞ Keep rules positive.

Clean up after yourself. *Instead of: Don't leave a mess.*
Tell the truth. *Instead of: Don't lie.*

☞ Keep rules general.

Everyone helps pick up. *Instead of: If you played with it last, you pick it up.*
Respect yourself and others.

☞ Keep rules to a minimum.

🏠 For home:
Ask before you take something from another.
Stay inside the fence unless with a parent.
Buckle your seat belt.

🍎 For classroom:
Be here on time.
Have everything you need to do your work.

Rules are often confused with principles which are very important to homes and classrooms. Rules involve behaviors we can define, recognize, and therefore enforce consistently. Principles are concepts (not behaviors) by which we guide our lives. (Please see section on Principles.) We teach and model these. Some principles include:

Speak for yourself and not for anyone else.
Listen to others, then they will listen to you.
Avoid put-downs; no one needs them.
Take charge of yourself; you are responsible for you.
Show respect; every person is important.[13]

These, too, need to be discussed, both in families and in classrooms, and then posted. They are guidelines, not rules, and need to be modeled and taught by adults each and every day. These principles are the major tests of our integrity. It is much easier to discuss and post them, rather than live them. The principles a child learns and comes to depend on must be the important foundations which help determine how she handles her life; I can think of nothing more important to teach.

Life Lessons

Limits tell children their safety, development and learning are important.

Both policies and rules are the precursors to laws. There are some behaviors which are digressions and are not acceptable - for everyone and all times.

Policies and rules, like laws, inform us of the right things to do. Whether or not we abide by them is always our choice; this is self-discipline.

Structure and general guidelines can make any type of group living, home or classroom, more pleasant and efficient. Expectations are known and understood by all.

Principles are used to guide our lives; these, too, are about self-discipline.

"IT IS YOUR RESPONSIBILITY TO feed the dog."

"IT IS YOUR RESPONSIBILITY TO leave gas in the car after you've used it."

"IT IS YOUR RESPONSIBILITY TO pick up the dress-up clothes when you are finished playing."

"IT IS YOUR RESPONSIBILITY TO put your cup in the trash when you're done with lunch."

"IT IS YOUR RESPONSIBILITY TO turn your work in on time."

"IT IS YOUR RESPONSIBILITY TO ask for make-up work after you have been absent."

🍎 "IT IS YOUR RESPONSIBILITY TO make sure your homework gets finished, stays safe, and is returned to me on time."

These phrases tell clearly and concisely about responsibility and ownership; they make argument difficult. They also help keep us from lecturing and giving commands and are assertive and respectful. We must stop being afraid to tell children what their responsibilities are. We must also be willing and able to hold them accountable for their actions and responsibilities. This is how children learn to be responsible.

Life Lesson

This phrasing plainly teaches responsibility and ownership.

🏠 "YOU DO NOT HAVE THE RIGHT TO hit your brother."

🧍 "YOU DO NOT HAVE THE RIGHT TO hurt anyone in this class with your hands or your words."

🍎 "YOU DO NOT HAVE THE RIGHT TO speak disrespectfully to me or anyone."

Have you ever said, "We don't throw!" Not so, some of us do. This is a very weak statement as well. Have you ever caught yourself saying, "I will not tolerate...!" I have only said this right after what I do not tolerate (hitting, rudeness, bad language, etc.) has occurred. Which, of course, means I have just tolerated or permitted it. (Technically, making me sound foolish.) More importantly, "I will not tolerate" is about me and my values. "You do not have the right" is about the child, correct principles, rights, and responsibility - far more important lessons. Further, "You do not have the right" carries greater authority. "Big deal" is a possible answer to "I will not tolerate." It is rarely heard in response to "You do not have the right." Clearly, this phrasing is inappropriate for small digressions. "You do not have the right to leave your bed unmade" sounds, and is, absurd. Keep the truth in the phrase and only use it with rights and responsibilities.

Life Lesson

This phrasing teaches the concept of rights and responsibilities; it can also teach the difference between rights and privileges.

Anger Without Destruction

Sometimes it seems as though my children lead me to the brink of disaster and then push me over the cliff. I wish I could always be calm, but I cannot. It seems I am not alone.

From the *Statistical Handbook on the American Family*, by Bruce Chadwick and Tim Heaton (1992) come the following statistics:

Percent of Parents Who Yell				
Frequency	Children Age 0 - 4		Children Age 5 - 18	
	Men	Women	Men	Women
Never	19%	17%	10%	7%
Seldom	36%	31%	33%	29%
Sometimes	40%	44%	47%	51%
Very Often	6%	7%	11%	14%

This table clearly suggests not only that there is much yelling taking place but that parental yelling increases as our children get older. For parents of children from ages 0-4, 46% of men and 51% of women report yelling at their children sometimes or very often. By the time children are 5-18 years old, these percentages of yelling increase to 58% and 65% respectively. It would be much more comforting if this trend were reversed and suggested that parents tend to improve their skills and reduce their yelling as they become more skilled, veteran parents. Unfortunately, the statistics suggest otherwise.

Instead, the table most likely reflects both increased frustration and the absence of new skills culminating in a developed habit of yelling. Most of us recognize that raising our voice is not nearly so effective a discipline tool as refraining and speaking more softly. Yet, we fail to develop skills to do so. As adults, we need to learn to take care of our own anger. Time-out for us, is one method of dealing with our anger. As well, Jean Clarke offers another helpful tool, time-in, in her book, *Time-In: When Time-Out Doesn't Work*.

We do get angry with our children. We may question whether we *should* get mad at our children or students. The real question is *will* we get mad at them. Of course we will. And it is in their job description to frustrate the older generation. We may question also whether we should show our anger. The helpful question is: can we *not* show our anger? Anger always shows through in our tone or body language. Each of us has heard someone shriek, "I am *not* mad!" Right.

Perhaps more important and disconcerting is *what* is being screamed at our children. Let us take a close look at how we can each reduce yelling and still vent our anger without destruction.

The real problem we face is that when we are angry, we many times destroy character and self-esteem. This we do not want to do. When my hands are pulsing with "Neck, neck" as I move toward the offending child, I know I need skills and words which express my anger without destructiveness. I also need to carry a high degree of authority. If I am this angry, *something* has happened.

Once I witnessed one child throw scissors past another's ear just missing the second child. You can bet this got my attention. What do I want to accomplish with my discipline? I need the scissors never to be thrown again. Our words can carry a great deal more authority than we sometimes realize. Often, words coupled with appropriate touches of authority are sufficient.

What exactly are appropriate touches of authority? How can one add authority to words? Here are several suggestions.

Tips for Maintaining Authority

1. Move to the child. It is by no means necessary that every time you discipline a child with words that you must move to her. It is, however, necessary when a situation requires you to carry considerable authority; simply moving to the child lends an extraordinary amount of authority. Remember a time in high school when you committed some small infraction, and suddenly you realized that the teacher was now standing beside your desk? Remember that "oh-oh" feeling in the pit of your stomach which told you this was a bigger deal than you had expected. And this before your teacher ever said anything; she simply arrived.

2. Lower the tone of your voice from your general speaking range. Lower voices carry more authority. Higher voices weaken authority; try not to squeal in anguish or fear.

3. Lower the volume. People lean forward when we speak softly; they lean back when we yell. Yelling implies we are out of control; speaking softly indicates we are fully in control.

4. Speak slowly and clearly. This gives both of you time to think about what is being said. Speaking slowly also implies that what is being said is extra important.

5. Drop or rise to their physical level. Speak directly, face to face, on their level so that your body suggests that there will be no miscommunication. Directness, not intimidation, is the key.

6. Do try to make eye contact. However, do not get distracted by this issue. Several types of children fail to make eye contact:

• Children from many cultures are taught to show respect by looking down rather than looking at an adult speaking to them. Their body language is expressing respect as they have been taught. Many Asian, Native American, Middle Eastern, and Hispanic children are included in this group. This is not the time to change their cultural values.

• Children who realize that what they have just done was wrong also may put their heads down and fail to make eye contact. (The last time you did something you wished you had not, what did you do with your head?) Again, their body language speaks their embarrassment and chagrin with what they have done. This, too, is a good message.

• Children who have learned to expect emotional or physical abuse may also put their heads down. They await the next blow, be it verbal or physical.

• Children who wish to express defiance, not caring, or not owning what they have done also look down - more vigorously than the first three groups who drop their heads rather than sharply looking away. This group intentionally thrusts it down to send the message, "I'm not listening; you can't get to me." For two major reasons, it is helpful not to address this missing eye contact. (Bear with me for a moment; I know this sounds strange.) First, with truly defiant children, it is virtually impossible to make them look at you. Lifting chins only results in diverted eyes. "Look at me; *look at me!*" only begins a power struggle which you will very likely lose. Plus, you have been very effectively distracted from a dangerous issue (throwing scissors) to a less important issue (eye contact). Yes, disrespect is a big issue, but not as critical as throwing scissors. Defer the concern with disrespect to be dealt with at another, more appropriate time. Limiting ourselves to one very important issue is extremely helpful. Second, eye contact is not critical. Ear contact is. They are sending the message, "I am not listening." Their body language is slightly confused and inaccurate. They are not looking; they are listening. And at present we are dealing with the thrown scissors. There is no escape. Yes, you want eye contact, and you try to make eye contact, but it is not the critical issue. Throwing the scissors is the critical issue.

7. Sometimes it is helpful to touch a child while we are speaking. Some children turn this touch into a distracting issue and scream, "Don't touch me!" It is important that as parents or teachers we recognize whom we may touch and whom we should not. All teachers, especially male teachers, must be careful about how and whom they touch. If you do choose to touch while you speak to someone, it is called anchoring. Anchoring is a counseling technique which recognizes that the words being spoken at the time of the touch are most likely to be weighted and remembered or anchored. As we look at some "anger without destruction" phrases, it will become obvious that it is important to anchor at the end of the statement, not at the beginning. This delay also helps us to avoid grabbing.

In a low, firm voice, close to the child, at eye level:
🏠 "WHEN YOU throw the scissors,
    I AM concerned,
    BECAUSE someone could get seriously hurt;
    I EXPECT you never to throw the scissors again."

If the child is very impulsive, a more appropriate phrasing is:
🏠 "WHEN YOU throw the scissors,
    I AM concerned,
    BECAUSE someone could get hurt;
    I EXPECT you to ask permission before you use the scissors."

🏠 "WHEN YOU CHOOSE not to do your chores,
    I AM irritated,
    BECAUSE everyone in the family needs to contribute;
    I EXPECT you to do your chores without being told."

For the child who has changed the issue from whatever misbehavior has occurred to the higher level and more important, "I don't have to own my behavior" (remember, owning behavior and accountability are key to discipline):

🏠 "WHEN YOU CHOOSE not to own your behavior,
   I AM concerned,
   BECAUSE you own everything you do;
   I EXPECT you to hold yourself accountable."

🍎 "WHEN YOU continue to shout your question,
   I AM irritated,
   BECAUSE others need a turn, too;
   IT IS IMPORTANT that you let others speak."
   OR
   "WHEN YOU continue to shout your question,
   others miss their turns;
   IT IS IMPORTANT that you let others speak."

🍎 "WHEN YOU continuously speak out in class,
   everyone's learning is disrupted;
   I AM CONCERNED
   BECAUSE YOU DO NOT HAVE THE RIGHT to disrupt others' learning.
   I EXPECT you to raise your hand and wait to be called."

🍎 "WHEN YOU hurt others,
   I AM concerned,
   BECAUSE you do not have the right to hurt anyone;
   I EXPECT you to solve your problems without calling names (without hitting or without manipulation)."

Depending on the situation, the last sentence can begin with IT IS IMPORTANT THAT, YOU DO NOT HAVE THE RIGHT TO, IT WOULD BE HELPFUL IF, or I EXPECT.

There is one other situation when this type of phrase is very useful and necessary. As discussed previously, sooner or later almost all children and students roll their eyes, walk away, or mumble "whatever" during a disciplinary interaction. Their message in each case is that they do not need to listen to us. This supercedes the misbehavior which started the interaction because our authority is undermined and must be regained. The following is one form of phrasing to use:

"WHEN YOU CHOOSE not to listen to me,
I AM concerned,
BECAUSE everything I have to say to you is important;
I EXPECT you to listen and learn."

Our feelings may range from irritation to fury to scared to death. Behind each of these is usually a far more helpful and benevolent emotion, concern. All of us listen to concern more readily than we listen to anger or irritation.

When a teacher calls me about one of my children and is angry with him and tells me, "I can't get Kris to be quiet in class; he's disturbing everyone," I tend to turn into Mother Bear, whose job is to protect her offspring. In reaction, I judge this teacher harshly and think she is a weak teacher. I deal with her harshly by saying, "What type of discipline do you have in your class that you can't keep one child quiet?" Anger begets anger. On the other hand, when a teacher calls me and is *concerned* about my child and reports, "Kris is talking a lot in class; I'm concerned that he's disturbing the other children and that he is not learning all he can," I am appreciative and recognize her for the wonderful teacher she must be. After all, she is concerned about *my* child. Rather than attacking, I am cooperative; I reply, "What can I do to help?" There is a big difference. Each teacher had the same concern and the same problem with my son. Only one of these teachers handled this situation, and me, helpfully. Only one do I perceive as a good guy, on my side, caring about children and about my child and me. The other teacher I feel I must push and fight. And that is exactly what happens.

These dynamics, anger giving rise to anger and concern producing concern, occur between all people. Understanding them is especially important when talking to parents about their own children and when disciplining children who are our biggest challenges, those who are emotionally and physically abused or from dysfunctional families. These children are accustomed to having people react to their mistakes with anger. We become just another person who is mad at them, and some of these grown-ups get very nasty and hurtful when angry. Children know the rules of this *Anger Game*. The child does something wrong or annoying, the grown-up gets angry, the child becomes defiant or disrespectful, the adult blows up and attacks, the child pretends not to care. Genuine concern comes as a surprise. We have altered the game format. These children know how to respond to anger; they do not know how to respond to concern. This can be helpful in breaking a cycle of behavior. Further, it is very difficult to fight with someone who is concerned with your well-being.

Each of the phrases above, as most of the situations we will need to handle, can genuinely and more helpfully use the feeling term CONCERN. Please feel free to change any of the phrases to, "I am CONCERNED...." Use this phrase in times of your own anger, with dangerous incidents which must never be repeated, and with most troubled children and students. It is rare for this latter group to hear concern from anyone. Concern is almost always the real reason for, and the actual source of, our anger.

How will a child generally feel after a strong statement like this? Embarrassed, ashamed, bad? Is it our job to make a child feel bad? No, our job is not to *make* any child feel worse. However, it is our job to *allow* a child to feel badly about something she has done. In the above statements, the parent or teacher is never disrespectful, never belittles or shames the child. Rather, the adult descriptively shines a light on exactly what the child has done and allows the child to draw her own conclusions and feelings. We do not make the child feel bad with put-downs, negative or disrespectful comments; rather, the child makes herself feel bad when she understands and owns exactly what she has done and its results. These negative feelings about what one has chosen to do are called emotional homework. Emotional homework yields some of the most powerful, long-term behavioral changes. This child says to herself, "That was stupid; I wish I hadn't done that. I feel awful. (Pause) Of course, I'd never have to feel this way again if I never throw the scissors again. I am *never* throwing those things again!" Now that's good thinking.

Do we need to do anything more after these words? That, of course, depends on the situation. The caution is with regard to adding a punishment which will create resentment and lead the child to stop considering what he did (in other words, what a jerk he has been) and begin to consider what you have just done to him (in other words, what a jerk you are). Punishment can stop the process of emotional homework. However, sometimes additional disciplinary action may be needed. If, for example, the scissors were thrown by a very impulsive child, the last part of the phrase needs to be changed to "I EXPECT you only to use the scissors with my permission." In this case, we could also move the scissors to a place where the child cannot reach them and will have to ask before using them. As well, place this type of child at a table or place by himself when cutting to avert temptation and unpredictability; supervise him closely.

Most importantly, follow up with some form (words or action) of reconnection and affirmation - a smile, a pat, or a hug - that tells the child that it was a tough mistake, but we're still connected; he still has value. Or simply tell the child, "It was a long day and a tough lesson, but you learned it. It takes a lot of courage to learn from a mistake."

Our modeling of ANGER WITHOUT DESTRUCTION, of being respectfully assertive, is a lesson of great magnitude. Dr. Haim Ginott, in *Between Parent and Child*, stated that learning how to handle anger is the work of a lifetime. We are all pretty good with our children until we get angry. Learning how to handle anger and direct it helpfully without hurt demonstrates a very high level of maturity and development. This phrasing demonstrates one very appropriate and important way to handle anger. And not just with children!

Life Lessons

Anger frequently masks concern. Expressing the concern rather than the secondary anger is far more helpful and productive.

Children learn to do emotional homework and begin to understand that some behaviors are just not worth the aftermath of feelings which accompany them. A conscience is a most helpful item to develop.

Life Lessons

Children learn that when a mistake is made, their job is to take ownership of it, learn from it, and prevent it from ever happening again.

Parents and teachers carry authority without needing force, ugliness, or disrespect. So, too, can a child.

Life Messages

I have value even when someone is very angry with me. Concern overrides anger. I am valuable.

I can learn from my mistakes. I can solve problems.

KEYS TO AUTHORITY

- **"Don't start what you can't finish."** Always follow through with what you started. Choose your battles wisely.

- **Belief in yourself.** Our body language (including tone of voice) reflects directly how much we believe in what we are saying and how important it is. It is critical that we are sure of what we say and how we say it. With correct principles and life lessons guiding us, we can be certain.

- **Concern.** Concern for another's welfare and well-being is far more powerful and helpful than anger.

You may want to pause here and do the following exercise, an opportunity to apply "Gaining Cooperation" skills.

⌂   **Gaining Cooperation Practice -**
                                    Parents

Determine your "first-thought" response; then select a response likely to generate cooperation.

1. Sue throws a fork at her younger sister.

2. Erica has left her clothes all over her room again.

3. Manuel has left a huge mess after fixing a snack.

4. You need someone to close the door; you have no idea which child left it open.

5. Tamisha approaches you whining.

6. When you all arrive home from the grocery store, Haley and Scott leave the car without helping unload the grocery bags.

7. The gas tank is almost empty after Jill has used your car.

8. The babysitter reports that your children misbehaved while you were gone.

Gaining Cooperation Practice - Early Childhood Educators

Determine your "first-thought" response; then select a response likely to generate cooperation.

1. Sue throws a crayon at another student.

2. Erica has left her shoes and coat all over the classroom again.

3. You ask Manuel to pick up the items he has been working with; he tells you he didn't use them last.

4. The class misbehaves while you try to talk to a parent.

5. Tamisha approaches you whining.

6. Everyone but Sally and Scott are helping to pick up toys.

7. Jane refuses to wear her coat outside when it is very cold.

8. Whitney is bugging her neighbor again.

❧   **Gaining Cooperation Practice -**
                                    Teachers

Determine your "first-thought" response; then select a response likely to generate cooperation.

1. Sue throws a pencil at another student.

2. Two or three students are talking while you are teaching.

3. Stacy is beginning to clown around or verbally disrupt the class.

4. The class misbehaves when a substitute teacher takes over or when they go to the restrooms.

5. Tamisha approaches you disrespectfully.

6. Jane says her baby sister tore up her homework.

7. Kendra is not participating, has no book or pencil, and refuses to work on the assignment.

8. During class or in the hall, a student says, "I don't have to listen to you!"

7:
Respect as a Second Language

As you begin to alter your language, please keep in mind that this can be a very frustrating change. Most of us will be entering and using RESPECT AS A SECOND LANGUAGE. It will literally feel like a new language. Making this change requires practice and concentration. First, we have to catch ourselves using the disrespectful barriers common to us; this can be most discouraging. Many workshop participants have reported to me how very difficult this listening to ourselves process can be. Old habits die hard. People who get through this stage without hurting self-esteem are those who tell themselves, "Last week, I wasn't even aware of what I was saying. This week, I am a whole lot smarter. Next week, this will get easier and I will be better." They do not dwell on how frequently they hear disrespectful barriers; they focus on changing. They view change as a step by step process.

The next step in this change or learning process is using respectful alternatives. The actual application of this skill takes practice. Finding respectfully assertive phrases takes time to become a more natural process, particularly when we are tired, frustrated, or angry. This is, for all practical purposes, learning a new language. The term RESPECT AS A SECOND LANGUAGE is not used lightly. It would be difficult for any of us to try to use a foreign language exclusively - even with the use of a dictionary. This is the same type of frustration and obstacle you will be facing. However, considering the benefits of addressing people the way we wish, receiving more cooperation, and beginning to break the cycle of diminishing respect, this practice and struggle are well worth the effort, and the only way to gain the return to respect we now so acutely need. No one I know has accomplished this task without real effort; thus, true commitment is critical.

☞ Choose one of the phrases which you like and which seems most natural to you and add it to your speaking. Only after you have become comfortable with the first, add a second. Trying to add three or four at once usually creates frustration. Simply trying to be more respectful is quickly forgotten.

Adding Respect to Children's Language

We have addressed making our language more respectful. The next obvious question is how we can help our children become more respectful. Teachers across the nation report that in the last two generations, both children and adults have become progressively less respectful. Yet, when I talk to parents and teachers, I hear no lessening in the strength of their value for respect. We are lacking skills. We too frequently move from nice and passive to ugly and aggressive. We miss respectful assertiveness. Part of our job as parents and as teachers is to rediscover and reteach these skills. There are four keys to adding respect to the next generation's language.

KEYS TO ADDING RESPECT TO CHILDREN'S LANGUAGE

☞ **Be respectful.** Keep respect constantly in our own language. Always work with others from a perspective of respect. Modeling (what we practice, not what we believe) is the most powerful teaching tool we have. Respect continues to be modeled far too infrequently.

☞ **Insist upon respect.** Insist that they approach everyone with respect. Neither accept nor overlook incidents of disrespect.

☞ **Maintain dignity.** Avoid violating anyone's dignity during all interactions, especially disciplinary interactions.

☞ **Teach.** Take time to teach RESPECT AS A FIRST LANGUAGE to young children. Teach RESPECT AS A SECOND LANGUAGE skills to older children. Help children with more respectful phrasing; guide them through reapproaching, interacting, and problem solving with respect. Respect is now like a second language. We have to learn it, and so must they.

8:
Gaining Cooperation Summary

Although at times we manage to manipulate or force cooperation, cooperation is not something we *take* from others. The last time you cooperated with someone, what caused you to do so? You liked the other person, you wanted to contribute, to make life easier, or to help. In short, we all cooperate *because we choose to do so.*

> **Cooperation is a *gift* from others; they choose whether or not to bestow it upon us.**

With our words, body language, and actions, we can engender resistance or cooperation; this choice is ours. Our task, then, is to help make cooperating feel more comfortable than resisting. Generally, we feel that another's lack of cooperation is their fault. We overlook our part and our ownership of the approach we use. Our approach, the words and body language we select, is a decisive factor in determining whether or not cooperation takes place. It is the only factor we control.

Respect is more than language, more than phrasing; it is a perspective from which we determine how we treat others. This perspective directs our language. The perspective we select might also be called our attitude. It is the place where respect is born and brought into true existence. Being genuine is essential.

All that has been discussed in this chapter is summed up by the words of wisdom found in the Golden Rule, a correct principle: Do unto others as you would have them do unto you. In other words, the Golden Rule asks, "Do you choose to treat others, including children, in ways you do not wish to be treated?" The question of integrity reappears here. Are you who you want to be, who you want others to perceive you as being, who you want your children to be? Do your actions match your beliefs?

Believing in the Golden Rule is one thing, living it, another.

PART IV - DON'T START WHAT YOU CAN'T FINISH

9:
Discipline Strategies

We have looked at words and phrasings which help to gain cooperation. But no matter how wonderful our words are, they will not always work. And with the under three year old set, taking action will always be a large part of discipline. We have now arrived at Step Three of Discipline: "Take the action necessary. Do what you've said you would do." The caution, DON'T START WHAT YOU CAN'T FINISH, was discussed previously. In order to avoid unending testing and loss of authority, it is necessary that once we have started discipline on a specific issue, we follow through.

Choose your battles wisely. Try not to say no arbitrarily. Take time to determine what is really important and what is not, not just right now, but for the future. Will it matter in two years, in twenty years? This judgment call, the choosing of battles, is difficult for many of us. When in doubt, talk to other parents or teachers; listen to what several people feel is important. Listen to your own little voice inside. Remember, no one knows you or your children better than you do. So when your little voice speaks, truly listen. It is usually one of your own principles speaking to you.

What, then, are some strategies we can use, actions we can take that teach life lessons and correct principles *and are effective, too?*

Disciplinary Consequences[14]

Consequences, as a disciplinary tool, continue to be misunderstood and misused. A consequence, by definition, can be anything that follows an event or an action. This could conceivably include rewards and punishments, neither of which is a form of discipline. Thus, we will use the term DISCIPLINARY CONSEQUENCE to limit the concept of consequences to true discipline actions only. The consequences included here will always be *fair, reasonable, direct, and related*. This type of disciplinary consequence will also always *teach* the lesson the child requires at the time. Consequences also teach ownership of not only behavior, but also of the results and effects of the behavior. Disciplinary consequences very effectively teach the fundamental principle:

You are responsible for what you choose to do and for what happens to you and others as a result of your decisions and actions.

Disciplinary consequences are frequently confused with punishments and rewards. These other systems of child management use the word consequence to describe punishments (check mark, name on board, loss of unrelated privilege) and rewards (marble in the jar, green card, checks). The use of the term consequence in this text is strictly limited to actions which are fair, reasonable, direct, and related to a specific antecedent behavior, not simply any action taken. True disciplinary consequences must also teach the lesson needed. Making a child pay or rewarding a child are distinctly different from allowing a child to experience the related and fair or naturally occurring consequences to her behavior. Disciplinary consequences always teach a related lesson concerning the specific mistake or misbehavior; they clearly link behaviors and outcomes. Unlike punishments, they are never arbitrary or spiteful.

Early in my career, I was invited to a preschool to deal with a four year old boy whom we will call Frankie. The preschool's concern about Frankie was his continual practice of riding a tricycle into a wall in a huge gymnasium-type room. His teachers were concerned about his safety and the wall's appearance. Despite numerous measures taken to change this behavior, Frankie continued to smash into the wall.

I arrived just ahead of the time period when Frankie's group played in the large room. As expected, Frankie was the first child to get onto a tricycle. Before he started moving, I stepped in front of him and introduced myself.

"Hi, Frankie, I'm Mrs. Swift."

He did not know me. Now it is time to tell the truth and identify the problem respectfully.

"Frankie, your teachers tell me that you have been riding the tricycle into the wall. And they also tell me that they do not want you to do this."

No response from Frankie, except a disdainful look that says here we go again. So I proceed.

"Here's the deal, Frankie."

Now it is time to set up a disciplinary consequence by linking one behavior with its consequence and a second behavior with its consequence.

"You have a choice. You can choose to ride the tricycle and keep it away from the wall

Behavior 1, simple description, linked to:

and continue to ride the tricycle for as long as you like until snack time when they are all put away.

Consequence 1, notice I qualified "as long as you like" with "until snack time...."

Or you can choose to ride the tricycle into the wall

Behavior 2, which he already knows about, linked to:

and not get to ride the tricycle until tomorrow morning."

Consequence 2, fair and related.

It is easy to see how one can turn Consequence 1 into a reward - "If you keep the tricycle away from the wall, I'll give you a sticker." Or how Consequence 2 can be altered to punishment and control - "You can choose to ride the tricycle into the wall, and you won't get to go to story time with all the other children."

Have you ever noticed that what you say and what they hear are often two different things? Now it is time to check.

"Frankie, what did I say?"

Teens may hear this as condescending; it is best used with younger children.

Frankie answers, "You said if I ride the bike into the wall, you're going to take it away."

That is not what I said; he has taken my words of discipline and turned them into a threat (barrier to cooperation) with shades of control.

"Close, but not quite. I said that you have a choice; what happens is all up to you. You can choose to ride the tricycle and keep it away from the walls, and you will be able to ride the tricycle as long as you like until they all get put away at snack time. Or you can choose to ride the tricycle into the wall and not ride the tricycle until tomorrow. What did I say?"

I tell him the truth. Once again, I link chosen behaviors with the disciplinary consequences.

Frankie mumbles, "You said if I ride the bike into the wall, I can't ride it until tomorrow."

Close enough; he is not terribly happy at this moment.

Since I have used a very appropriate discipline tool for this child and situation, and because I do carry a great deal of authority, and because I have set this disciplinary action up beautifully, one might assume that Frankie will, of course, keep the tricycle away from the wall. However, all of us who deal with real, live children realize that this is not what is going to happen. All children with self-respect and courage who face a new person and technique test us. Frankie, like other children, needs to find out if I mean what I say. He could ask, but they never do. The only way he can discover this is to run the tricycle into the wall. Sometimes we fail to expect this testing, this learning the lesson the hard way. Sometimes we let this testing behavior get to us and make us angry. When the child tests us, we become angry and say, "Why did you do that? Didn't I tell you not to?! How could you be so foolish? I told you I'd take that bike away!" We need to remember that it is the child who must deal with the consequences; we need to be able to stay emotionally disengaged from the child's decision. The child has made a mistake in judgment. Thus, when Frankie did decide to find out how much authority I actually carry and if I mean what I say, he ran the tricycle right into the wall and then looked for me to see what I was going to do. I was already on my way to him.

I looked at Frankie and said these very important words, "I see you made your choice (or decision)." Frankie's eyes got a little larger at this point, but he is still not terribly worried. For he, as do all children, carries with him at all times, an imaginary duffle bag full of distractors, excuses, and reasons for having done things. Frankie reaches in and says to me, "I didn't do it." I have just seen him do it, but I do not have it on video tape. It is not my job to prove he did it. In addition, this is a great distractor. Please realize that IQ testing is going on right at this moment and it is not Frankie who is being tested. If I am foolish enough to fall for it, we will spend our time arguing about whether or not he ran the trike into the wall, rather than following through with the discipline. Besides, I know he did it; he knows he did it; he even knows I know he did it. Do not bite.

"You made your choice,"   *I simply restated.*

"I won't do it again," Frankie quickly replies.   *Another distractor. This is **not** the time to ask, "Just how stupid do you think I am?" Someday a teenager will tell you. Neither is it time to back down and say, "Good, ok. You've learned your lesson." This teaches children they can get away with things once, say the right phrase, and avoid discipline. As discussed previously, not following through diminishes our authority.*

"I'm glad, because tomorrow you'll be able to ride it for the whole period."   *At this point in time, Frankie decided that I might be a problem.*

If you are thinking that Frankie's next distractor will be a tantrum, think again. This is a sophisticated four year old. If he throws a fit, he will give up possession of the tricycle; he is way too smart for that. He clamped on to the tricycle with both hands. It is time to take him from the tricycle. Yes, I pried his little fingers from the handlebars (physical assertion, not aggression), left the tricycle sitting where it was, and began to carry Frankie out of the room. He is kicking, hitting, and screaming - trying to do his best to hurt me. How do I feel as I carry him past the very teachers who hired me to solve this problem? I feel just fine for several reasons. And you, too, need to feel fine when you discipline, otherwise you simply will not do it. First, I have treated Frankie respectfully, fairly, and justly. I have never once violated his dignity. Second, I could have described this scene when I was first told about Frankie, the tricycle, and the wall. He has been riding the tricycle into the wall for three weeks; he is not going to learn this lesson easily or happily. He will, of course, choose to learn it the hard way. No one should be surprised by this choice. Third, I have not failed. It is not time to judge whether I have been successful. That time comes tomorrow with his second approach to the situation under the new guidelines and after the lesson has been taught. Fourth, I have done this child a favor. As much pain as Frankie is in presently, it is the least amount of pain he is going to experience learning this particular lesson. The earlier the lesson is learned, the lower the amount of pain - physical, emotional, social, and financial.

When I tell this story in my workshops and I ask how people think I am feeling while I am carrying Frankie from the room (or how they would feel while they were carrying him out), they throw out words like "humiliated," "sad," "mean," or "embarrassed." Perhaps that is how many of you reading this feel also. Let's address this directly. Ask yourself why would I feel humiliated, or sad, or mean or embarrassed taking the action this child needs to become a more cooperative and contributing member of our society, a child who is learning that his actions have consequences, that he will need to think about the decisions he chooses to make. I have given this child a gift. When we give a child a gift for his birthday, or for Christmas or for graduation from one of life's passages, we usually don't feel humiliated, sad, mean or embarrassed. And this gift to Frankie has so much more value, is so important to his future. I feel great. Give yourself permission to feel great also.

Let us look at the long range picture. The specific lesson Frankie is learning is to handle a tricycle safely and appropriately. More generally and for the long term, what I have begun to teach Frankie is a Life Lesson. Whether he will learn it forever in this first trial or whether we will only begin to build the foundation for this lesson is yet to be known. Either way, we have *invested* with our discipline. The Life Lesson is: If you choose to handle a vehicle - any vehicle - safely and appropriately, we will permit you to continue operating it. However, if you choose to handle this vehicle unsafely and inappropriately, we will wait until we think you are more ready before we allow you to use the vehicle again. You do not have the right to hurt yourself, others, or objects with carelessness or recklessness. Frankie can learn or begin to learn this concept at the tricycle level reasonably inexpensively. Or he may end up learning it at the car level at the cost of another person's life - a far greater price, with far more pain. I have given this child a gift, the beginnings, and perhaps even the completion, of a very important life lesson. Considering some of the other options for learning this lesson, his pain, as great as it is to him right now, is minimal compared to what it might have been. Not a bad gift. Of course, Frankie does not see this, nor is he going to thank me now. Nor will he think of me on the day he is driving carefully through a school zone and consequently manages to avoid hitting a child who dashes into his path. But I have contributed to his life, his self-discipline, and his well-being. So I need to understand the worth of what I have done. I feel good while I carry this very upset child out of the room - very good.

Evaluation of this disciplinary procedure comes the next morning when he again heads straight for the tricycles. It is here where Frankie altered his thought process and thus his behavior. Each morning prior to my intervention, Frankie asked himself this question, "Do I want to ride the bike into the wall or not?" The answer was, "Yes, I love smashing into it!" Today his thought process is more helpful, "Do I want to ride the bike or not? Yes, I love the bike! Of course, I have to keep it away from the stupid wall in order to be able to ride it." So be it. After disciplinary consequences, his question changes from the behavior level to the consequence level. Rather than choosing between behaviors (to crash or not), Frankie chooses between consequences (to ride or not). I have given him an opportunity to learn to make decisions at the outcome level rather than the behavior level. When he is sixteen and deciding what he will do, he may have learned to ask himself questions at the outcome or consequence level rather than at the behavior or temptation level. For example, rather than simply checking to see if he wants to go with his friends to the lake from the party, he may ask himself whether he wants to get in a car with a drunken driver and risk his life. Do you know what we call kids and adults who ask themselves questions at the outcome level? Self-disciplined. To paraphrase: One small step for Frankie, one giant leap for self-discipline.

Here are some additional examples of disciplinary consequences.

⌂ "YOU HAVE A CHOICE;
YOU CAN CHOOSE to play nicely (cooperatively) AND continue playing with your friends, or
YOU CAN CHOOSE to continue bothering them AND have to stop playing with them and play by yourself."

⌂ "YOU CAN DECIDE to pick up your toys AND you will keep possession of them, or
YOU CAN DECIDE to leave them, AND I will pick them up and keep them until Friday."
Better still:
"You can pick up your toys, AND you've done your chore; or you can leave them, and I will pick them up, AND you will owe me a chore. Your choice of chores will be gathering up laundry or cleaning up after supper."

🚶 "YOU CAN CHOOSE to keep your hands to yourself AND continue working at this table, or
YOU CAN CHOOSE to put your hands on other people AND move to another table."

🍎 "YOU CAN redo this paper AND raise your grade, or
YOU CAN leave it as it is AND earn the failing grade on it."

☞ Paint a picture of *linked* actions and consequences with your words. Note the AND in each clause. Take a child down both complete paths. Each time the first choice links one behavior to its consequence, and the second choice connects the alternative behavior with its consequence. In this way, we help children choose between desired consequences (passing or failing) rather than between desired behaviors (doing more work or doing no work). This helps a child perceive and be more comfortable with the reasons behind the more appropriate choice.

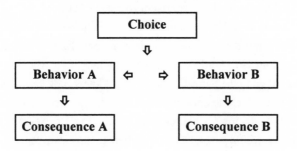

Another helpful phrasing for disciplinary consequences involves a WHEN YOU, THEN YOU sequence.

 "WHEN YOU pick up your room,
(THEN) YOU may read (leave, go out and play, watch television, go on to your next activity, do what you want)."

🧍 "WHEN YOU pick up your lunch box,
(THEN) YOU may play with the blocks."

🍎 "WHEN YOU have finished your class work,
(THEN) YOU may start your homework (read your book, play the math games, start your project)."

Unless a child is tired or ill, he cannot handle doing *nothing* for very long. Keep in mind, holding you up or working against you as you get agitated is doing *something*. If you can remain detached, your child will have nothing to do. This "when you have completed the necessary task(s), then you can go on to your fun activities" is a wonderful lifelong lesson (work first, play after) as well as an effective tool for the present. It is *not* the phrasing of choice when *you* are in a hurry.

☞ Consequences are most effective when they are immediate and inevitable, not harsh.

Trying to find and use the biggest consequence often backfires. When my children were in pre-school, I became irritated with them because their room was yet again a mess. Knowing that the once-a-year, very popular, big event Santa Claus parade was happening later that morning, I pronounced that when their room was cleaned up, we could go to the Santa Claus parade. I knew they very much wanted to go, but I overlooked two very important factors. First, they were so excited about the parade that it was virtually impossible for them to stay on task. Second, only a mean, evil, wicked mother would not take her children to this wonderful event. Good mothers take their little Santa Claus-believing children to the Santa Claus parade. It was not acceptable to me to not take them, especially for not having picked up their room well enough. Consequences must be fair, not harsh to be most effective and helpful. In addition, consequences must be tolerable to the parent. Never set up something you are uncomfortable following through with, because your bluff will be called. And yes, I helped them clean up their room (to keep me legitimate) and then took them to the parade. I am not going to Mommy Hell over the Santa Claus Parade!

☞   When you catch yourself asking what can I use to get this child to do what I want, you have crossed over into manipulation, rewards, or punishment.

☞   Consequences easily become threats ("IF YOU ... I WILL..."); when imposed in anger, these aim to make the child pay, not learn.

☞   Forcing or inventing consequences usually fails and frequently involves punishment, control or rewards. ("You can choose to pick up your toys or to get a spanking." or "If you ride the trike in the street, I will take it away from you." or "If you pick up, I'll let you have a cookie.")

☞   As wonderful a tool as disciplinary consequences are, no tool is appropriate in every situation. Other tools will be needed as well.

☞   As children age, they can be involved in establishing consequences; they are then more likely to cooperate and to make more appropriate decisions.

> **Life Lessons**
>
> Consequences help children learn to think ahead to effects and repercussions of behaviors. They teach children to own both behaviors and results. Children learn to make decisions based on consequences or outcomes rather than behaviors.
>
> Children learn to work or finish important tasks before play.
>
> Children learn that when they behave appropriately, responsibly, and maturely, freedom and privileges increase. They move and grow into their lives.

Guide to Remedy, Amends, or Contribution

When a child makes a mess, breaks or loses something belonging to another, or hurts someone, it is important that we help him understand the need for repair, restoration, or restitution. Our focus too often is on what went wrong rather than on what needs to be done to fix it.

🏠 "The milk is spilled. Do you know where the dish cloth is?"

🏠 "I'm glad you had a good time. The dress-up clothes are all over the floor. Now you need to put them back in their box. Will you start with the ones on your bed or those on the floor?"

🏠 "When you use my car, you do not have the right to use up all the gas. I need at least enough gas to get to work."

🏠 "Did you enjoy lunch? Me, too. Now it's time for us to clear the table."

🧍 "Oops, the paint spilled on the floor. The sponges are back by the sink."

🧍 "You sat on his crayon. Can you find him another green one in the box?"

- "Your test tube is broken; you will need to bring money for a replacement tomorrow."

- To the student who has ruined another's pen:
  "Do you have an extra pen in your desk?"

Life Lesson

Here is a wonderful opportunity to help children learn the concept: Whenever you undo (harm, break, damage) anything or make something wrong (lose, disturb, alter), it is your responsibility to make it right again (fix, replace).

I bet many of you did not realize that how you handle your 18 month old spilling juice and how much gas is in your gas tank when your child turns 16 are related. They are. One of your first opportunities to teach remedy and amends is with spills. We begin to teach that when you undo something, you need to replace, fix, or clean it. Some children learn this lesson by age two; others take longer. However, once learned, it works in most situations. The teen who discovers that he has used up all of the gas in your car returns to the gas station and (no, she does not fill up the tank) puts in a couple of dollars of gas. When you get into your car the next morning, you have fuel. No problem exists and therefore, no discipline is necessary. Well, actually, discipline did take place - the afternoon before. It was self-discipline and the goal of all our disciplinary practices.

Jean Clarke in *Time-In: When Time-Out Doesn't Work* discusses making amends quite thoroughly. She suggests five excellent guidelines for determining amends to others:

1) The amender must put forth the effort.
2) Amends should support family or classroom values.
3) Amends should help the child become a better person.
4) The amend should be related to the problem.
5) The amend must be satisfactory to the victim.

Occasionally we are unable to make true amends - as when an antique is broken or a personal memento is lost. This, too, can be an important life lesson. While playing with a ball in the living room (against house rules), my son broke one of three graduated glass candle holders which had been a wedding gift. He very willingly cleaned up the glass and offered to buy me a new one. The set, of course, was not to be found anywhere. Replacement was impossible. Saddened though he was, he learned that making it right is not always possible. It is far less painful, both emotionally and financially, to learn this with a ball and a glass candle holder than with a car and a child. When you kill a person by driving carelessly, you cannot replace him or make amends - *no matter how badly you may wish to.* This is one of life's harshest lessons: best to learn it early and inexpensively.

We begin teaching children to contribute by maintaining themselves and taking care of their own needs and business, such as getting dressed and picking up their own toys. As children get older, we add that it is also their responsibility to contribute to the family. By teaching our children how to do all household chores, we are able to send them off to college or work with adequate survival skills. We want it to be a luxury to bring home laundry, not a necessity. We do them a disservice by not helping them learn. After all, do you want your own child to marry someone who neither knows how to do chores nor expects to do them?

We also start teaching them to contribute to larger arenas of their lives. As noted previously, no matter what group we belong to, family, classroom, school, church, organization, nation, planet, we need to contribute to its general welfare and maintenance. No group can afford parasites. No one has the right to be a long-term or permanent parasite; short periods of no contribution in times of great duress and need are, of course, acceptable.

Taking care of only our own life and our own problems is not enough. Each of us finds himself in need of help and contribution from others at various times. This is perhaps the best use of a *credit system.* Healthy marriages and good relationships of every kind build a surplus of contributions; one never knows when the tables may turn and the resources be needed. We need to have enough resources.

🏠 "Our whole house needs cleaning today. Would you rather vacuum the carpets or mop the kitchen floor?" If they ask why they have to do it, *tell them,* briefly.

🧍 "It's time to wipe off all of the tables."

🍎 "After all of the cutting we've done for this project, we need to pick up all the scraps on the floor."

🍎 "It's time to clean up the lab."

Life Lesson

Contributing teaches a truth: people need people.

When you do something wrong, frequently what you need to do is make it right.

Life Message

I can solve problems.

Problem? Think!

When children face problems, we have an opportunity to build self-esteem and confidence and send the message, "I can think for myself." Too often, we move in with our own solutions and generate resistance or sabotage or helplessness. It is critical that we let children practice thinking and problem-solving skills on *child-size* problems so that their skills have a chance to grow and develop with their problems, which seem only to get larger as we age. Further, children become comfortable with the fact that problems are part of every-day life and relationships; the key is to stay calm and work together to find a plan that just might work for everyone.

🏠 "You both want the same toy (as you take possession of the offending toy); this is a problem. What are some ways to handle this situation?" *(Until you take possession, no one will listen.)*

🏠 "Both of you feel it is your turn to ride in the front seat. Don't try to convince me; work it out between you. You have fifteen seconds, or I will solve it; my solution is for you both to be in the back."

🏠 "You each want to watch different TV shows (as you turn off the television and take possession of the remote control). How can you two solve this?"

🏠 "You both need the car; when you've worked out a solution, come get the keys."

⌂   "Here is a list of the chores the three of you need to do by noon. You determine how you will divide them, and let me know who is responsible for what before you begin."

⚐   "You both want the same chair. What can you think of to do about it?"

⚐   "You both need the computer; let's work out a solution that is agreeable to both of you."

🍎   "You both want to sharpen your pencil. The rule is only one person at the pencil sharpener at a time. Decide who should stay and who needs to return to her desk. You have ten seconds or both of you will have to sit down."

🍎   "You both want the same report topic; everyone needs to have a different topic. You have until tomorrow morning to work this out. I'll be here right after school if you want some help."

☞ Help guide them through alternatives and problem solving until you find a solution agreeable to the parties involved.

☞ Young children or children who have *not* learned or practiced problem-solving skills need to be taught these skills by modeling or walking through problems appropriately *before they are left on their own to solve problems.* Problem-solving skills need to be taught, walked through, and modeled. Over and over and over again. Abandoning children by saying, "It's your problem, you solve it," may lengthen the learning process or allow unhealthy practices like manipulation or coercion to develop.

Life Lessons

When we have a problem, we need to think, work together, and come up with a plan, which is mutually acceptable to all involved.

Children learn that helplessness is not acceptable or necessary.

Life Lessons

Problems will always be with us. Our job is to accept this and take care of them as efficiently and cheerfully as possible. Grace is a wonderful virtue and a skill in itself.

Life Messages

Children who have conquered problems build the belief system: I can think for myself and I can solve problems.

They are also immunized against discouragement and even suicide. These children understand that life is filled with problems, but these can all be worked through, by oneself or with help from others.

Use Humor

Humor is a wonderful way to change moods and slide through troubled times. In our family, humor is the lubricant which helps us keep functioning; without it, we truly would be lost and life would be uglier. When I am too tired to get into *real discipline*, I often reach for humor. Children almost always respond positively. It is important to keep the humor within the child's level; it is easy to go over a child's head. Humor is aided by our bond; I would only ask a child who feels absolutely safe from physical harm from me if he wants to continue in his present life-form. Not having previously established this sense of trust and safety would prevent me from using humor of this nature.

The most frequently asked question I receive about using humor is, "How do you find it?" I truly do not know. Drawing upon shared experiences and stories can help. I do know that it is worth working on and developing. Especially if you are ever going to live with teenagers. Here are some examples.

To the child who gives you an evil look:
🏠 "That look is ugly, but it's not up to your regular standard. I know you can do better." (It is very hard to make ugly faces when you are laughing.)

Sometimes by the end of the day, after struggling to get to bed, none of us feels very loving; yet I hate to miss this nightly opportunity.

⌂ "The Mommy Handbook says we have to kiss goodnight, but it doesn't say we have to enjoy it." (I confess I frequently refer to this non-existent product of my imagination.)

⚱ Tickle a child into changing his mood and his mind.

🍎 When two students are talking or one is clowning around, walk near them and hold up a small stop sign; you won't need to say anything.

> ☞ Always avoid sarcasm, derision, mockery, belittling, and ridicule - anything which makes fun of a child. Using humor consists of fun with them, not fun at their expense.

> **Life Lesson**
>
> Life and people do not always do as we would wish; a sense of humor helps our mood, our attitude, and our health.

Take Action - Physical Discipline

For a time, in my seminars, I would say tongue-in-cheek, "Some of you are saying to yourselves - physical stuff *finally!* " I no longer say this because physical abuse has risen to such a disturbing level. Our generation, as parents, caregivers, and teachers, needs to wipe out physical abuse. In part, this means we need to abandon striking, slapping, shaking, shoving, grabbing, biting, spanking, in short, hurting children in any way. Physically hurting children is an extreme form of punishment which we have for years known creates resentment and backlash. It is remarkably short lived, stops working, and destroys relationships. Furthermore, it is *not effective*. Children become immune and impervious. If it were effective, one would not have to keep doing it, nor keep increasing the severity. Step by step, increment by increment, a parent moves toward abuse. And keep in mind that many victims of physical abuse become adult perpetrators and perpetuators.

Hitting also teaches appalling lessons and flawed principles. Too many people have learned to operate their lives on flawed, potentially harmful principles that say: 1) we solve problems with aggression and pain and power, 2) if someone does something, however minor, that you do not like, you do have the right to hit or hurt that person, and 3) aggression and violence are respectable ways of solving problems. We need to be teaching our children the correct principles in the following life lessons.

Life Lessons

You do not have the right to hurt anyone even if you do not like them or do not approve of what they are doing (except in self defense, defense of others, illegal actions, extreme situations).

Actions speak loudly. Taking disciplinary action sends the message that we mean business. We can mean business without being mean.

What do we mean by physical discipline? The adult gets up and takes action and is physical in response, not just verbal. Although this type of technique works with all ages of children, it is especially helpful with young children (1-7 years) and tired children. Some examples follow.

- Walk a child to her bedroom, to her chore, to a destination.

- Take several children to bed by "train" - place hands on the waist of the person in front of you and travel locomotion style.

- Carry a child piggy-back to the bathtub.

- Put the hockey stick left out *again* into the shed.

- Remove yourself from whining or disrespect.

- Remove a child to her bedroom or outside or another area of the house.

- Remove an "offending" toy.

🏃 Sit a squirmy, distracted, or aggressive child on your lap at circle time.

🏃 Take the hand of a child who runs when she needs to be walking. (Have her verbally commit to walking all the way to the play area before you release her. Give only one opportunity to get it right.)

🏃 Involve a child in songs by helping him with hand motions.

🏃 Put objects which seem to lead to trouble in the cupboard.

🏃 Stand by the bathroom door when a "creative" child washes her hands or on an I-am-finding-all-kinds-of-trouble day.

🍎 Walk and teach near a student or group not attending well. Walk throughout your class frequently.

🍎 Begin walking a student to the gym.

🍎 Help walk a child away from trouble.

🍎 Gently put your hand on a student's shoulder to quiet him down or to bring back focus. Alternatively, lightly tap his desk or paper.

🍎 Meet your class as they return from gym or recess.

🍎 Stand by your door or in the hall during passing periods. This action significantly changes hall behavior in a school where teachers do this consistently.

Outsmart Them

Outsmarting children is difficult but not impossible. It is also one of my favorite strategies. Included in the concept of outsmart them is *do no harm and take no advantage*. Manipulation is neither involved nor allowed. This strategy simply means out think a problem or situation. Not a bad lesson to teach a child; of course this one will return to undo you when you are the problem.

⌂ As a bedtime ritual, read to your children IN THEIR OWN beds, AFTER bath, toilet, and teeth brushing. BRING one drink. For a time, we read to our children on the couch and then had to get them to their beds; this change of venue tended to unsettle them and make them ready to play again. Children settle down and settle in when reading; take advantage of this situation (not the child) by reading to them where they can fall asleep. Sometimes a child's second wind can last longer than ours.

⌂ "No" is the answer to any question asked or any request made when you are on the phone.

⌂ Buy an alarm clock; let *it* wake up your child.

⌂ Use a timer to tell them when to take turns, when to get out of the bath, when to come in from the backyard. A child can argue with you, but there is no arguing with a clock. (There is tampering with it, though. Sometimes to complete this outsmart them arrangement, the clock must be placed out of reach, or you will need to set the kitchen timer as well.)

⌂ Send them outside! I mean *allow* them to play outside.

⌂ Call a friend. Call a friend for each of them.

⌂ Choose your neighborhood wisely, when possible.

⌂ For fighting: Place them on a couch or in two separate chairs and tell them they can get up when they give each other mutual permission.[15] Explain mutual permission. Or place them on two different chairs and tell them when they think of a solution, they can move their chair closer to the other child. When they have several solutions, they will be close enough to each other to talk and decide which solution they like best. Then they may call you and tell you their plan.[16]

⌂ When things get noisy, ugly, or out of control, call for Absolute Silence for five minutes. Or play the see-who-can-be-quiet-the-longest-game.

⌂ Play a child's tape in the car or at sleep time. Use coordinating tapes and books. To paraphrase, you can lead a child to bed but you cannot make him sleep. Give the mind something to do so the body can be quiet.

⌂ On long trips, plan stops to eat, outside if possible, to run and get rid of built-up steam. Take along new or special used-only-in-the-car toys and activity books. Check your local children's book store for activity ideas.

⌂ Have Santa or his elf helper visit (unseen, of course,) early in December and bring Christmas crafts, puzzles, books, and other fun things to do. It is awfully hard to wait for that one big night. Do the same for other long awaited, eagerly anticipated occasions such as Halloween and birthdays.

⌂ Give transitional warnings. These are frequently suggested for young children; they also prove most helpful with older children, even teens.
   "We need to leave the park in five minutes; choose whatever you most want to do and go and do it; otherwise, you won't have time to do what's most important to you."
   "At noon, the (rented) video game has to go back to the store."
   "Your room needs to be finished before we leave in ten minutes."

Early childhood educators incorporate the outsmart them concept as well as any group I have ever met:

🚶 Allow children to bring a cuddly toy from home for nap time.

🚶 Have lots of activities, as well as soft space for quiet times.

🚶 Give them several opportunities to play outside or do gross motor activities.

🚶 Sing with them when you move from one room to another or when you get caught and need to wait in line.

🚶 Add hand motions and finger play to songs, rhymes, and stories. Use these to keep "busy" hands occupied.

For clean up time:[17]

👤 Have the children line up side by side and on all fours as a human comb and comb a play area completely clean. Explain the phrase "go over with a fine tooth comb."

👤 Toys and game parts get mixed up. Collect them and then tell the children that the "lost toys" are sad and want to go back to their homes and families. Play it up.

👤 Use a large piece of cardboard as a scoop to pick up toys with lots of small parts, such as blocks and Legos.

🍎 "No" is the answer to any request made while you are talking to another student, teacher, or parent.

🍎 Questions which interrupt inappropriately are not answered.

🍎 When a student is not paying attention, move to the student, make eye-contact, and ask a question looking directly at this student. At the very end of the question, slide your eyes to the student behind or beside the one not attending, and using the second student's name direct the question to him. The student not paying attention knows you caught him and is grateful for at least twenty minutes, and you have lost no valuable teaching time.

> **Life Lesson**
>
> Gentleness, respect, consideration, and thinking are healthy, acceptable methods of influencing others; manipulation is not.

Determine What Child Needs[18]

Interestingly, parents and teachers rarely consider this action a disciplinary one. Many times, meeting a child's needs will avert or short circuit a problem quickly and easily. No one ever said we had to make child-rearing more difficult than it already is. This technique is frequently used with babies and toddlers; it can also be helpful with older children. What types of needs can we meet? Bodily comfort for young children -

hunger, discomfort, wetness, position change, temperature adjustment, boredom, over-stimulation, and fatigue. There are also emotional needs such as attention, affection, affirmation, emotional safety, and understanding. As well, there are needs stemming from frustration and thwarted efforts which require problem-solving help. Providing developmentally appropriate activities and materials also meets needs.

- Give attention, even in small amounts, throughout the day. Leave extra time at the end of the day, at reunion times, and at bedtime. Schedule regular times to be together.

- Help with big jobs such as cleaning a bedroom. It is difficult for children to stay with a task which seems overwhelming. Working with them helps. I only work as long as they are working; I explain I am here to help, not to perform single-handedly.

- Be sensitive and perceptive! Listen and watch.

- Provide a small climbing apparatus inside or allow them to play with sofa pillows and cushions.

- Select one floor level cupboard and place all of your plasticware in it; allow access to small children.

- Teach your children to say, "I need a hug," when they need some attention. Stop what you are doing and hug them when they ask.

- Take your children for an outside activity (walk, play in the yard, go to the park) at least once each day. They need to blow off steam and use up their energy. (Turn off the television.)

- Be affirming; encourage and teach others to be affirming.

- Help with problem solving.

- Be available at times of crisis and major need.

- Use developmentally appropriate practices (DAP).

🚶 Provide water and sand play, gross and fine motor activities, quiet times, social times, and rest periods.

🚶 Help direct the peg into the hole. (Help with problems.)

🚶 Provide comfortable areas in quiet places for children who need time away from others.

🚶 Be sensitive and perceptive! Listen and watch. Be affirming; encourage and teach others to be, as well. Help with problem solving. Be available at times of crisis, major need.

● Address various styles of learning; incorporate all into your teaching and activities. Involved students are well-behaved students.

● Allow all children to go to recess; they need the break. Breaks are necessary, not earned.

● Teach students non-irritating ways to seek your attention; teach them appropriate and inappropriate times to approach you.

● Include activities with group discussions and movement throughout the day. For all students, most especially middle school or junior high students, provide learning opportunities which involve group work. Direct what they talk about instead of trying to keep them quiet.

● Be sensitive and perceptive! Listen and watch. Be affirming; encourage and teach others to be, as well. Help with problem solving. Be available at times of crisis and major need.

Life Lesson

You do not have the right to be disrespectful, hurtful, or ugly anytime. Even when you are frustrated or angry, you still need to find ways through or around obstacles. Others may even be willing to help you.

> **Life Message**
>
> I am valuable and likeable and important.

Trade or Substitute

This, too, is a common discipline tool with young children, yet it can be helpful with older children. This tactic simply involves substituting an appropriate item or activity for an inappropriate one.

- 🏠 When the baby wants to "make rain" over the kitchen floor with his sipper cup of juice, substitute plain water for the juice and the bathtub or the backyard for the kitchen.

- 🏠 When a child is frustrated because he wants to take a good spoon out to dig in the sand, give him an old spoon, a trowel, or a plastic shovel.

- 🏠 When your eleventh grader wants to go into the city or to a basketball game in another town, let her use the more reliable family car for the evening rather than the older one she usually drives.

- 🏠 Instead of quitting work, find a different, better job.

- 🏃 When the child wants to go down the slide head first, remind him to go feet first with your words or a gentle physical position change.

- 🍎 Offer all of your students, including the class clown, the opportunity to act out a scene from their books rather than write a book report. Or allow them to build a representation of an event from history.

> **Life Lesson**
>
> We do not always get exactly what we want; but if we can be flexible, we end up with more options and more pleasure in life.

Limit the Environment Rather than the Child

Some of you are thinking, my child will learn not to touch the items on the coffee table. Others of you are thinking, my child will never learn not to touch (at least not for years). It is just not worth my constant vigilance. Some of you are blessed with both types of children.

Children are remarkably different. What works best with one does not necessarily work well with another. Parents, too, differ in values and expectations. What works best for one parent may not work well for or even be acceptable to another parent.

When limiting the environment is acceptable to you, it becomes a discipline tool which can ease life rather than make it more difficult. Especially when children are young, postponing a life lesson and making your life easier is a valid and helpful option - at times. When a child is young, a lesson (not touching breakables) may take repeated disciplinary action to learn. If, on the other hand, a parent waits a month, six months, a year, the lesson may be easily, quickly, and relatively painlessly learned. *Timing in this case is the parent's choice.* Do not hold off on lessons which will help keep a child safe or prevent a child from being obnoxious and unlikeable. Do not wait on lessons for over-indulgence reasons. Limiting the environment, rather than the child, is one method of accomplishing this.

⌂ Always childproof for danger. No one, no matter how careful, is vigilant every second, and seconds are all it takes.

⌂ Childproof for precious items and ease of life. Sometimes when a cherished item is broken, it is difficult to remember that people are more important than things. Some items are themselves a hazard to young children. We had a beautiful glass table which we did not use for several years because it was exactly the wrong height for wobbly, carefree toddlers.

⌂ Remove temptation. Children are about as good with temptation as we adults are - in other words, not very. Out of sight frequently can be out of mind and out of trouble. Chocolate candies left on the counter beg to be eaten. A ponytail just within reach says, "pull me, pull me." And a car left running, implores "drive me, just take one little spin around the block!"

- Fencing in our own backyard eased my life more than almost anything else ever did.

- Invite a playmate to come play.

- Go to a park; life is always better at the park.

- Keep scissors in a cupboard or closet.

- Watch when they paint; paints talk to young children - "Taste me; try me on your clothes or body or in your hair; I would look great on your buddy; I would look great on the hamster."

- Create an "office"in your classroom where students may go to work quietly and without distraction. Only purposeful workers go to this office.

- Take possession of toys and small objects which come out to play during work time. Return at the end of day. If they come to play again, return at the end of the week, six-weeks, or semester, or request that a parent come to claim them.

- Move your desk. Move their desk closer to you or away from other students. Separate the talkers.

Life Lessons

Temptation is very difficult to resist. Sometimes it is helpful to remove it from sight or access.

Simply altering our environment can make life easier and smoother.

Redirect

This strategy involves diverting or redirecting children. Redirection can take place as problems arise or to prevent their occurrence. Redirection is the single most common form of discipline for children three and under. Generally it is a gentle and subtle form of discipline.

🏠 When you see frustration start to build, help a child change to a less upsetting activity. For example, when a child is becoming annoyed with the block tower that keeps falling, suggest: "Let's look at your books for awhile."

🏠 To the child getting louder at the table: "Use your inside voice." Make sure you have demonstrated and practiced this inside voice, or it is not fair to ask for it.

🏠 To the child about to hit in anger: "Use your words, not your hands." Make sure you teach what types of words to use.

🚶 When a group of children playing with dolls start to get too noisy, begin to sing softly a lullaby. They cannot resist helping to put the "babies" to sleep.

🚶 When a child is standing and waiting for a favorite activity, suggest: "It's not your turn to paint yet. Would you like to play with the clay or the blocks?"

🍎 "Tackle football is not allowed. You may play touch football or flag football though."

🍎 When a student who is supposed to be working is off in space, walk by and point to the place on his paper where he needs to resume working.

Life Lessons

When a door is shut, frequently a window opens.

A little bit of flexibility goes a long way.

Empower Yourself

As the saying goes, he who hesitates is lost. Life is filled with incidents where we simply do not know what is the best thing to do. Many of these predicaments occur when we need to discipline a child. Whether we lack confidence, skills, or vision, we end up feeling powerless or helpless, in short, victimized. When we feel helpless, we are most likely to turn ugly and return to our worst old habits or to stop trying altogether. Neither of these is helpful. Just as we never want a child to feel helpless, we also wish to empower ourselves with the knowledge, "I can think and do for myself. I am capable." It is, however, unrealistic to expect always to know what to do as a parent or a teacher. A truly critical concept for each of us is the realization that it is the wise person who *STOPS AND THINKS* when in doubt or bewilderment. This can be accomplished in two ways. First, when we are faced with a new situation, it is perfectly prudent and excellent modeling to tell a child: "I am not sure how I want to handle this, but as soon as I decide, I'll get back to you. Until that time, no one plays with the paints."

Take time to collect your thoughts, talk to your spouse, or check a resource. The child, having read your irritation, exasperation, or anger, spends time stewing over what she has done and what will happen. Clearly, this has limited usefulness with very young children who generally cannot remember what they did five minutes ago; children under three require a more immediate response.

Children often repeat misbehavior. This gives us a warning. The second way to empower ourselves involves repeated behavior. Forewarned can be forearmed. It allows us to determine how we will deal with a child the next time the behavior returns. When confronted with a repeated misbehavior, it is most beneficial to take a quiet period (during naps, at bedtime, after school, while driving) and simply think about what is bothering us the most. Then we need to determine what lesson needs to be learned and how we can best teach it. By developing a plan, we avoid becoming trapped as helpless victims and slowly going crazy or getting angry. The next time we are confronted by the repeated behavior, we are ready with what we want to say and what we need to do. This works well when a general feeling of malaise is present. What is helpful is discovering exactly what is bothering us and what we want to do to change it. Again, merely having a plan decreases stress. In short, we need to be prepared.

In the classroom, it is sometimes helpful or necessary to put off discipline until a natural or scheduled break in the lesson or day occurs. Problem solving sometimes needs to wait because it requires extra time. However, delaying discipline is a technique which can be abused. When possible, discipline is more helpful the closer it occurs to the incident. This strategy is for new and innovative behavior by a child which throws off or surprises the parent or teacher.

Life Lessons

No one knows everything. And we are not supposed to!

When in doubt, wise men and women stop and think before taking action. Take *NO ACTION* when angry.

Being prepared is good for more than scouts; it is a life skill.

Enhance Self-Esteem

There are numerous important reasons for building self-esteem apart from discipline. However, building self-esteem is also a powerful discipline technique. There is a direct relationship between self-esteem and discipline. Children with low self-esteem have issues to deal with, for example: proving themselves, being the best, always looking good to others, manipulating others, obtaining and using power. They are also more difficult to discipline. A child with high self-esteem may need only a glance, a gesture, or a quick word to return to appropriate behavior; children with low self-esteem typically require more intervention. To summarize:

The greater the value the child places upon self,
> the lower the probability of misbehavior (fewer digressions),
> the higher the probability of cooperation (easier discipline), and
> the greater the frequency of self-discipline (much less need for outside intervention).

Life is simpler when self-esteem is solid and high. There is age-old wisdom in the adage "An ounce of prevention is worth a pound of cure." Prevention is a wonderful investment. By building and affirming self-esteem, we make discipline incidents and procedures easier, and we prevent a remarkable number of incidents all together. We reduce both the frequency and intensity of discipline. What a tremendous bonus.

Neither parents nor teachers can afford to overlook the importance of their relationship with children. Each of us remembers a high school teacher we liked and one we did not. Not only did we learn more from the one we liked (kids don't learn from people they don't like), but we also behaved much better for the teacher we liked (kids don't behave for people they don't like). Healthy families work together, so do healthy classrooms. We do not need to be best friends with our children and students. We do, however, need to be affirming, fair, and respectful. When strong relational bonds are built, children more easily and more frequently choose to work with us. When bonds are weak, or when children do not like us, they choose to work against us and drive us nuts for the fun of it. The older the child, the more sophisticated and capable he is at making life together difficult. The less emotionally healthy, the greater the difference between how a child behaves for an adult she likes or with whom she has a strong bond and one she does not like and with whom she does not have a relationship. Good, strong bonds are an essential ingredient of discipline. Affirming self-esteem is one key to building bonds; the second key is respectful treatment. How much a child perceives we value and like her contributes to the strength of our bond. How we treat a child both during, and outside of, discipline determines the strength of our bond.

The bond between adult and child is a critical ingredient of discipline with children of all ages. As children enter the teen years, the bond reveals its importance. At the beginning of their middle school years, I asked each of my children how many of their friends liked their parents. Each answered that most of them liked their parents. When I inquired again at the end of their middle school years, the answer had changed to only half. When the bond is weak, when children do not really like a parent or a teacher, it becomes very difficult to discipline effectively. A healthy, strong bond eases the frequency and degree of discipline. Taking time and effort to build bonds is a valuable investment. It can make a tremendous positive impact in discipline.

During the teen years, a strong bond can be the difference between "living is easy" and "life is hell." Apart from all of the discipline that you have given to your child up to her teen years, no factor is more important nor contributes more to the ease of dealing with a teen than a strong positive bond. Child-rearing is, or at least can be, about relationship building. If our children do not learn to forge healthy relationships in their youth, when and how will they master this important life skill?

Life Lessons

Life is easier when we are nice, respectful and affirming. Bonds are built, and people are more likely to work with rather than against us.

Other people are valuable. Other people are likeable, and can be depended upon and trusted.

Life Message

I am valuable. I am likeable.

10:
Problem Solving

The best way out of a problem is through it. - Unknown

Problem solving is a wonderful discipline tool used when we sense a child is choosing to work against us, or at the very least is not choosing to work with us. It is also extremely helpful in cases of repeated misbehavior. Problem solving with children teaches children important problem-solving skills and lifelong lessons. It offers children an opportunity to practice and flex child-size problem-solving skills on child-size problems. This, in turn, allows their skills to grow just like their minds and their muscles. Actually, problem-solving skills may be the most important set of skills we ever teach our children. We are presently facing huge problems in the nation and the world. If the problems of today are to be successfully dealt with, this next generation is going to need remarkable problem-solving skills. It is our job to ensure that they have them. Repeated practice will be necessary. Fortunately, we can count on children to provide myriad opportunities for practice. In truth, conflict is our partner. Learning to handle conflict respectfully and creatively is one of our most important lessons. There are six steps to problem solving.

Define the Problem

It is at this first step into problem solving that we often fail to sufficiently engage the child. It is crucial that we describe the problem we see from *both* our and the child's viewpoints; when we only include our viewpoint, the child has no reason to enter into problem solving. Further, he has reason - we want to change him and get what we want - *not* to enter problem solving. Always include the child's vested interest or reason for wanting a particular problem solved. Here are some examples:

🏠 "I am wondering if you feel not getting along with your brother and having him bug you so much is a problem?"
Instead of:
"I'm tired of you and your brother fighting all of the time."

🏠 "I don't like having to remind you about your chores, and I bet you're tired of my nagging. Let's see if we can find a way to settle these issues of chores and nagging."
Instead of:
"You never want to do your chores. Let's find a way to work this out."

🚶 "Sometimes you need a specific color and someone else is using it; we need to look for some ways to help everyone get the crayon he wants as quickly as possible."
Instead of:
"You are going to have to find a way to share these crayons."

🍎 "The noise level in here is too high, and you all need to talk to your table partners to finish your projects. How can we solve this?"
Instead of:
"We have to do something about the noise level in here!"

Take time to listen to the child's point of view and to her feelings about the situation. Her point of view is as important and valid as the adult's; not taking enough time to listen can result in the child's leaving or sabotaging the process or in working on the wrong problem. Paradigm shift as a communication tool is very helpful here. Make sure you understand (not agree with, simply understand) where they are coming from. Take a moment to demonstrate your understanding of their viewpoint. It is the most helpful tool in reducing emotions and building real communication. Simply stated, at the very beginning put yourself in their shoes.

After the child has spoken, if you feel it will be helpful, talk *briefly* and *respectfully* about your viewpoint and feelings.

Transition Phrase: Are you ready to think about things we might do to solve this problem?

Brainstorm - Generate Ideas

Invite the child or children to work on finding solutions. Someone who has been involved from the first step, identifying the problem, and who has helped with solutions is far more likely to follow through with the agreed upon solution than someone who has not.

It is important not to pass any judgments or make any criticism during brainstorming. Judgments stop the generation of ideas. All ideas need to be accepted for the time being. Often it is helpful to write down all of the ideas at this stage.

One of the early problems my family used problem solving on was to determine the children's bedtime and avoid the stalling and ugliness which had developed. The first idea my son Kris came up with was, "We'll just go to bed when we're tired." Clearly, to me this was not acceptable for a two and four year old. However, it was also obvious that we needed more ideas. If at this time I had said, "No, that won't work" or "I don't like this idea," my sons would have stopped thinking of more ideas. We wrote this first thought down and searched our minds for more ideas. Remember, you are not looking for the single best option; here you are simply looking for ideas, so be as creative as possible.

Transition Phrase: Do you feel we have enough ideas to begin evaluating them?

Evaluate Options

Now it is time to evaluate the ideas - after many have been generated. Together, decide which ideas or portions of ideas you all feel comfortable with and which you do not like. Star or highlight the ideas you like best. Take time to make improvements on these promising ideas. Look for your shared interests and mutual gain; they are there. Now is the time to modify, amend, or mix ideas. Be careful to avoid put-downs at this stage.

"I wouldn't be comfortable with that."   or   "I can live with this one."
Instead of:
    "This one is dumb."

Transition Phrase: Do any of the solutions stand out as the best choice?

Select the Solution That Meets Everyone's Needs

When we select a solution that meets everyone's needs, we greatly increase the odds that everyone will follow through and comply with the decision. There is, however, a vast difference between a solution that meets everyone's needs and a compromise solution. Often, we stop at compromise rather than seeking further to find mutually agreeable. In *Getting to Yes*, Fisher and Ury suggest focusing on interests rather than positions to find a solution that meets everyone's needs. They tell a story about two men quarreling in a library:

> One wants the window open and the other wants it closed. They bicker back and forth about how much to leave it open: a crack, halfway, three quarters of the way. No solution satisfies them both.
> Enter the librarian. She asks one why he wants the window open: "To get some fresh air." She asks the other why he wants it closed: "To avoid the draft." After thinking a minute, she opens wide a window in the next room, bringing in fresh air without a draft.

We can learn much from this story. First, interests help to define the problem more clearly - to clarify the *real* problem (gain fresh air versus avoid draft), rather than the problem first stated (open window versus closed window), which involves positions. Second, if the parties involved had stayed with positions, the best solution they would have devised would have been a compromise position (window half open), where each gains some of what he wants and each loses some of what he wants. Neither is satisfied with the solution. Although it is no longer being addressed, in reality, there is still a problem. Third, in order to discover interests, the librarian asked, "Why?" ("Why do you want the window closed?" "Why do you want the window open?") Sometimes asking "Why not?" ("Why don't you want the window closed?" "Why don't you want the window open?") can be helpful as well. Lastly, the librarian used an important skill to invent the solution; she took a moment to *think*. She invented a solution for this specific problem.

Focus on interests, not positions, to define the core problem and uncover mutually agreeable solutions that last.

Transition Phrase: Are you ready to plan who does what by when?

Make a Specific Plan

Determine what steps need to be taken to get this plan into action. Decide who will be responsible for what - specifically. Set a time frame for completion of actions. Without the specifics of who, what, and when, excellent plans may fail. Be very clear. Write it down - now.

Transition Phrase: It might be helpful to think about how we'll know if your solution really works.

Provision for Review - Plan a Failsafe

How will you know if the solution really works and if you have been successful? Determine the critical factors to success. Agree to try the plan for a short, specific time (three days, a week, a morning), and then to evaluate progress. If the plan is not working, if all parties are not satisfied, return to the first step.

Transition Phrase: I will check with you next Thursday.

Three additional tips for problem solving include:
1. Look after everyone's interest, even those absent. Be nice.
2. Deal fairly: no lion's share or special interests. Be fair.
3. Deal straight: no hidden agendas or deals. Be honest.

No matter how calmly you try to referee, parenting will eventually produce bizarre behavior, and I'm not talking about the kids. *Their* behavior is always normal. - Bill Cosby, *Fatherhood*

11:
Temper Tantrums

Temper tantrums can be extremely difficult and time-consuming to handle. Traditionally, we have been taught to ignore them. There are serious concerns about ignoring a child having a temper tantrum. The first concern centers on the reason children have temper tantrums. We must be very precise about what we label a temper tantrum because there are two very similar-looking behaviors that appear to be tantrums; only one qualifies as a true tantrum. In the pretend tantrum, a child is in perfect command of himself and is seeking attention or his own way. We generally get that feeling in the pit of our stomachs which says, "This does not ring true; it seems false. This feels like a performance." It *is* a performance. The key factor here is that the child is in command of himself and is directing his behavior.

When a child is in the midst of a true temper tantrum, he is no longer in command of his actions. Real temper tantrums are not to seek attention; they may, however, be an effort to get one's own way. True tantrums are the result of frustration and anger. Children enter these tantrums because the blocks fell down, they cannot get their shoestrings tied, they want a cookie but are not allowed to have one, they do not want to pick up toys. In short, they have been thwarted.

It is helpful to consider what happens physiologically to a child, or anyone, when anger takes over. Anger, like fear, triggers adrenalin. This triggering is an ancient survival mechanism. When a caveman, walking through the jungle, hears a saber-toothed tiger above him, his survival depends on the quickness of his response. Adrenalin enables reflexive action - no thought, no decision-making to slow down response time. The caveman either flings his spear or runs like crazy. Fight or flight. In order to deliver this reflexive action, adrenalin increases heart rate and respiration. Have you ever noticed how much stronger a child having a temper tantrum is? Perhaps more significantly, adrenalin shuts down the left hand portion of the brain to allow the right hand portion, where reflexive action is controlled, to dominate. The problem becomes clear when we realize that the left hand portion of the brain, which has been overridden, controls reason, logic, and language. This is why trying to reason with a child having a temper tantrum never works.

Perhaps the most important thing we can say to ourselves when dealing with anyone who is angry is, "No thinking person is home." Our first job is to help get the thinking person back. Neither discipline nor problem solving can take place until the thinking person, in command of the left hand portion of the brain, returns. Ignoring does not help this important return. We must consider the message that ignoring a child in temper tantrum sends: "As long as you are in control of yourself, I will be there for you; but if you get out of control (and truly need my help), I will not be available to you. You are on your own in a time of great need." If my husband should happen to ignore or abandon me when I am really mad, I'd become even more furious. How about you?

Researchers have compared the brain wave patterns of many different groups of children, among those were children in temper tantrum. The brain wave patterns of children in temper tantrum most closely resembled the brain wave patterns of children in epileptic seizure. None of us would ever consider abandoning or ignoring a child during a seizure. Truly, there is no thinking person home.

In addition, many children begin to hurt themselves, others, or things (furniture, walls, toys) in the course of a tantrum. None of us allows this; we intervene immediately. Thus, we have not been ignoring. We end up teaching - teaching children to do the temper tantrum exactly the way we do not want it. We teach them to hurt something or someone in order to get our help and our recognition that there is a problem.

There are two important steps to handling temper tantrums. First, we must help the child calm down, reduce the anger, and get back the thinking portion of his brain. This is the difficult step because what works with one child may cause another child to go deeper into anger. Some children like to be held and rocked or to be hummed to; these types of activities which involve motion or music are right brain controlled. We must go through this right-hand, controlling side of the brain to help restart the left-hand, reasonable side. Motion - swaying, rocking, and patting all help us calm down. Lullabies have been used for their calming effect since the beginning of time.

Unfortunately, some children are made angrier by our touch or proximity. It is better to allow these children space as long as they hurt nothing. Allowing a child space is vastly different from ignoring a child and refusing to help. Still other children need to use up the energy the adrenalin has given them. These children run, stomp, pound, and jump.

It would be wonderful if there were an easy way to determine what works best with any given child. However, trial and error is the only method to find out what works. The first step in dealing with a child in temper tantrum is to find a way to help him calm down.

Step two is to return to the initiating event and take appropriate disciplinary action or problem-solving steps. We want to teach the child that the temper tantrum will neither prevent him from doing what he did not want nor get him what he did want. In other words, if the temper tantrum was about not wanting to pick up toys, this child will return to pick up the same toys. If the tantrum was initiated by blocks falling down, then yelling, crying, and hitting someone else will not get the blocks back into position. Temper tantrums do not get you what you want, nor do they solve problems. This is an important lesson children, and some adults, must learn.

Learning to handle our anger appropriately is a job all of us continue to try to complete. We must help children begin to recognize developing anger and begin to learn how to handle it. Skills develop over time. A three year old may appropriately stamp her foot; a nine year old needs to use appropriate verbal skills or to isolate herself for a time until she can cope better. We cannot rid our lives of frustration and anger; we can learn to handle them appropriately, respectfully, and responsibly.

Time-out

This leads us directly to time-out. Despite what you have been taught, time-out, by itself, is *NOT* a discipline tool. It is, however, a truly indispensable tool used *prior to* discipline or problem solving. First, let us investigate the confusion surrounding time-out, then we will address the remarkable tool itself.

When time-out is incorrectly taught as a child management tool, it is suggested that we place a child in time-out, generally a chair, for any and all digressions. What lesson does sitting a child down in a separate place for *any misbehavior* teach a child? It can teach that a child can do something negative to someone whose actions they do not like. It can teach resentment, and it can teach attention-seeking. But it will not teach any correct principles or helpful life lessons which are required for DISCIPLINE.

Time-out improperly used as child management falls into the category of *punishment.* It has been confused with *isolation,* which is a discipline tool used specifically as a consequence for a child having difficulty getting along with other children. Isolation (not time-out) is suggested for use when a child who is not upset is having difficulty getting along with friends playing together. Picture this, Amy tries to color on Martha's Mother's Day picture. Martha realizes what is about to happen, and in trying to prevent Amy from ruining her picture, Martha pushes Amy off her chair. Martha is not upset; she solved her problem. Amy has not ruined her picture. Both children require discipline. Both may be separated from their friends at the table because each is having difficulty working nicely together. The consequence involved is: You have a choice. You can choose to play appropriately at the table and continue staying with your friends, or you can choose to try to mark on your friend's papers (play inappropriately) and play at another table by yourself (away from temptation) in *isolation.* This is a specific technique for a specific type of misbehavior. It teaches an important life lesson about getting along with other children or needing to play by yourself. It also teaches about avoiding temptation where possible.

What then is time-out? As the word itself suggests, originally time-out was a gift of time and space given to *upset* children. The key is that the child is in emotional distress. It is time away from regular activities. Misbehaving children do not go to time-out: upset children do. They enter time-out, which can be a chair or set place, but need not be, to calm themselves down, to find the thinking person. I have seen time-out chairs called sugar chairs, where one goes to find one's sweet self. I have seen benches with banners behind them declaring, "Please don't talk to me; I am trying to get myself back together." These all represent time-out.

Time-out, to be most helpful, must be followed by discipline or problem solving. Once the child is calm and able to think, discipline (when you pick up the clay, then you may get out the building blocks) or problem solving (how will you handle this problem the next time?) can take place. The issue which caused the distress or temper tantrum must be addressed, not ignored.

☞ Time-out is an excellent tool for helping children calm down, often the first step for dealing with tantrums. Redirection is a common form of discipline which follows time-out with younger children. Problem solving is most common with older children.

During a seminar, a pre-school teacher asked me about having used time-out slightly differently. Near the end of one of those extremely long days, she found herself quite upset with one particular student. As she started to walk toward this student in need of discipline yet again, she realized that what she was about to say was unhelpful and hurtful. Rather than continue toward him, she walked herself to the time-out chair and sat down in it. She asked me if she had done the right thing. I asked her to describe what had happened when she sat down. As expected, her entire classroom settled down, became very quiet, and stared open-mouthed at their teacher in the time-out chair. So far so good. After a short time in this chair, the teacher felt calmer and returned to teaching. I asked her if in the next few days anything unusual had occurred in her classroom. It seems that the next day, one of her students found himself very mad at another student. The teacher watched as the irate student eyed the other, clenched his fists, and then slowly but deliberately walked to the time-out chair and sat down - just as his teacher had done the day before. A short time later, after calming down, he went back to work. The teacher asked me if this was alright. I answered that it was wonderful. She had modeled what we all need to do when we are angry - take time to calm down before we proceed. In other words, use time-out. It is fine when we offer to provide time-out for angry children; it is even better, a sign of maturity, if they provide it for themselves. Great modeling tends to produce great lessons.

Time-out teaches an extremely important principle: When we are angry and bent out of shape, we have the right to do nothing - absolutely nothing. We must first calm down, then and only then can we make decisions and take actions. We tend to regret almost everything we ever say and do when we are angry. It is better to be silent and inactive and need neither to regret our actions nor to apologize for them. Situations involving domestic disputes are a leading cause of police officers' deaths. These extreme examples involve someone who is very angry and has failed to learn the correct principle of time-out.

Time-out is a gift of time and space which teaches: Take no action while angry. First take time to calm down.

Each of us needs to learn how to use time-out and then how, on our own, to place ourselves in time-out. Remember, time-out is not for misbehavior; time-out is for distress. It is a gift.

It may prove helpful to work through the exercises on the following pages.

Discipline Practice - Parents
Pre-School & School Age

For each situation described, respond to the following questions: 1)How do I feel right now about this child? 2)What do I generally say? 3)What might I specifically say or do that would be more helpful?

1. Mark and Rob are fighting over who will hold the television remote control.

2. You look up and see Sheila smack Shaquille.

3. Robbie does not want to go to bed; he wants to play longer.

4. Maria says she will not eat her cauliflower. She means it!

5. Joshua has forgotten to make his bed again or left out his toys again.

6. You leave your two daughters for fifteen minutes while you talk to a neighbor; they have eaten candy, destroyed the family room, and one of them is hurt.

7. Petra is bothering her brother again.

8. Sally tells you that the two other neighborhood girls won't let her play.

Discipline Practice - Parents
Teens

For each situation described, respond to the following questions: 1)How do I feel right now about this child? 2)What do I generally say? 3)What might I specifically say or do that would be more helpful?

1. Mark and Rob are fighting over who will get the car.

2. You look up and see your teen push your youngest child.

3. Despite your reminders and requests, Shaquille still has not taken out the trash.

4. It is 10:00 p.m.; your daughter tells you she forgot about her science homework.

5. Joshua needs new jeans; he wants the most expensive designer jeans.

6. You leave your oldest son in charge of starting dinner while you run to the store. When you return, you find him on the phone with no dinner started.

7. Carmen continues to put down her younger brother.

8. Sally tells you that her older brother is making fun of her new swimsuit.

☃ **Discipline Practice -
Early Childhood Educators**

For each situation described, respond to the following questions: 1)How do I feel right now about this child? 2)What do I generally say? 3)What might I specifically say or do that would be more helpful?

1. Mark and Rob are fighting over who will use the blue crayon first.

2. You look up and see Sheila smack Shaquille.

3. Robbie is fooling around during circle time.

4. Petra says she will not go to a different center; she wants to continue building block towers. She means it!

5. Joshua has left toys all over, again.

6. Carmen just scribbled all over Sarah's picture.

7. Melissa is bothering Sheila, again.

8. Sally tells you that Gunther just took her ball.

Discipline Practice -
Teachers

For each situation described, respond to the following questions: 1)How do I feel right now about this student? 2)What do I generally say? 3)What might I specifically say or do that would be more helpful?

1. A student is not participating, has no book or pencil, and refuses to work on the assignment or open his book.

2. A student is beginning to clown around or verbally disrupt your class.

3. Right before class starts, Maria tells you that Chen just took her book.

4. During class, a student says, "I don't have to listen to you!"

5. A student contradicts you on a point of information.

6. You notice a student moseying along; you tell him to hurry or he will be late for class. He says, "yeah, right, whatever," and continues his slow pace.

7. Juan and Rob are fighting over who will use the pencil sharpener first.

8. You look up and see Danella smack Terry.

12:
Discipline Summary

To do things today exactly the way you did them yesterday saves thinking. - Woodrow Wilson

Of course, nothing will change or improve either. Thinking is necessary to discipline children. There is no easy way out.

There you have it, over one hundred different phrases and actions to handle various situations and children. Still, we have not covered it all. I know you were hoping I would be "THE ONE" - the one who would solve all of your discipline concerns, the one who would fix the children, the one who would make life with children easy. I wish I could place my hand on your forehead and "heal," but I cannot. THE ONE does not exist. The magic cookbook approach has not been written and cannot be. We all hope for that one guaranteed formula - if you will just do this, this, and this, your children will be perfect or at least turn out fine and your life will be easy.

Being a parent, rearing children, being a teacher, running a classroom, disciplining - all require *thinking*. There simply is no way around this fact. We must make judgment calls (what to ignore, who is telling the truth, how important is this issue?) almost constantly. Further, we must determine what each child needs to learn, decide exactly what principles are important to us and our future, and find and use words or actions which effectively teach these principles and improve behavior. This is not easy. It is, in fact, extraordinarily difficult. In addition, the job continues to change. The children are constantly changing. Parenting a toddler is not the same as parenting a teen. Being a parent or a teacher is a process oriented job. No one is ever completely formed. We change constantly throughout our life. This is the reason all of us, even the brightest, most principled, most caring of us, struggle with discipline. There is, however, good news.

Using DISCIPLINE FOR *LIFE!*, investment discipline, discipline based in respect, discipline based on correct principles can and will make life with children easier, more fulfilling, more joyful and enjoyable, more relaxed and comfortable now and in the long run. Your integrity *can* be intact. You *can* be competent and confident. You *can* be who you want to be!

Our goal or vision for our discipline program must be clear. If it is not, we are headed into a *future we allowed to happen rather than one we shaped.* It is critical that each of us takes time and determines what principles we believe in and wish to teach to our children. We must be aware that life lessons are always being taught - *whether or not we are aware of them.* It is far more prudent and beneficial to be aware.

We can no longer afford only to fight fires. It is our job to stop and check what we actually are teaching and to teach only what we believe. Our own responsibility and ownership are clear.

There is yet one last level of discipline. The first level regards discipline as what we do to change children's behavior. It merely addresses changing behavior right now. We certainly do not want to throw this level away, it is critical for effectiveness. But there is danger in staying at this level only. We can too easily move off the path of true discipline into rewards, punishment, or control and teach flawed principles which can and will return to haunt us. Built upon this layer is the second level of discipline which views discipline as more far-reaching in that it teaches: lessons, life lessons, correct principles to guide lives, healthy relationships, and respectful communication. *We teach a lesson every time we discipline, whether we are aware or not. We must be aware of what we are teaching.* The third level, which is built on the first two layers, considers that discipline, specifically how each of us chooses to discipline, tells who we are. My disciplinary actions identify and disclose who I am quite clearly and certainly. Regardless of whether I am tired, frustrated, or stressed, whether I have taken time to learn and develop skills, whether I like it or not, and whether I am aware of it or not, I own how I discipline. Whenever we discipline, we teach and we reveal who we really are. This brings us right back to our own integrity - which is where I started. We must ask ourselves, "Do I act on and practice what I believe in, or are my beliefs and actions on two different courses?" Do I, or do I not, have integrity?

Integrity is one of several paths. It distinguishes itself from the others because it is the right path, and the only one upon which you will never get lost. - M.H. McKee

Discipline truly is about *teaching*. A child in need of discipline always creates an OPPORTUNITY FOR LEARNING and thus for TEACHING. True discipline must ask, *What lesson needs to be learned here; how can I best teach it to this child?* True discipline is based on correct principles.

Of course, we need to be wise about what we select to teach. Among the most important are those included in the Corsini Four-R System (C4R):

FOUR R'S

RESPECT - the key to cooperation, dignity, and worth. A skill and touch in sore need of modeling.

RESPONSIBILITY - the foundation under all of discipline is ownership of behavior, the belief that *I am responsible for what I choose to do and for what happens to me and others as a result.* We not only have the right to choose our behavior, we have an obligation.

RESOURCEFULNESS - the liberator who empowers us to take charge of our lives in new ways. No more helplessness!

RESPONSIVENESS - the deterrent that keeps us human and humane. Some of our darkest periods in history were led by those who had an abundance of the first three traits, but none of this one.

Please keep in mind the Law of the Harvest:

If we compel children to submit by trying to control them, we will reap a future where violence and abuse of power continue to grow. They will simply ask, "Who can stop me?"

If we continue to reward children, we must accept a future filled with people who care only about themselves, who make decisions based on immediate self-interest, and who are willing to manipulate others to accomplish their own purposes. They will ask, "What's in it for me?"

If we constantly punish children and make them pay, they will become resentful, bitter people who frequently find it necessary to work against others. Further, they are controlled only by outside forces, who must be watching and able to do something *to* them. All that will matter is, "Will I get caught?"

But if we *TEACH* our children how to conduct their lives responsibly, respectfully, healthfully, and if we *TEACH* our children healthy life messages (I like myself, I can think for myself, I can solve problems), we will reap also what we have sown. Here and only here does our future look much brighter.

Sounds great, makes sense, but will it work? Yes, it will - **one step at a time**.... Can we truly **get it right with children**? Yes.

And let us not forget that teachers and learners are frequently interchangeable, that the "official" learners frequently teach the "official" teachers. In one of my favorite Mothers' Groups, the Remedials as they called themselves, we were privileged to watch the unfolding of a child teaching his parent an important, thousand time lesson. One mother freely admitted she was into control, controlling what took place in the family and her business (she is a CPA - surprised?) to ensure things were perfect or nearly so. She had grown up the "good one, the successful one." This was her job description and had been for her life. She made things happen and happen correctly. She felt obligated to own most of what happened around her. Her son's thousand time lesson was that he owned his behavior and choices. One can see how he might fight this with his mother being so willing to own so much. Yet, Chris struggled mightily over ownership of his homework, and his chores, even his poor choices of behavior. It was in tears of frustration and heartbreak, after yet another incident, that Chris was gently brought to a new level of thinking by another mother, Leslie. After her statement that she simply did not know how to get him to accept responsibility and ownership, and the group's response that she couldn't *get* him to she could only allow him to do so, there was a pause. Chris said she knew this in her head but that allowing, rather than trying to force, would be difficult; however, she would try. Her love for her son is absolute and ever apparent. It was then that Leslie asked her what lesson she thought her son had been given to her - *to teach her*. There was silence and a very long pause. We had moved to another level. Not only do we teach our children, they teach us. Almost meekly, Chris confided, "I don't have to control everything, that I don't own everything, that perfect is not my job." This was a group filled with wisdom. Life is a series of encounters with people who will teach us much if we only let them and are open to the lessons. It is my firm belief that our children teach us the toughest lessons, the most important for our own character development. For our children, we are most willing to fight our own personalities, struggle with and overcome our weaknesses, and revisit and finally learn our previously missed lessons. I do wish someone had told me when my first child was born that a master teacher had just entered my life. I had no clue at the time.

The Law of the Farm is true for us and for children as well. J.G. Hubbard summed it up this way: "One thing at a time, all things in succession. That which grows slowly endures." Parenting, teaching, learning to deal with children helpfully is a process. We must acquire patience and meet this challenge one step at a time. Growth takes time.

Our legacy: The next generation will be closer to where we need to be, not farther into chaos. It has been noted that Buckminster Fuller described our job as that of the trim tab on a sail boat. With slight adjustments to the trim tab, the rudder moves. With adjustments to the rudder, the ship moves. Our legacy will be a nation closer to harbor, not farther out in the stormy sea. One child at a time, one day at a time, we move closer to safe harbor. Our generation may not get the ship to harbor; we can, however, teach the next generation well enough that they will get home safely. Not a bad legacy.

The future will depend on what we do in the present. - Gandhi

THE LESSON OF THE PIE

We have looked at discipline closely; we have considered the absolute seriousness of this vast, crucial undertaking. And we have looked at many ways to help teach our children the important life lessons they will need. But let us never overlook the lesson of humanity and laughter and fun. Some of us get lost in the job of parenting or teaching; we take it and ourselves much too seriously and lose ourselves and sometimes our children in the process. My absolute favorite and most cherished discipline strategy comes from, of all places, a television commercial viewed years ago. Here is my memory of this commercial.

On a bright, summer day a mother and daughter have just returned from grocery shopping in the family station wagon. The daughter is helping her mom carry in the grocery bags when she drops one, the one with the fresh apple pie. Her mother turns and sees the calamity, but before she speaks, this scenario is interrupted to talk to us about the importance of children and parenting.

If we stop here, many of you, having taken the message about life lessons seriously (as I meant for you to), will anticipate what needs to be done. The daughter just needs to understand that she is responsible for her action; she has simply made a mistake for which she needs to make amends. She could replace dessert by baking or fixing something else for the family. Mom may or may not help depending on her other duties and the lesson she wants to teach (self-sufficiency or help in times of need). Sounds good. But the producers of the commercial were far wiser. *Sometimes wisdom and humanity are very hard to find.*

When the commercial returns to the car scene, the mother and daughter are sitting on the tailgate happily eating the smashed pie. They remembered another important life lesson: "When life gives you lemons, make lemonade," or more apropos, when you smash a pie, eat it fast. Mom understands that her child is considerably more important than the pie, and that special moments need to be recognized and treasured.

By no means does this book cover all the lessons your children will need. Please do not overlook the most important ones - the humane lessons, the lessons which understand that our children are *gifts*. For our children are people, too. We are allowed to have fun with them and enjoy them. In fact, it is essential that we do so. Perhaps to the enjoinder, "stop and smell the roses," we should add, "stop and smell the children." Well, perhaps, "stop and enjoy the children." Like the roses, children do not last long. They grow up. They find lives for themselves. And we will miss them. My oldest son has now gone off to college. His room is immaculate; he isn't there to mess it up. I hate this clean room. I now love the messy one; it signifies that he is home, if only briefly and temporarily. I miss him. Our children are a special gift and presence. The elderly, read experienced, venerable, and wiser than the young, understand this. They take time with children; sometimes, they simply sit and watch them. They understand just how precious a child is. Life offers no more precious gift.

One last note on love. My husband has spent years demonstrating and teaching love to me. What he has taught me is that really loving another means putting their interests first. He is right. And this is not easy to do. Yet, with our children, it is critical. It is the essence of discipline. If you are taking time to read this book, you love your children. Please act on it.

PART V - BUILDING SELF-ESTEEM

13:
The Importance of Self-Esteem

This above all: to thine own self be true, and it must follow as the night the day, thou canst not then be false to any man. - William Shakespeare

Why Self-Esteem is Critical

The final discipline technique to be addressed is ENHANCE SELF-ESTEEM. The strong links between discipline and self-esteem are clear. The better, more respectful and humane, the discipline, the higher the self-esteem. The higher a child's self-esteem, the more infrequent her misbehavior and the easier the discipline. This is a major reason to try to build self-esteem. More important, however, is the fact that the higher self-esteem, the healthier the child and later in life, the adult.

Do you ever wonder if something is missing? Do you ever find yourself believing you are worthless or incapable? Do contentment, joy, and confidence elude you? Do you wish you could be someone else? You are not alone. And sadly, more and more children feel this way. When I talk with teachers across the nation, they concur that self-esteem is declining - conspicuously, both in adults and children. This is an alarming trend. As self-esteem declines, so too does our nation. Our nation needs positiveness, confidence, and courage; these traits are correlated with high self-esteem.

Keys to Life

In *The Psychology of Self Esteem*, Nathaniel Branden says,
There is no value judgment more important to man, no factor more decisive in his psychological development and motivation - than the estimate he passes on himself. The nature of his self evaluation has profound effects on a man's thinking processes, emotion, desires, values and goals. It is the single most significant key to his behavior.

This is a powerful statement. It mirrors Dorothy Briggs' assertion in *Your Child's Self-Esteem* that:

> Self-esteem is the mainspring that slates every child for success or failure as a human being.

If you agree with these statements, then a crucial job for every parent and every teacher is affirming and building self-esteem in each child. None of us had children or chose to work with them in order to make them feel worse. In fact, a cardinal trait found in most caregivers and educators is that they chose their profession because *they want to make a positive difference in children's lives.* I have seen a poster in a school which read - All children have the right to discover that within them they have the power to learn how to learn and how to think and how to handle their lives with courage and confidence. As teachers, we owe our students at least this much. As parents, our responsibility is even greater for we are the single most significant influence in our children's lives. As Dorothy Briggs notes, "Helping children build high self-esteem is the key to successful parenthood."

It is also the key to successful teaching. As the book by Aspy and Roebuck entitled *Kids Don't Learn From People They Don't Like* suggests, how we view, value, and treat children affects how much they learn from us. Each of us remembers a year in high school when we had one teacher we adored and one we did not like at all. We learned more, our grades were higher, and we enjoyed and behaved in class more with the teacher we liked - no matter what the subject. Alternatively, we learned less with what seemed like more effort, had difficulty paying attention and behaving, and loathed class with the teacher we felt did not like us and whom we, in turn, learned to dislike.

Most importantly, high self-esteem is a key to emotional health. Liking ourselves and feeling capable are the foundations on which emotional health rests. High self-esteem is simply the key to our lives. How can a child recognize her own goodness and her gifts if her parents do not? If her teachers do not? This is clearly a monumental responsibility, not to be taken lightly. Our job then is to help children feel better about themselves, not worse. How can we do this?

Research, among it the work of Stanley Coopersmith, shows that self-esteem develops from the quality of the relationships between a child and those (parent, care-giver, teacher, grandparent) who play a significant role in his life. Children, at one time, were considered to be blank slates upon which we write. The environment, it was believed, shaped the child entirely. Yet, any parent of more than one child and every teacher realize children differ from each other from the start. We will not revisit the nature-nurture debate here. Nature certainly contributes; we each come into the world unique. Nature provides the groundwork, the clay (some malleable, some less so, some light and full of sun, others gloomier and full of clouds); nurture provides the molding and shaping. It is indisputable that environmental factors, other people, circumstances, and events, modify the original model. Nurture does affect what nature gave us. Another perceptive analogy describes us, parents, caregivers, and teachers, as the mirror our children look into to learn who they are and what value they have.

What do we want then? A child who is deeply and quietly happy to be himself.

Every child, despite her uniqueness, has two basic psychological needs: to feel lovable and to feel capable. Many experts agree that these two basic human needs translate into two convictions:

I am lovable: **I have value because I exist**
I am capable: **I can handle myself and my environment**

Notice that what is important is not that the child is loved but that he feels loved. Parents cannot simply love a child in their hearts; they must be able to demonstrate this love so that a child truly feels loved. Each child from infancy needs to be told with words and actions that she is lovable and important. Parents must accept this responsibility.

Sadly, not all do. That is when teachers become even more important in a child's life. Teachers are the second most important influence on a child's life. Many caregivers and teachers spend more time and have more interaction and communication with a child than his parents. For some children, a teacher is the only positive person they regularly encounter. We must be aware of what messages we are actually sending, and we must become very skilled at sending the correct messages. Do we view and thus portray diaper changing time as a nuisance job to be finished in record time? As a time to send the message, "I wish you weren't here; your existence is not important." Or is it a loving time, a time to tickle, stroke, and talk to your baby? A time to send once more the critical message that your baby is loved, important, irreplaceable? No one expects you to enjoy the diaper part, but it is critical that you enjoy the baby part. *Take care that your baby does not receive the diaper's message!*

When your toddler tries a new skill, perhaps climbing a chair to be closer to you and the counter where you are working, do you send a you-are-not-capable message: "Get down off that chair! You'll fall and get hurt!" Or do you send a more affirming message, "You did it! And you were careful."

There is no doubt we are the mirrors from which our children learn who they are and how much value they have. It is the child's feelings about being lovable and capable that develop from our messages that help a child build self-esteem.

Three Categories of Self-Esteem

We discussed earlier that there are three LIFE BELIEFS (convictions or attitudes which children need to develop about themselves). These were: I like myself, I can think and do for myself, I can solve problems.

These three important LIFE BELIEFS parallel the three categories of self-esteem; these are Existence, Accomplishment, and Mistakes.[19]

I like myself	⇨	**Existence**
I can think and do for myself	⇨	**Accomplishment**
I can solve problems	⇨	**Mistakes**

The connection between these three areas of self-esteem and the two convictions based on human needs is also clear. I Am Lovable coincides with the area of Existence. The conviction I Am Capable involves both successes - Accomplishments and the other side of the coin, failures - Mistakes.

Two of the categories are concerned with what we do, with actions. The area of Accomplishment focuses on success - challenges we master. The third category, Mistakes, deals with our actions that have failed or gone awry. Each of us has experiences in both categories. It is a common misconception that the more accomplishments achieved and the fewer mistakes made, the greater one's self-esteem. Not so, self-esteem can be built and affirmed in all categories, including times when mistakes take place.

Quite significantly, though often overlooked, one section of self-esteem is not dependent upon actions. Self-esteem in Existence has to do with the fact that we each have value simply because we exist. We do not have to *do* anything to obtain this. We care about and care for a baby, *any baby*, deposited on a doorstep, not because of what the baby does (hardly!) but because it is there, it exists. This child has value simply because she has entered our lives, because she *is*.

Existence is the most fundamental and foundational area of self-esteem, upon which the other two areas are built.

The other two areas, Accomplishments and Mistakes, are built upon this first area. Without this primary one, self-esteem built solely on the other two is always unsteady, at risk, and mercurial. Self-esteem built without the stabilizing effects of affirmed existence is extremely vulnerable. Arthur Miller describes our tendency to determine value based on success:

> Success instead of giving freedom of choice, becomes a way of life. There's no country I've been to where people, when you come into a room and sit down with them, so often ask, "What do you do?" And being American, many's the time I've almost asked that question, then realized it's good for my soul not to know. For awhile! Just to let the evening wear on and see what I think of this person without knowing what he does and how successful he is, or what a failure. We're *ranking* everybody every minute of the day.

In our culture, as in many cultures, we overuse and overrate Accomplishments. (Just watch television, read the newspaper, listen to the first questions of people just meeting.) We place entirely too much significance on our successes. Consequently, we misuse the third category Mistakes; we lower our value when we make a mistake. As well, we sabotage and then proceed to under use and underrate the value we have based purely on our Existence. As soon as a baby is born, we check to see if the baby can focus and track with his eyes; we get excited when the baby lifts her head or smiles (even if it is just gas). We are always waiting for the next accomplishment, and we quickly march right through the value of existing without ever noticing it or acknowledging it. Many of us do this on a daily basis. This is most unfortunate and detrimental.

Each of us knows a child or an adult whose self-esteem is built almost entirely on Accomplishments. These people are stressed constantly, and their value is at risk continuously. Why? We all know about mistakes. Everyone makes them. Everyone. When is the next mistake coming? No one knows, but we all know with a certainty that it is waiting just around the corner for us. When a child whose value rests on Accomplishments does well, self-esteem seems high; in truth, it is artificially high. But when that child is not successful (misses the catch, comes in second, gets a low grade), self-esteem plummets. And we then spend much time and energy trying to raise self-esteem back to its previous level. Unfortunately, we might again focus mostly on accomplishments further causing and aggravating the next fall. I call this the roller coaster of self-esteem, because self-esteem is up and down and all over the place. A child really does not know his own worth because it is so variable. If, on the other hand, a child has 80% of his value based on Existence and he happens to make a mistake, his self-esteem can drop only a little - down to the 80% base level. And fairly quickly, on its own, self-esteem returns. For this child, self-esteem is fairly constant; his self estimation is clear, expected and predictable.

Let us look at the game of baseball, a game of heroes and goats. Much of the time during the game, the play is elsewhere. You are either up to bat or you are not. The ball is in your area or not. But when the play is in your area, you are on display. Have you ever been a center fielder? You frequently have a fly ball arrive in your field. If you catch it, you are a hero - at least temporarily. If you drop it, you are a goat.

Imagine two center fielders: one whose self-esteem is built largely on accomplishments and one who has 90% of his self-esteem built on existence. The first fielder catches the ball, makes the out, and returns to the dugout like a returning king; of course, some of his teammates may not feel like bowing down in homage. This may cause some squabbling and dissension on the bench. The next inning this same fielder may not be so lucky. The ball flies toward him; he puts out his glove, and the ball hits and then bounces out of it. He returns to the dugout at the end of the inning like a wounded bear. Depending on his age and personality, he sulks, cries, swears, stomps the dirt, or yells at somebody else. He is less than pleasant to himself, his coach, and his teammates. Often his game goes downhill from here. And let's hope this was not an away game, because this child is not a joy to have in the car on the drive home. It is quite understandable; this child's estimation of his own worth has been yanked around by outside events from very high to almost nothing. He is bound to be stressed and disagreeable. In truth, this child really does not know what he is worth; his value is always changing, always at risk. Is it any wonder he grasps at any accomplishment to feel good? Or that he is willing to lie or cheat or make excuses to feel good? ("The sun was in my eyes. I couldn't see the ball.")

Briggs, in *Your Child's Self-Esteem*, notes that "whenever personal worth is dependent upon performance, personal value is subject to cancellation with every misstep." Pretty scary.

Bryan Forbes formed an interesting truth in the twist of a phrase: "Nothing recedes like success."

Let us return to baseball and our second center fielder. This is the one who understands he is valuable simply because he exists; this allows him to also understand baseball is a *game*. When he makes a catch, he returns to the dugout happy and accepts the hoorays and pats from his coach and team; after all, it is fun to catch the ball - to accomplish and succeed. It is also short-lived, and that is alright, too. This player does not get lost in it. He might even tell the second baseman about her great play. Inevitably, another inning, another fly ball, this time, a missed catch. This child's estimate of his value drops - a little. That is all it can drop. And without question, he wishes he had caught the ball. He walks back to the dugout wondering if maybe what the coach said about using two hands merits trying. He may sit down quietly for awhile, but pretty soon he recovers. He walks over to his friend the catcher, with whom he is spending the night, and asks, "Do we really get to order pizza tonight? What's your favorite place? Do you like Canadian bacon on it?" He is back, and he is whole and valuable. And we will not mind having him with us; he is primed and ready to have a good time.

OVER-EMPHASIS ON ACCOMPLISHMENT

Stress on accomplishment has taken a toll on many: both sexes are involved, but we continue to be especially hard on men. Too many of us have most of our self-esteem tied up in the most visible form of accomplishment or success - our jobs. It is easy to see why stay-at-home mothers, who technically do not have a (paying) job but work inside the home rearing children, can have difficulty maintaining self-esteem. We have convincingly taught ourselves that the dollars we bring home are inextricably linked to our worth. If our job is not good enough (high power or high status) or high paying enough, our worth is less. And, if we should happen to lose our job, we are in danger of losing most of our value as a person. Evidently, we are genuinely in danger.

Perhaps you are fortunate not to know anyone who has taken his own life. Many of us are not so lucky. I am not. The last two funerals I attended were for men who had committed suicide. One of the two men whose death haunts my thoughts had a dispute with his boss and lost or left his job. That afternoon, he took his own life. I do not pretend to know what goes through anyone's mind at a time like this, certainly many factors. But the timing of this suicide makes it difficult to dispute that not having a job was one of the contributing factors, perhaps a prompting factor. For too many men, no job equals no value. No value equals no need for existence. No need for existence equals no life. We must stop this type of thinking. However, it seems that rather than reducing it, we are now effectively spreading it to women. After this incident, which stunned and frightened every woman in one of my parent groups (no one is immune), each woman decided to make sure that her husband understood or began to understand that his value does not come from the paycheck he brings home, but from the fact that he brings himself home each evening. As we all know, previous bias or learning can be difficult to override. Nevertheless, we must stop over-emphasizing accomplishments.

This was still too expensive a lesson.

OVER-EMPHASIS ON APPEARANCE

Much as we try not to, it is evident that we continue to treat boys and girls differently. They *are* different. Testosterone and estrogen are two very different hormones. Male and female "nature"are different; male and female "nurture" need not be. Many arenas of life are affected by these dissimilarities. For example, research shows us that, generally, boys seek a teacher's notice more aggressively than do girls. As a result, teachers, quite inadvertently, tend to call on boys more often. This is certainly not the only occurrence where the adage "the squeaky wheel gets the grease" is given life.

What we seek is beneficial treatment for each child. The issue at hand is providing the necessary affirmations of self-esteem for every child. All children need to receive many different affirmations encompassing all three areas of self-esteem. Which affirmations we choose to offer a child may unintentionally be determined by his or her gender rather than by his or her individual needs. Previously we discussed how boys are more at risk for linking most of their self-esteem to success and accomplishments. They receive more affirmations in this area of self-esteem, and as a result, assume accomplishment is most important in establishing self-worth.

By contrast, girls generally receive more affirmation messages that highlight the importance of appearance. We are far more likely to tell a little girl than a boy that we think she is pretty, that her hair looks nice, or that her outfit is lovely. For some of us, it may even be difficult to imagine saying these things to a boy. Furthermore, we are less likely to validate a girl about her ability to cope, her accomplishments, or her successes. We seem more comfortable allowing a girl to be helpless than we do a boy. Some girls fail to receive enough messages that they can *do* things, and that they can be and should expect to be capable, effective and productive. Sadly, as a result, some females tie most of their value into their looks which, as we all recognize, are destined to fade. Little of their value comes from their abilities or their existence. Some take desperate actions trying to look beautiful, yet fail to develop skills that last a lifetime. We must ensure that we give all children positive messages about their abilities to cope, to think for themselves, to handle problems, to conduct and own their lives. It is important to remember that we most frequently fail to do so with our girls. It is critical that girls and boys receive affirmations in all three areas and based on their individual needs, not on our own unrecognized gender bias.

The second and third categories of self-esteem, Accomplishments and Mistakes, are inextricably tied together. We all know we feel better about ourselves when we do something right. Accomplishing feels good and builds our self-esteem. However, the other side is that doing something wrong, making mistakes, frequently makes us feel less valuable, less good about ourselves. *This is not necessary.* Interestingly, the area of Mistakes provides the opportunity for the most dramatic and quickest increase in self-esteem. Consider how it feels when we accomplish something or get something right easily and quickly. Most of us feel good and enjoy the success. However, each of us has messed something up, missed what we needed to do, and had to grapple and struggle with a challenge. Perhaps we had to learn, acquire skills, seek help. But in the end, we finally conquer our mistake and make things right. (Let's just say we got parenting or teaching right.) How does it feel when we straighten things out? When we get things right which previously we had gotten wrong? Wonderful! It is more fun to beat a tough adversary than a weak one.

When we compare the three categories of self-esteem, we realize that:

Existence is the foundation of self-esteem. Without self-esteem in this area, a child is at risk and will have difficulty building lasting self-esteem in the other categories.

Accomplishment is the most fleeting area, and when over-affirmed has a tendency to overshadow and place at risk the other two areas of self-esteem.

Mistakes provide the quickest boost to self-esteem, yet it is the most abused area, for we often reduce self-esteem within this category.

It is necessary to learn how to affirm children in all three of these categories of self-esteem. It must also be clear that the one area of self-esteem that everyone needs first and foremost is Existence - the one we so frequently and habitually overlook and skip by without ever noticing. Let us begin with this essential realm of self-esteem.

14:
Existence

LIFE MESSAGE: I Am Valuable - I Am Lovable - I Am Likeable
TRAIT: Positiveness

> The healthy child is true to himself; this gives him personal integrity. He does what he can with what he has and is at peace within. The unhealthy one lives by borrowed standards. At odds with himself, he masks his unacceptable parts and judges himself and others accordingly. - D.C. Briggs

Self-worth must not come just from achievements; it comes from our acceptance of each child just as she is. Each child must have fundamental worth *separate* from accomplishments and mistakes. We must help our children realize that they have value simply because they exist.

At bedtime one night, I rather foolhardily asked my younger son a seemingly innocent and easy question - one to which I was certain he knew the answer. "If I could choose from all of the children in the world, whom would I choose to have for my child?" Now because I had already told him a million times that I loved him, I assumed he would blurt out the only answer conceivable - him. Not so.

He looked at me and disclosed, "Probably one like me but better behaved." (Well, yes, there is some emphasis on good behavior at our house.) I was astounded and saddened; the answer was so very clear to me. How could *he* not know? Easily, I had never told him. I did not recover as quickly as I would have liked.

I responded, "No, really, who would I choose?"

"A good one, one who behaves all the time," he said.

I finally recouped, and I told him my heartfelt truth. "No, Tim, I would choose you without ever needing to look at any of the others; *I would choose you.*"

"I don't always do the right thing; I don't always behave," he reconfided.

"I know," I said. "That doesn't matter at all, and it isn't the point. The point is that you are my first choice for a child; I want you; I would choose *you.*"

He thought about it for a moment and then asked me why. I should have seen this one coming. Don't ask the first question unless you know why. Luckily, I did.

"Because you are my son, because you are *you*, because although you don't belong to me, you belong with me. We are family. No one can ever take your place." He thought again for a moment, digesting what I had said, I thought.

And then he, of course, asked, "If you could only choose one, would you choose me or my brother?" I should have seen this one coming, too. By now, I was thinking as fast as I could. I found this truth more quickly.

"I'd choose two - both of you. I would not go away with only one. I came with two; I take two away. Period." He accepted this answer.

The point is that to believe in himself, a child must not have to question his worth as a person. - D.C. Briggs

Telling our children we love them is truly important, but it is not enough. We need repeatedly to reaffirm their value based purely on existence. How can we do this?

Greetings

Greet them at each reunion and acknowledge them throughout the day.

Greeting - it seems so simple. We underestimate its power, and we, at times, fail to do it appropriately. First, greetings have power. One of my early career positions was not fun. The working environment was polarized and negative. I remember feeling down and less than valuable. I had naively expected that my boss would always appreciate me. I sought reassurance and solace at my friend Linda's house at lunch times. Linda was always glad to see me; bless her heart. But it was her baby daughter Sarah who always managed to greet me first. Sarah was still in a walker and raced to the door when she heard the knock and my entrance. With a big smile, she greeted me with, "Hi Malm!" - the best she could do with my very difficult name. I always felt better immediately. For Sarah, like her mother, was just glad to see *me*. What a gift.

My husband, too, has taught me about greeting. My work with parents takes me out evenings. Tired, I arrive home. My husband has been known to hear the garage door open and come to the back door, open my car door, take my briefcase, and tell me he is glad I am home. He often offers to make me a cup of tea or cocoa. The long day washes away - at least partly, and I realize how very glad I am to be home and that someone cares about me.

Do you know who are the best greeters in the world? Dogs. They are the only ones who will get up from a nap, walk over to us, and with all their body language (tail wagging) tell us they are glad to see us. Inevitably, we put down our things and reach down to pat them. And somewhere in our minds and our hearts, we think, "At least *someone's* glad I'm home."

A preschool teacher at one of my presentations told me that when the young children arrive in her classroom, they always come over to her and show her their shoes or shirts or hair bows. She wondered how she should respond. Should she tell them how beautiful their hair is or how nice their shirt looks? We probed the incidents and determined that the children were not seeking praise. What they wanted and needed was *reconnection* to her as they were leaving Mom or Dad and *acknowledgment* that each was important to her. They were checking the emotional climate. Is it safe? Is it nurturing? Is it affirming? It is not just attention they wanted, but affection and affirmation. What they want and need to know is that they are important and lovable, that they belong here, and that they are emotionally safe - not that their shirt is cute. She decided that a hug or a smile and an "I'm glad you're here today," were what was most helpful.

Our greetings to others tell much about us and our feelings toward the person being greeted. If you are a teacher busily looking for a file you need for today's program and one of your favorite parents, Mrs. Sunny, walks by your room, I will wager you will stick your finger in the file cabinet to hold your place and turn and call out your greeting. This parent brings sunshine into your life, she will respond with a smile and friendly retort which makes you smile, and you always have time to collect a little sun. But when Mrs. Grumpy walks past, most likely you just stick your head farther into the file cabinet; after all, you are busy preparing for class. We do not take time to add darkness to our lives, and Mrs. Grumpy is always down on something or someone. Of course, no one is ever glad to see Mrs. Grumpy; that is one of the reasons she *is* so grumpy. Choosing between Mrs. Sunny and Mrs. Grumpy, guess who *needs* the greeting more. For, of course, Mrs. Sunny will be greeted by everyone; Mrs. Grumpy by almost no one. Mrs. Sunny's self-esteem is high; Mrs. Grumpy's is low to non-existent. Keep in mind, we have just sent Mrs. Grumpy a strong message that *she is not even worth a simple greeting*. As well, until someone helps Mrs. Grumpy begin to see herself as valuable, it would be foolish to expect her to change.

When a teacher greets his favorite class, he smiles, relaxes, and talks to many of them. ("Hey, Jimmy, how are you doing? Melanie, you sound happy! New shoes, Kate?") But let the trouble-making, difficult class come along, and the greeting changes. ("Joe, get your hands away from her hair! Quiet, you're too noisy! Monica, don't push; wait your turn!") Yes, we tell them who they are to us and help shape who they will become. And once again, guess who needed us more.

We count and frequently begrudge every speck of attention and affection we give to the difficult children; yet, without ever counting it, we dispense far more time and energy to the easy, likeable children. When we are not greeting at reunion, we are acknowledging them throughout the day. We are sending messages to children all the time. Unfortunately and unhelpfully, we tend to interact differently with different types of children. I will never be called into a classroom to take a look at a charming child (Master Sunshine) who almost magically is given lots of attention, affection, and time. But I do get asked to help with a child (Miss Clouds) who gets these same items obnoxiously with temper tantrums, aggression, or inappropriate behavior. It is arresting that with some children we give away our affection and affirmation, and with other children we count everything they *steal*. Did we not choose to have children or to work with children to give away our affection, affirmations, and attention? Didn't we wish to make a positive difference in individual children's lives? Or only the easy, sunny ones? It takes a good deal of courage to face this last question.

It is Miss Clouds, the less socially skilled child with low self-esteem, who needs us to make a positive difference in her life. She does not need fewer affirmations; she needs to be taught how to engender them. Master Sunshine needs less (than Miss Clouds) from us; his life is already great, and everyone else is busy trying to make it even better.

Further, we must get better at greeting and at affirming Existence at these wonderful opportunities. Some of us too often say, "Hurry up, I'm in a hurry." The message here is that I don't have time for you. (Why did I have you if I don't have time for you? Who and what more important do I have time for?) When we first see a child after school, many of us still ask, "What did you *do* today?" We have moved right into Accomplishments and completely overlooked Existence. And our children inevitably answer, "Nothing." If we are concerned about their behavior at school, we ask more invasively, "Were you good today?" or "Did you play nicely?" or "Did you hit anybody today?" or "Did you eat your lunch?" Not only are we off target, but what an opportunity we miss. We miss an opportunity to reconnect, to let them *know* how very important they are to us, to affirm their value in Existence. What if we simply gave them hugs and smiles and told them the truth, "I'm glad to see you!" As parents, we need to stop missing these daily opportunities which cement our relationship and our child's estimate of herself and her worth. What we say first to a child, our greeting, will be what they believe is most important. Which is more important? They exist still or they behaved well? If you have any difficulty with this answer, ask any parent who ever lost a child. These parents know the answer.

🏠 "Good morning."
  Instead of:
    "It's time to get moving!"

🏠 "I'm so happy to see you. I missed you!" Big hug, big smile.
  Instead of:
    "Did any teacher have to talk to you today?" OR "Move! I'm in a hurry."

🏠 "Welcome home. It's nice to have the family all together."

As teachers, we have the opportunity to help those children receiving little affirmation at home to improve their view of themselves and their own value.

☺ "I'm glad you're here today, Scott. Welcome back, Julie."
   Instead of:
      "Put your coat on the hook."

🍎 "Hi, Maria, how's it going?"
   Instead of:
      "Did you do your homework?" OR
      "You're not going to repeat yesterday are you?" (Remember, you're bad!)

Parents remind me of how stressed and hurried they are when they pick up their children. Perhaps try a deep breath, a pause, and a reflection. You are about to see the person or persons whom you love most in the world. You likely either had them in pain or painfully worked through a bureaucracy to get them; they are the most important people in your life. And you get to see them. Surely, somewhere, you can find within a smile, a hug, and a "I'm glad to see you." If perchance you think your children do not notice how they are greeted, think again.

Greeting happens to be one of my stronger areas; I do tend to greet happily and affirm Existence. However, one day after school, I pulled up to pick up my son at middle school. I watched through the glass doors as he talked with his friends and talked with his friends and talked with his friends. Through elementary school, we parents tend to make the rules. In middle school, the children also begin to set rules for us. Now, I know the rules. The first rule is that parents may not do any uncool things, anything which might embarrass the child. Mothers do not go into the school and fetch middle-schoolers. However, as time ticked away, I became increasingly irate. After a full five minutes, I decided to break the second rule; yes, I honked my horn. My son looked out for the first time, grabbed his stuff, and came quickly out to the car. I, of course, started my tirade-lecture (yes, this is a Barrier to Cooperation), "Picking you up after school is a gift. I provide a service for you. There is absolutely no reason for me to lose five minutes of my time because you don't bother to look outside. My time may not seem valuable to you, but it is real important to me. Blah, blah, blah, blah, blah...." When I finally finished, there was a short pause; then my son grumbled, "So much for, 'Hi, Tim! Glad to see you.'" They notice.

Teachers also share information. First, they are already too busy, and they do not have time to greet all of their students. But there is time to greet some of them each day. One suggestion is to try "targeting" students, especially, needy students. One technique is called the Two-Minute Intervention. For at least ten days, select one student to greet and converse with at the beginning or end of class, at recess, in the hall, or at lunch. Show interest and warmth to this student for one or two minutes per day. Watch your relationship change; watch the child bloom. Each of us has two minutes per day to give to a needy student.

The second point teachers make is that I have never met so-and-so; we'll call him Eric. Eric is described as a dreadful child, very, no, extremely difficult to like. Reportedly, no one likes Eric. We overlook that without the Erics of this world, we would be less skillful teachers; for it is the difficult children who challenge us and keep us on our toes and keep us seeking and learning new information and skills. As well, many people could handle our jobs if only easy children were involved. It is the difficult children, the troubled children, the dysfunctional children, who require us to be skilled, trained *professionals.* We are not making plates here; if a mistake is made with a plate, it becomes a second and sells for less. We cannot afford the luxury of seconds in our work. No child is a second. Although we get many chances with each child, in the end, we do not get another chance with youth and early formation of self-esteem and estimate of personal value. It is imperative that we maintain a high professional level of skill when we work with children. The Erics ensure that we do not slack off - not for a moment; with them in our room, we cannot. So the next time your difficult student appears at the door, you will be able to say in all sincerity:

"Hi, Eric, I'm glad to see you." And silently, remind yourself that if Eric weren't here, you might slack off and not do your best work today. And being an excellent teacher is truly important to you.

The hard truth is: Until you find a way to love him, he will be unable to find a way to love himself and begin his journey to "I am lovable."

We must also make sure we affirm Existence throughout the day, not only with greetings when we first meet. At home, bedtime, mealtime, and quiet times are great times for affirming. At preschool, nap time, lap time, line time, diaper time, and quiet times are available. For schools, recess, breaks, individual work time, passing periods, and individual tutoring times work. For our own children, smiles, hugs, hair ruffling, and pats play an important role. Teachers now must be aware of how they touch children and the ramifications, and of who hates to be touched. Male teachers must be even more careful. However, smiles and affirming words are available to everyone.

> **Life Lesson**
>
> Our first words tell others what we believe are the most important issues or their attributes. Greetings, though short, speak volumes.

> **Life Message**
>
> I am valuable to someone else. Others are glad to see me.
> I am likeable.

Take Time

Take time to *be* together.
Take time to listen to their thoughts, concerns, and interests.
Take time for play and fun.

Why is this strategy, this "time thing" as my friend Shauna calls it, so difficult to accomplish? Most likely because we have so little time. Dolores Curran in her eye-opening book *Traits of a Healthy Family* notes that:

"Lack of time, then might be the most pervasive enemy the healthy family has."

I agree completely. Each year seems to bring more and more busyness to families. More insidious, each year brings more acceptance of this fast-paced, stressful lifestyle. We are becoming increasingly desensitized to this pace and to the stress which inevitably accompanies it. We need to take back our lives. Life does not need to be crazy.

An acquaintance recently returned from a trip to England where afternoon tea is a daily ritual, where the pace is, as she described, civilized and healthy. She wants to return. It made such complete sense. I have been fortunate to spend a week in Mexico with women friends - all mothers. Although we enjoy the beach, the mountains, and the quiet reading times, without exception, our favorite part of the day is sunset. It has grown into an inviolate ritual - margaritas on the porch which overlooks the sea and faces the setting sun. Perhaps surprisingly, it is not the margaritas which are important. It is the pause, the time for each other and for our souls which we cherish. What grabs us is the contrast to 6:00 p.m. at home where we are racing around chauffeuring children, trying to get done what we did not find time for earlier, and throwing together dinner. Again, here is a ritual of a guaranteed, calm, soothing time in the afternoon. Interestingly, what to some cultures is expected (long, relaxing lunch in France, tea time each afternoon in England, siestas in Spain) is considered unnecessary or sinful here in the United States.

Another friend, Jenny, arranges to sit with a cup of tea or coffee when her children arrive home from school. She looks forward to this little break. She is calm and focused as her children sit down with her and reconnect and talk about their day. Where is it written, "Thou shalt take no time for yourself or your family. No time for peace, solace, rejuvenation."

Do you sympathize with these feelings: a continual sense of hurry and urgency, a lack of control due in part to too little time to get everything done, a perception that time is getting away from you, and a longing for a simpler life? The expectations we have allowed ourselves and society to place upon us have raised our stress levels and stretched the fabric of our beings and families to drastic, unhealthy levels. Yet, most men continue to be trapped by the job status + money + power = your value myth, while most women are caught by the "you can have it all" fantasy as opposed to the more truthful "you must *do* it all." More and more, in order to be a good parent, it is expected that our children take numerous lessons, participate on all sports teams, and be organization members; in short, they must fill every waking moment with all-important structure. *We have included and indoctrinated our children in our crazy pace!* No pause, no relaxing, no playing, no time off for good behavior - no time off period. All too often the very organizations which strive to strengthen families (church, scouts, volunteer organizations) actually become part of the time stealers. We do not have time to *be* a family; we are too busy *doing*.

Yes, we must learn to prioritize our time; but more importantly, we must limit our activities and expectations, carefully select personal and family activities, and set our personal values for our own and our family's time. We must no longer buy into the myth that the more involved a family is the healthier it is. I now sometimes catch myself wondering why an extremely involved family *needs* to be so involved and when it finds time for itself and for regrouping, rejuvenating, relaxing, and rebonding. I wonder to myself, how do they manage? And at what cost? Dolores Curran reports that the 551 professionals she surveyed reported definitively that "the healthy family spends more time *together,* and not more time involved in activities that steal members from one another." The shift to less involvement and more family time has begun. Not only professionals, but families as well, are beginning to recognize the family's need for time together. As a family we must turn to our own structure and members for affirmation, support, healing, renewal, and meaning.

Perhaps we need to listen to Nobel prize winner, Mother Teresa's words:

I think the world today is upside-down, and is suffering so much, because there is so very little love in the homes and in family life. We have no time for our children, we have no time for each other; there is no time to enjoy each other.

This author would most respectfully add so very little love *demonstrated* in the homes and in family life. Love is not just a feeling. It is actions. It is how we treat someone. In order to be able to take time, many will first have to make time.

Of course, necessary to this time together is the development of a sense of humor and play, an ability to select activities fair to all, and the capability to treat one another with dignity and respect. Not to worry, these skills help us tremendously outside the family as well and are certainly worth the effort.

● Take time to be together

Have you ever experienced being with someone who, although is physically present, clearly is not there: a spouse watching a football game, a parent preparing dinner, a child playing video games? It is not enough to be present physically; we must learn to be present emotionally, to be available, to be tuned in to what is happening to others. Each of us carries our own duties, interests, concerns, and stresses; it can be difficult to move out of our own space and move into another's. Still it is critical that we take time to be there for each other.

● Take time to listen

Listening is one of the most important and recognizable ways that we connect with one another. Real listening takes place in the other's time frame and is rarely convenient or planned. It also involves his topics, interests, or concerns; too easily we transform the conversation to ours. Paradigm shift as a communication tool is the most sophisticated and powerful form of listening. Truly, it is the last parenting or dealing-with-people skill I would ever give up both personally and professionally. It is too important and too helpful to miss. It is the tool with which I have in fact built and maintained communication with my husband and my children. It gets me out of difficult situations with grace, dignity, and speed. Specifically, being able to shift into another's perspective and demonstrate understanding of it, reduces emotion, increases genuine communication, builds trust, credibility, bonds, and understanding, and gets to and through problems faster than any other skill. Paradigm shift as a communication skill is available on the third program of the Discipline For Life - One Step at a Time parenting audio series or in the teacher training audio or video programs.[20] It is a tool worth spending time developing.

If you have never spent time communing - just spending time in front of the fireplace or taking a long walk together or sitting on the back porch talking about anything and everything and nothing - with one of your children, you have missed some very special moments and some easy closeness and bonding which ease the tough times and build a bridge for getting through them.

⌂ Take a walk with a child, daytime or nighttime, and make special memories for both of you.

⌂ Play golf or go fishing with a child. Where else can you find so much concentrated time together?

⌂ Take one child to lunch or dinner or weekend breakfast.

⌂ Leave extra, padded time each night to tuck them in, be together, and talk.

⌂ Schedule time with each of your children each week.

🜊 Early childhood teachers can use snack time, nap time, play time to *be* with and listen to an individual child.

🍎 Teachers can use recess, lunch, passing periods, extra curricular organizations, coaching time, and after school time. If you are a coach or organization sponsor, you have additional time with specific groups of students.

● **Take time for play and fun**

Some of us have a gift for creating fun; some of us do not. If you have difficulty finding fun or play activities, you might want to try one of the numerous books which give dozens to hundreds of ideas on fun activities for grown-ups and children to share. After all, if we do not manage to enjoy our children, why did we have them? The planet does not need a larger population, and few of us still need help bringing in the crops. Pleasure, fun, *joie de vivre* - joy in living is a need we all share. No matter who we are, there will likely be more than enough dark times. It is part of our job as humans to help create moments of delight, enchantment, fun, joy, merriment, and happiness. What else are we going to remember when we are old?

⌂ Read a longer "chapter" book with your school-age child.

⌂ Shop together. Simply browse and share ideas; spending money is not necessary or the point.

⌂ Play basketball together (no coaching), throw a ball back and forth (no tips).

⌂ Plant something together.

⌂ Cook or bake together.

⌂ Watch their television program and discuss it afterward.

⌂ Make something (craft, sewing, hobby) together. Remember whose project it is, and let them take the lead.

⌂ Play cards, checkers, chess, board games.

⌂ Create and build traditions - holiday, weekly, personal, bedtime, weekend.

⌂ Every now and again, simply live in the moment.

⌂ Laugh - it is good for you!

Early childhood teachers create fun frequently and well.
🚶 Join in their games and activities.

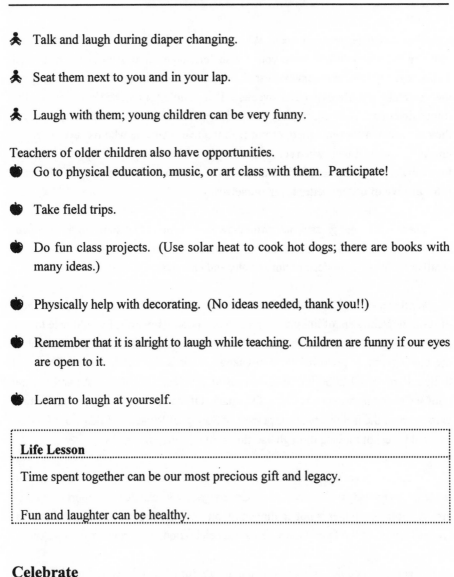

❮ Talk and laugh during diaper changing.

❮ Seat them next to you and in your lap.

❮ Laugh with them; young children can be very funny.

Teachers of older children also have opportunities.

❊ Go to physical education, music, or art class with them. Participate!

❊ Take field trips.

❊ Do fun class projects. (Use solar heat to cook hot dogs; there are books with many ideas.)

❊ Physically help with decorating. (No ideas needed, thank you!!)

❊ Remember that it is alright to laugh while teaching. Children are funny if our eyes are open to it.

❊ Learn to laugh at yourself.

Life Lesson

Time spent together can be our most precious gift and legacy.

Fun and laughter can be healthy.

Celebrate

Celebrate rather than reward. Show with actions how much you value them.

Sometimes it is my children who teach me. Neither of my children enjoys homework; neither goes lightly to the task. But when my sons first started doing homework, I would occasionally take them a cold drink and snack while they were working. I always received a thank you and a big smile, and I knew in my head that this small act was appreciated. But it was not until the day when one of my sons brought me a cold drink while I was working in my office that I understood in my heart what these small gestures can mean. When my son carried in that first cold drink, I not only smiled and said my thank you, I also felt somewhere deep in my heart that someone really loved me, someone cared, someone cared enough to *do* something for me - to make my life easier and sweeter. This simple act touched my heart. Little things do count! As well, children love when we do a chore for them - especially if they are pressed for time, tired, or not feeling great. Anyone who has ever been ill, knows how good it feels when someone takes care of us in any way. Appreciation and love run deep. Whenever we do something for another without looking at what is in it for us, two of us feel better about ourselves.

There is a recent grass roots, ground-swell movement that sums up this concept nicely: *Practice random acts of kindness.* You may be amazed to discover how these small acts change attitude, emotional state, and character.

What is meant by celebrate rather than reward? Earlier we looked at the dangers of rewarding children, of linking rewards to behavior. However, I would hate to live in a world with no frills, no bonuses - without special things. We need only to remove the contingency of good behavior to change rewards into celebrations. The good things do not need to be linked to actions or accomplishments. Just hand out the bonuses sometimes in celebration. Of what? Of the fact that we are a family or a classroom, of the fact that time has passed, of Spring, of Winter, of Friday, of Monday, of good times, of moving through bad times, of nothing, of life.

At the end of each grading period, take the family out to dinner to celebrate having made it through yet another six weeks. Generally, one week later the report cards will arrive. Going to dinner is not contingent upon - did not depend upon - good grades. Every member of the family goes. This is a celebration, not a reward.

"Get out of trouble" coupons come in handy for both children and adults. I give them for birthdays and just every now and again for no reason. There are also "get out of a chore" coupons which are great for the children, less so for you since you will be doing the chore.

At preschool, young children love stamps, stickers, and stars. I would never want to take these precious items out of their lives. However, giving them only to the "good" children is not helpful; it discourages some, and teaches flawed principles. Instead, give them out as the children come through the door - to celebrate their arrival and to affirm Existence. Or give them out after nap time to celebrate another welcome back and return.

With elementary children in the classroom, place the box of stars on your desk and let each child decide if he wants to put one on his paper. The child who believes his paper is wonderful will take one and so will the child who is sad today or did not do great work. One of these children needed the star more; guess which one. Usually it is the one who, before, did not receive one. This child needs his existence affirmed. He needs to believe he has value regardless of his current level of accomplishment.

For older students at the beginning of the grading period, hand out "A" coupons or "No Homework" coupons which turn a failed paper or missing paper into a 100. Even high school students love bonuses. We never get too old to celebrate.

Life Lessons

Responsiveness is learned. Doing for others feels good and strengthens our bonds.

There is much more in life to celebrate than success.

Celebrations are fun regardless of what is celebrated. Fun is important.

Find and Acknowledge Each Child's Uniqueness

Each child is truly unique. As parents and as teachers, we must learn to appreciate each child as an individual. From color of hair or eyes or a smile like Grandpa's, from determination (stubbornness!) to easy-going, from practical to idealistic to creative, from filled with joy to filled with too much sorrow, from born old to forever young, from gifted to uncoordinated, from polished to rough-edged, from dependable to care-free, there are so many ways to see uniqueness and distinctiveness. Each of us wants to be understood and wants to be liked and accepted as we are. (How many relationships have failed because one party could not change the other?) We need to make sure we know the characteristics of our own children and the children in our classrooms. Each of us wants and needs to be special to someone. And we want to be liked and accepted as we are...warts and all.

> **Life Lesson**
>
> One of the more important yet most difficult traits we ever develop is tolerance.

> **Life Message**
>
> I am somebody. I am special. I am valuable.

At home, we have special nicknames for our loved ones; most of which we do not use in public. But we only take time to select affectionate nicknames for people we love. These, too, help us to build our bonds and to affirm uniqueness and value. Using nicknames or special names can also help us bond with our children. Most of us have a name used only by family members and close friends; sometimes it is a name never used in public. My closest friend in high school and I still instantly identify each other on the phone by nicknames used only between us. She lives far away, and I do not see her enough, but she will always be special to me. I know because only she calls me --- well, never mind. My husband rarely uses my full formal name except in public when he is calling me across a crowded room. At school, coaches often use nicknames.

> ☞ Nicknames must not be put-downs. Only affectionate names are included.
>
> ☞ As your children get older, *never* use family nicknames in public! As children age so should their nicknames.

> **Life Lesson**
>
> With a few people, we have a very special, very strong bond. These are the important relationships in our lives.

Teach

Ask questions. Educate them on their own value.

Be clear with children. Tell them more than that you love them and care about them. Help them understand how and why you value and love them. Students also need this type of guidance from teachers. When a child seems to believe his value is dependent upon accomplishments, disrupt this belief system.

🏠 When they drop the ball in center field and when they catch it, ask: "Do I love you more when you catch the ball or when you drop it?"

🏠 "Do I love you more when you get A's or C's on your report card?"

🏠 "Do you have more value when you behave or when you don't?"
The correct answer: "Neither, it doesn't matter. I love you the same either way. I always love you. You have amazing value all of the time."

🏠 "What's the difference between winning and losing?"

🏠 "What's the difference between getting a first place ribbon and a third place ribbon or getting no ribbon at all?"
The correct answer: "Winning's more fun."

🏠 "If I could choose from all the children in the world, who would I want to be my child?"
The correct answer: "YOU!" If they ask why: "Because you're you. Because we belong together. Because we are a family."

🧍 "Do I like you more when you behave or when you misbehave?"
The correct answer: "Neither, it makes no difference. I always care about you."

🍎 "Do you have more value when you get A's or C's?"
The correct answer: "Neither, it doesn't matter. I care about you just the same. You're always important to me. You are valuable either way."

🍎 "If I could choose from all the children (or classes in the world), who would I choose to have in my classroom this year?"
The correct answer: "You and you and you..." until you have included them all. OR "I would choose this exact class, just like it is." As children get older and wiser, change the questions from "Do I...." to the even more important "Do you believe you have more value...."

Telling your child you love him but do not like him can be hurtful and dangerous. Our children not only need to be loved, they need to be liked. How can I be lovable and not likeable is a question children cannot answer, nor can I. Quite frankly, we each want to be likeable, not just lovable. Too many of us have relatives we love (because we have to or are supposed to) but whom we do not like. We really only want to spend time with those we like and enjoy. Check your own really good friends; you love them and you like them. Our children want and need both.

Try:
> "I do not wish to be with you right now. I need some space for myself."   OR
> An appropriate discipline technique to change the undesirable behavior.   OR
> Descriptive Criticism (See Descriptive Criticism in Mistakes Chapter.)

Instead of:
> "I love you, but I don't like you."   OR
> "Get out of my sight!"

When we further discuss criticism, we will learn how confusing and dangerous to self-discipline the concept, "I like you, but I don't like your behavior" is. However, most of us have been taught this "Separate the deed from the doer." Using Descriptive Criticism will get us entirely out of this bind.

Life Lesson

I have value simply because I exist. I am valuable and lovable always, not just when I behave or perform.

Most Precious Gifts
These invaluable gifts are love, time, understanding , and an unwavering belief in each child.

What more does anyone need emotionally? If you love me, you give me time freely and make sure you have time for me. If you give me time, you will come to understand me. And if you understand me, you will believe in me.

● One Key to Encouragement:
We are frequently told we must be encouraging; yet it continues to be difficult to know exactly how to accomplish this. One very important key is unwavering belief.

Hopefully, each of us has had at least one person in our lives who has always *believed* in us, who becomes a touchstone for us. Unwavering belief is deeply encouraging.

Periodically in the growing years, a child may meet someone whose confidence in her abilities will not only surprise her, but will have a profound impact upon how she views herself and her ability to tackle new challenges. Here is a story about the gift a very special camp counselor gave a young and frightened child.

At age nine, Vicky, previously a competent swimmer, had a near drowning experience in a pool. Not unexpectedly, her confidence in her ability to survive, let alone enjoy, water play vanished. The following year she attended a summer camp where swimming was a daily event, indeed a requirement for many of the things she wanted and loved to do. Fear, anxiety, and disappointment became her constant companions. In order to paddle a canoe, her greatest passion in life, Vicky had to swim 200 yards. She was convinced that she could not meet this requirement: she could not swim 200 yards. She told them so with conviction.

There was, however, a young waterfront counselor, named Kim, who believed that things were not so bleak. Over a period of several days, she took on Vicky's fears and anxieties in what was a difficult battle. Each time Vicky refused to try and insisted she could not swim, Kim would calmly and gently reaffirm her belief that Vicky could. Furthermore, Kim added, she was prepared to help at any time. Finally, a compromise was struck. With Kim's continual but quiet insistence, Vicky got into the water with Kim at her side coaching her through what seemed the most perilous 200 yard journey of her life. You are probably not at all surprised to discover that this swimming episode was ultimately successful. Despite a few momentary panics, Kim's patience and belief that this child could conquer this challenge prevailed.

Seven years later, Vicky was herself a qualified lifeguard and had long since forgotten how scary the water had once been. It was not until much later that she realized that in the darkness of those days when she had felt helpless, stupid, and terrified, Kim's unwavering belief had been a beacon of light. Kim's gentle and reassuring manner had made all the difference. Years later, as a parent, Vicky would marvel at the wisdom of this young university student and be thankful for her priceless gift - belief.

Trait: Positiveness

A final note on the positiveness which accompanies self-esteem firmly built in this area of Existence. Generally these children are recognizable on sight. They include the new child in the neighborhood or in the classroom who arrives and before she has ever spoken a word, her entire body language says, "Hi, you'll like me!" And you know what, you will, starting right now. These children and adults are easy to like. They have found another key:

If I like me, you will like me. And if you like me, I will like me even more. And on and on and on.

Of course, sadly but inevitably, the reverse is true as well:

If I am not sure I like me, you probably won't like me much. And if you do not like me much, I will begin to like myself less. And on and on and on.

We help determine which spiral they will travel and become.

Self-esteem built on Existence is the most stable; it is value we can depend on to be there for us regardless of circumstance or fortune. It is also the foundation for building self-esteem in the other two areas. Every child and every adult requires an understanding and certainty of his own worth.

Self-esteem based on existence is a requisite for emotional health.

15:
Accomplishment

LIFE MESSAGE: I Can Think and Do For Myself - I Am Capable
TRAIT: Confidence

E arlier, we looked carefully at the relative importance of each of the areas of self-esteem. This second area was determined to be the least important as well as the most problematic. It too often becomes the center for all self-esteem and thereby weakens the foundational area of Existence, and destroys the quick-improvement area of Mistakes. We determined that too much investment in this area is not only detrimental to the other more important areas' development but also dangerous to the individual. We also looked at how precarious and unsteady self-esteem built in this area is, and how vulnerable it is to quick collapse. We must also keep in mind that most of the skills we have been taught that affirm self-esteem concentrate on this area.

However, we have all heard that "Nothing succeeds like success." Undeniably, we know that we feel better about ourselves when we succeed or accomplish. Even though this is the weakest domain of self-esteem, it is, nevertheless, one of the areas. With a final caution to keep from over-recognizing and over-affirming this area, let us look at ways to build self-esteem helpfully in this second category of self worth.

Praise or Descriptive Appreciation[21]

It seems everyone has heard of praise and is aware that praising children is important. Most of us were taught that good parents or teachers praise children; better parents or teachers praise even more. Yet, as with most communication skills, improvement can be made and needs to be made. Our concepts need to be re-thought. Communication skills (discipline and dealing with people skills included) are not unlike technology. We start with an idea, and we work with it for awhile, and then we make improvements and remove the *bugs*. Not so long ago, we had to go through an operator to phone our neighbor. Today we can call on a mobile phone, send a fax, or leave a message on an answering machine. The bugs are out and improvements have been made. Many communication skills have benefitted from improvements through time. It is time to review praise.

Originally, the use of praise was encouraged because we understood that everyone enjoys *occasional* acknowledgment of jobs well done. Further, it was recognized that saying something positive to a child was better than saying only negatives - especially if we are not skilled at helpful criticism. Even more importantly, it was recognized that saying something positive to a child was far superior to saying nothing at all. Too many children were receiving no positive acknowledgment. Neither negativity nor lack of acknowledgment helped self-esteem. However, praise, like almost every communication skill, had some rough edges that can indeed use some smoothing. It is time to tackle the fine-tuning of praise. First, let us locate the bugs.

Several concerns about praise, as it has traditionally been taught, have surfaced over the last several years. Praise is often used as verbal reinforcement. Many of the concerns discussed earlier which apply to reinforcement in general also apply to this verbal reinforcement. It can be manipulative; most of us were taught that one of the reasons to praise behavior is to get a child to repeat the desired behavior. This is manipulation. During live seminars, I have asked thousands of participants to raise their hands if they enjoy being manipulated by others. No one ever raises a hand. Next I ask them to raise their hand if they believe and teach the Golden Rule, "Do unto others as you would have them do unto you." Everyone raises their hands. And each is trapped by her own integrity. Why? Because if we practice what we teach and believe, we treat others as we wish to be treated and do not treat them in ways we do not wish to be treated. We are no longer free to manipulate anyone, because we, ourselves, do not like to be manipulated.

Another concern is that we have been taught that praise must take place immediately to be effective and, thus involves immediate gratification. Deferred gratification, the ability to wait for what we want, patience, is a truly helpful principle and virtue. As well, praise is externally motivating rather than internally motivating. Intrinsic motivation carries far greater strength than extrinsic motivation. We need children and adults who are self-motivating. Through such external motivation, children tend to become dependent upon praise. This praise dependence is a problem for many children since they ultimately need more and more praise. One teacher described her class as praise junkies. When a student answers a question in class and the teacher does not respond with, "Yes," "Good," or "That's right," many pupils do not know what to do or think - even when they were quite sure their answer was correct. This leads us to children failing to develop a sense of evaluation. As with internal motivation, it is ability to evaluate internally that is critical. Democracies require voters who can evaluate and judge ideas, issues, and candidates; without voters with these skills a democracy is destined to founder. Deferred gratification, internal motivation, and evaluation are signs of growing maturity, self-discipline, and initiative.

An additional concern involves our credibility. Praise, at times, may lack sincerity and believability, partly because we strive to give so much praise so often, and partly because we try to give praise to all children and leave no one out. Interestingly, the more superlative we become, the less believable our praise becomes. We give praise so often that our children or students sometimes tune us out. Our credibility is called into question. For example, every now and again my husband and I decide to go out to dinner - *alone* - without the children so that we can remember why we got married in the first place. I am no fool. I look differently from what I did twenty years ago, and truthfully, although I am getting better, I look no better. And there are women out there right now who look like I did twenty years ago; actually some of them have looks I never came close to ever. So, when my husband asks me out to dinner, I go into our bathroom and do things to my face and hair - improvements. When I finish, I look in the mirror to see how I have done. One of two things happens. Sometimes, and young women out there take heed, I see my mother. This is not good. Not by any means because my mother is ugly, but because she is old. She has *always* been old. Even when she was younger than I am now. (Everything is relative. Isn't your mother old?) About this time my husband comes back to see if I am ready. When he looks at me, he realizes I have worked on myself. Now he would tell you himself that he has a great deal invested in me and that he, too, is no fool. So, of course, he says, "Honey, you look great. Are you ready to go?" Now I have just looked in the mirror and seen my mother, his mother-in-law. There are only three questions I can ask myself: *Does he need new glasses again?* We just did that. *Has he lost his "eye" for women?* I doubt it. *Is his credibility or believability high?* No.

The reality is that sometimes the second option occurs when I look in the mirror. I realize I look about as good as I am ever going to again. I see me, not my mother.

This is good. My husband shows up about now and says - exactly the same thing, "Honey, you look great. Are you ready to go?" I love him dearly, but he knows, as do we all, what he is *supposed* to say. This knowledge weakens credibility. Children recognize this factor. Our credibility is too important to be compromised.

Another group of concerns about praise centers on the second reason we were taught to praise - to build self-esteem. This purpose, too, needs to be re-examined. It is possible that praise has caused more harm to self-esteem than benefit in the last several years. I realize that this is a very radical statement. But if you begin to consider that there are three areas of self-esteem requiring affirmation and that praise addresses only the weakest area (Accomplishments), compromises the quick-improvement area (Mistakes), and ignores the most important (Existence), the idea gains strength. Further, for many of us, praise is the only tool we have been taught to use to build self-esteem. As a result, too many children and adults have self-esteem built solely or largely on their accomplishments. Dependent upon unreliable, receding successes, self-esteem is shaky, erratic, and vulnerable. Lastly, when we see self-esteem falter in these children, we work hard to help them rebuild it - *using praise as the major tool, we end up in exactly the same bind and jeopardy!*

There is an additional false idea that praise in itself is what makes children feel better about themselves. This is simply not the case. The actual good thing that they have done is what genuinely builds their self-esteem.

> When children are working hard to do the right thing, little praise is necessary. Children know when they are being useful. This isn't to suggest that we shouldn't praise children for good work, but rather to say that the good work, not the praise, is what helps children feel good about themselves.
> - Mary Pipher

This suggests the importance of asking children how they feel about what they have done, rather than telling them how they should feel with praise. Our internal evaluation of ourselves is far more important.

One of these problems with praise, that of self-esteem being built exclusively in the area of Accomplishments, must be addressed by learning numerous affirming skills in the areas of Existence and Mistakes. We must affirm these areas much more often.

These concerns notwithstanding, we must still cope with manipulation, lack of evaluation skills, and praise dependence. These obstacles can best be overcome by fine-tuning our praise, improving it, and removing these bugs. Clearly, we will need to take out the evaluative aspect of praise, and we will need to find a way to avoid manipulation. The result is sometimes called descriptive appreciation; if you are more comfortable with the old term, you can easily continue to think of this skill as altered praise or improved praise. Descriptive appreciation differs from traditional praise in two important aspects.

First, it is descriptive only. No evaluation is involved; by contrast, traditional praise evaluates: Great! Terrific! Good Girl! I know some of you have one of those posters which give 100 ways to say "good" to your child. This concept of varying the way we say good is not nearly so helpful as descriptive appreciation. One hundred different ways to say "good" addressed only that we sounded canned and repetitive. It did not address praise dependence or external evaluation. What we say to a child about her (external evaluation) is not nearly so important as what she says to herself (internal evaluation) about who she is or what she has done. Descriptive appreciation is more powerful and empowering and runs much more deeply into the child's evaluation of herself.

Secondly, it is important that we change our intent from manipulation to expressing appreciation. When we manipulate, we teach and will reap manipulation. When we express appreciation, we teach responsiveness - the ability to respond empathetically to other people's feelings and needs. Responsiveness is a wonderful trait to develop in either child or adult. The roots of the term descriptive appreciation are clear.

To illustrate descriptive appreciation it is helpful to compare it to praise as originally taught. For example, a daughter has decided to knit golf club covers as a gift for her father's birthday. Any father who opens a hand-made birthday, or any birthday gift for that matter, knows he must respond. Praise is the response that tends to come to mind, "They're beautiful! Just what I needed. Terrific."

"Do you really like them?" asks his daughter. It is easy to understand how a child who has never before knit anything so complicated or given so much of herself in a gift might feel unsure of herself and her gift.

"Yes, they're wonderful - perfect!" To reassure her, father gets even more superlative, probably decreasing his credibility and increasing her doubt. Evaluations (beautiful, terrific, wonderful, perfect) often lack credibility and, hence may be perceived as less than genuine.

On the other hand, using descriptive appreciation, father may instead say, "These covers must have taken you hours and hours to knit. They're made of sturdy yarn; they'll protect my golf clubs. And they are the same color as my golf bag. Thank you for helping me celebrate my birthday."

"You're welcome," she replies, comfortable in the knowledge that he does like her gift, and more importantly, that she made a great birthday present. She says to herself, "I did it; I am a great knitter; I give great gifts; I helped my dad celebrate his birthday." Descriptions are difficult to dismiss; they evoke believability. How we employ descriptive appreciation follows.

Two Steps To Descriptive Appreciation
  1. Describe what you see or what has been done that you appreciate.
  2. Allow the child to evaluate for himself.

Here are some examples.

⌂ To the child who has cleaned up his room.
Try saying:
> "You put your books all on the shelf and your dirty clothes in the hamper. I can't find a single toy on the floor. And every corner of your comforter is off the floor - just like the policy says. It is a pleasure for me to walk in here."
> *Child may say to himself:* "I did it! I can clean my room. I did a great job!"
Instead of:
> "Your room looks terrific."
> *Child may say to himself:* "I hope she doesn't find the clean clothes stuffed in the drawer."
Instead of:
> "You did a great job picking up your room."
> *Child may say to himself:* "You made me do it. I didn't want to."

Instead of:

"Your desk is still a mess."

Child may say to himself: "Nothing is ever good enough."

🏠 To the child who has just given you a handmade potholder:

Try saying:

"You chose thick, thick quilted material for this potholder; it will protect my hand no matter how hot the pan is. It covers my whole hand. And it matches the colors in the kitchen. It is a wonderful feeling knowing you spent so much of your time to make me a gift to celebrate my birthday. Thanks, sweetheart."

Child may say to herself: "She likes it!" (least important) "I make terrific potholders, and I helped my mom celebrate her birthday. I help create happiness." (more important)

Instead of:

"This is so beautiful! I love it! You're so sweet to make me a present."

Child may say to herself: "I wonder if she really likes it." OR "Dad said I had to make you something."

🏠 To the child who has managed not to be ugly to his pestering baby sister.

Try saying:

"You have been trying to play with your blocks for fifteen minutes. You've given your sister a few blocks for herself, and you've gotten her favorite stuffed animal to distract her. You even moved your blocks to the table where she can't knock them down. And you've talked to her nicely every time. Not every big brother can handle a situation like this."

Child may say to himself: "I treat people nicely; I am nice. I am a good big brother. I can solve problems."

Instead of:

"You've been such a good big brother. I'm so proud of you."

Child may say to himself: "I'm not such a good brother; I'm just about ready to push her down and out of the way. I'm tired of her."

🏠 To the sixteen year old who has returned home on time.

Try saying:

"You win; you beat the curfew!"

Child may say to himself: "Just by a few seconds, but I did it."

"I'm glad to see you," is also an excellent alternative but not an example of this section's descriptive appreciation.

Instead of:

"You are so trustworthy!"

Child may say to himself: "If you only knew what we've been doing, you wouldn't say that. But you don't know."

Instead of:

"You're lucky - this time. Make sure you get here next time or, I mean it, you'll be grounded."

Child may say to himself: "Yeah, right, whatever."

⚘ To the young child who asks if you like her picture or if her picture is good.

Try saying:

"There is lots of bright green; it makes me feel like I want to go outside in the Spring time."

Child may say to himself: "She likes it." (least important) "I'm a good artist; I make terrific pictures!" (more important)

Instead of:

"It's beautiful; I love it."

Child may say to himself: "She says that to everybody." OR "I hate it; it didn't turn out the way I wanted it to. I couldn't make the bunny look like a bunny; it looks like a man, not an animal."

"What do you like about it?" or "Tell me about your picture; it looks like you spent some time on this." These are, of course, also appropriate responses, but not examples of this section's descriptive appreciation.

⚘ To the young children who have just finished cleaning up all the play areas before snack time.

Try saying:

"Just look at our room. Every one of the big blocks is on the shelf; the crayons are all in their baskets. The books are standing in the bookcase where they belong, and the modeling clay is safely zipped up in the plastic bags. It feels good to look around and see so many things back in their places. I feel lucky to be a member of this class. We are ready for snacks."

The children may say to themselves: "We did it! Our room is all picked up. We are ready for snack time." OR "I picked up lots of blocks. I contributed. I am part of this class. I'm glad I'm in this class." OR "Jenny and I picked up the crayons. We did a great job."

Instead of:

"You all did an excellent job!" "This room looks great."

The children may say to themselves: "I didn't do anything - again." OR "I just threw a couple of crayons in the basket." OR "There are a bunch of crayons under the piano bench that you haven't noticed. I don't think now is the time to tell you."

🍎 To the child whose work paper is one of the finest she has ever done.

Try saying: (or writing on paper)

"You used capital letters to start your sentences and periods to end them. You found places for three paragraphs, and your printing was very easy to read. You must be very happy with this paper and yourself."

Child says to herself: "I can do good work!" OR "It was worth the effort; I'm glad I worked hard." OR "I understand sentences - finally!"

Instead of:

"Good work!" "Terrific paper!"

Child says to herself: "I wish I knew what I did on this paper that makes it different from the others."

Instead of:

"It's about time. I knew you could do it!" (backhanded compliment)

Child says: "Thanks," weakly, with rolled eyes.

🍎 To the class who has continued working quietly while you talked to a parent or the principal in the hall.

Try saying:

"It is wonderful to realize I can be away from you, and you can keep working and stay quiet by yourselves. That's what self-discipline and responsibility are all

about. Thank you. I am proud to be your teacher."   OR   "Mrs. Stewart had
some important things she needed to discuss with me. It was very nice for me to
be able to take time with her when she needed it and not have to worry about you.
Thanks."

Class may say to themselves: "We can keep working. We are a good class."   OR
"I got most of my spelling done; I won't have to do it for homework."   OR
"I can work by myself. I am responsible. I am capable."

Instead of:

"You were so good while I was talking to Mrs. Stewart."   OR
"You are so responsible."

Class may say to themselves: "Aren't we good other times?"   OR   "Actually, I
was writing notes to Becky."

Life Lesson

Children learn to evaluate for themselves and to pat themselves on the back.

Life Messages

I am capable.
I like what I do; others like what I do.

These are the ways we can remedy praise without throwing the baby out with the
bath water. If someone had asked you when you were first learning about praise:
Would you rather teach children to look for a pat on the back for a job or deed well
done, or how to pat themselves on the back and begin to learn for themselves how to
evaluate?

I believe you would have chosen the latter. Praise teaches the first; Descriptive
Appreciation teaches the second.

● **Proximity Praise**

"I like the way Martha is sitting quietly."
"Will has *his* hands folded."
"Manuel is paying attention."

Many of us have been taught to use Proximity Praise. This is a strategy contrived to change mildly inappropriate behavior to more desirable behavior. For example, when Allison is not paying attention, we look at Jay who is sitting next to her and is attending and say, "I like the way you're paying attention, Jay." Three problems exist in this technique.

First, the phrasing "I like the way...." is weak and judgmental. Many students, especially as they get older, do not really care what we like; thus, this statement has little effect on them. In addition, the locus of judgment or evaluation is external not the more meaningful internal. Second, both phrases involve a comparison - one of the Barriers to Cooperation discussed in the Gaining Cooperation section. When we compare children, we are more likely to generate resistance than cooperation, and we also create competition, rivalry, and strife among children.

We need to ask ourselves the common sense question, "Why am I talking to one child when I am really trying to send a message to another?" The third problem is that we are talking to one child in order to send a message to a second child. This qualifies as something more than indirect; it is almost within the realm of dishonest, and at the very least faulty communication. Earlier, in the Section on Descriptive Language, we looked at the problems with indirect communication. When communication is this dramatically indirect, it is unhealthy. It is more honest, direct, fair, and helpful to speak to the child who needs the message. Put simply, *speak to the child you are addressing.* It makes more sense. Try saying, "Maria, you need to listen to me." Or move near the child not attending, or ask her a question, or involve her in the discussion.

● "I'm proud of you"

Happily, parents and teachers often find themselves realizing that one of their children has done something wonderful, something to be proud of, something out of the ordinary. Almost instinctively, we all respond, "I'm so proud of you." And many of us believed those to be some of the sweetest words uttered to us. We wanted our parents, our teachers, or any adult we respected to be proud of us. It is again helpful to fine-tune this phrase and remove a remaining concern.

I graduated from a small high school in my hometown. During my school years I rarely carried books home and rarely did homework (ask my friends). Book learning has always been easy for me. So it was with precious little effort, I managed to graduate with high academic standing. At graduation, many adults were kind enough to stop me and tell me how proud of me they were. Without question, they meant well. Even so, these remarks made me feel awkward. I was completely aware of how little effort I had exerted, especially compared to my friends. When someone would tell me how proud they were of me for my academic success, I always replied, "Thanks - I made the basketball team three years in a row." No one ever listened long or carefully enough to really hear me or grasp my point of view. I wanted to pass over the easy accomplishment about which I was not terribly proud or excited (academic success) and move to what I felt was the major accomplishment of which I was very proud and for which I had given great effort (basketball success). Six of us made the girls' basketball team our sophomore year; usually only two sophomores at most made it. The competition was stiff. I had worked hard and wanted with all of my heart to make that team. I still remember and appreciate the teacher who let me out of class to go check the just-posted list, and I still remember actually seeing my name. Academic success was important, and I was pleased about it. But making the basketball team my sophomore year and the two following years was my finest accomplishment. My point is that what I was proud of and what others were proud of were two different things. *And I was right!* It was my judgment, my evaluation which was most important; it is, after all, my life and my accomplishments.

The second thing I questioned was anyone else's right to be proud of me. Why were grown-ups, especially those who had contributed nothing to my academic success, proud of me? In my heart, I recognized that it was I who needed to be proud, that pride is in self, not in others. In the dictionary pride is defined as "a reasonable or justifiable *self*-respect" (emphasis added). I concur that pride is largely a feeling related to self, an internal evaluation. However, there is some room for confusion. The dictionary also defines pride as "a delight or elation arising from *some* act" (emphasis added). Notice it says some, not one's own, act. Perhaps it is fair game for someone else to be proud of us. Nevertheless, it is still important to remember that our pride in ourselves is more important than someone else's pride in us. With that in mind, we may want to take some opportunities to make the following modifications.

Consider changing, "I am proud of you."
To: "I bet you're feeling proud."
     "You seem awfully happy (excited) about that!"
     "I'm proud to be your mom (teacher)."

"I'm proud to know you (have you for a friend)."

"Being your mom is a joy!"

"I am so happy for you! How exciting!"

A final note to teachers who continue to be evaluated with forms which include a segment on praise. Many evaluators cannot distinguish between praise and descriptive appreciation. When they can, your score will be higher for using descriptive appreciation. When they cannot, you will still do well. In fact, teachers have stated that their ratings went up when using descriptive appreciation. The evaluators may not perceive the difference, but they hear plenty of excellent praise going on in your classroom. The result is a high rating in the praise category.

Self-imposed Victims and Learned Helplessness

Not being able to govern events, I govern myself. - Michael de Montaigne

Too many of us know people who do not direct their lives, who do not take responsibility for how they respond to what happens to them, and who do not choose their own paths. Each of us is open to two types of victimization. The first is perpetrated upon us; no one is safe from violation from the outside. Robbery, assault, rape, and abuse strike everywhere and anyone. Although we can take safety precautions, this is not the type of victimization we can prevent completely, nor a type for which we are responsible. Nor is it the type of victimization addressed in this section. The second kind of victimization is that which we do to ourselves and involves the portions of our lives which we can control, which we are responsible for, but which we allow other people and even events to regulate. This victimization is self-made; the helplessness is a learned posture or response.

We are not in control of, nor are we responsible for, others' actions. We are, however, responsible for our own actions and for our own responses to others' actions and events which take place in our lives. It is here where we tolerate, permit, and even excuse victimization or helplessness.

It is when someone passively *allows* or even actively *encourages* others to control his life, or when by abnegation or surrendering of responsibility invites negative occurrences or abuse that signifies this second type of victim. It is when someone chooses to allow abuse to occur or chooses to flirt with dangerous outcomes or consequences that this type of victimization takes place. Too many of us know someone whose life seems to happen *to* them rather than their taking responsibility for it and choosing to direct it. This is the person who always has an excuse at the ready whenever anything goes wrong. "I would have been on time for work this morning, but the alarm clock didn't ring." (If you don't set it, it will not ring.) "I would have gotten a better grade on my math test, but there was a great movie on television last night." (Watching the movie happened to you?) "The bartender never should have let me leave the bar that drunk. If he'd have stopped me, I wouldn't have wrecked my car." (Who chose to drink and drive?)

As is evident by the parenthetical comments, I have what seems to be diminishing sympathy for those who would blame others or events for the condition of their lives. There are many different levels and types of victimization. Some forms of victimization may fall into both categories. The Children's Defense Fund reported in February, 1994, that in one day in America, 2,781 teenagers became pregnant and 3,325 babies were born to unmarried women, and that 7,945 children were reported abused or neglected. The 1997 Yearbook reported the teen pregnancy rate had declined (~2,793 teens), but out of wedlock births were growing as a share of the teen birth rate. In this same yearbook, the number of children reported abused or neglected rose to 8,493 per day. These statistics include children victimized by others and children victimized secondarily or primarily by themselves. Some of those pregnancies were neither judicious nor premeditated choices. They were simply allowed to happen without effort to prevent them. Some of the abuse was repeated and might have been prevented *if, and only if, the child knows what abuse is and is able to speak out to a different adult.* We must teach children to take back their lives. No child can be blamed for or held responsible for being abused; some children, however, have taken responsibility for stopping abuse.

It is one thing to be surrounded by a war about which you can do precious little or to be a young child being manipulated, frightened, and abused. It is another matter entirely to blame a movie for a poor test grade. I do have great empathy and immense concern when I see a child taking the *Victim Path*. ("No one will play with me on the playground." "All of my friends are doing it." "I can't." "He told me to." "I was drunk.") More importantly, I also see glaring, vital opportunities to teach children how not to be victims and how to help themselves away from this Victim Path, and how to avoid a lifestyle of learned helplessness.

A crucial part of our job as parents or teachers is to teach children how to own their lives, their choices and responses, and to avoid becoming victims to themselves and by their own lack of knowledge, skills, or understanding. Each of us needs to learn responsibility and life-recovery skills. Each of us must learn to own our life and when necessary, to take back our life. *It is up to each of us NEVER to allow victims to continue down the path of victimization and learned helplessness.*

The Children's Defense Fund has adopted as its motto, "Leave no child behind." This motto applies well to the Victim Path.

Picture the self-allowed victims that you know. Are they emotionally healthy or happy? Victims rarely are. As a graduate student, I remember reading a research study which I recall to this day as the "monkey in the sidecar" experiment. Researchers were working with various pairs of monkeys trying to determine how intelligent and flexible they were. They placed one monkey in a little compartment (the control car) with a seat wired for mild electrical shock and with a panel in front with three buttons that could be lit up by the experimenters. They placed a second monkey in another compartment (the sidecar) separated from the first by a clear, plexiglass shield. This second compartment had no light-buttons on the panel; it did, however, have the same wired seat. Initially, the experiment sought to determine if monkeys were smart enough to figure out that when the light-buttons were turned on, an electrical shock followed in a few seconds. The lighted buttons also popped out. Both monkeys were simultaneously administered the same mild shock. And indeed, the monkeys soon figured out the connection and showed signs of distress as soon as the lights came on. Further, the researchers wanted to know if the monkey in the control car would then try to push in the light-buttons and prevent the shock. Yes, they did. Looking for more intelligence, the researchers changed the format and rules and subsequently required the monkey in the control car to turn the light-buttons off in a specific sequence in order to prevent the shock. The monkeys managed to adjust to this new development. When the sequence was changed, the monkey in the control car learned to try new sequences until he got it right and prevented the shock. Whenever the first monkey used the correct sequence, both monkeys avoided the electrical shock; when he missed, they both received the shock. After the monkey had mastered one sequence for a number of trials, the researchers would randomly change to a different correct sequence. The monkey, intelligent and flexible, would work to find this new sequence until he got it right and again avoided the electrical shock. The last twist of this experiment was that no sequence was correct. Regardless of what sequence the monkey tried, both were shocked. Then the researchers returned both monkeys to the large habitat area where all of the monkeys were kept.

It was at this juncture that the researchers discovered additional findings unrelated to intelligence, but associated with victimization. Soon after, they found that they had to remove one member of each pair of monkeys from the monkey society for what they labeled as neurotic-like, aggressive, antisocial, and violent behavior. Can you guess which set of monkeys needed isolation? It was the monkeys who had been in the sidecar, not the monkeys who had been in the control car. This outcome provides us with several very important inferences.

First, it was neither the problem, nor its negative outcome or punishment, the electrical shocks (equal to both sets), which caused the harmful changes. The significant variable was the ability to try to deal with the problem versus inability to try to solve the problem. I believe that the monkeys in the control car were just too busy to break down or to deteriorate emotionally. Some of us may feel this is one of the main factors helping us stay sane; we do not have the time for a nervous breakdown! It is the ability to take action or to have some control over our destiny that helps us cope in a healthy way. When that ability is taken away, when we become passive, helpless victims with no control over our fate, we become emotionally unhealthy. Thus, it is not the existence of a problem, but the lack of problem-solving skills which disturbs us.

Second, this emotional distress is displayed in aggressive, antisocial, insensitive, callous behavior. We have known for years that many child abusers (both sexual and physical) were themselves victims of abuse. Helplessness or victimization too often brings about its reverse behavior. Those who had no control take control over someone else and perpetuate this ugly cycle. Those who were victimized become the perpetrators.

Lastly, we need to look at exactly what was needed to keep the first set of monkeys (those in the control car) emotionally healthy and stable and non-violent. It is not, as so many of us believe, simply finding the solution to the problem. Actually solving the problem is not necessary to emotional health. Remember, in the final stages of the experiment, the monkeys could not and did not avoid the electrical shock. They left the situation having failed.

It is not *solving* a problem which is required for emotional health. It is *trying to solve* the problem which is necessary. We do not have to succeed; we only have to take some action, any action. If it is not the right action, we need only try again.

God doesn't require us to succeed; He only requires that you try. - Mother Teresa

Thus, emotional health does not require a problem-free life nor continual success with problems. Emotional health requires only that we work on the problems, that we take control of our actions and responses, that we do not engage in or permit ourselves helplessness in any situation where we are not. How can we help children develop appropriate skills? Here are three ways.

When you blame others, you give up your power to change. - unknown

● **Take ownership of feelings**
Frequently I hear caregivers or teachers ask a child, "How did that make you feel when Tanya hit you?" Or, " Tell Jackson just how he made you feel when he took your pencil." It is helpful to teach children to tell another child how they feel about what has been done to them. This teaches responsiveness, empathy, and understanding. However, we need to be very careful about the phrasing. The above phrasing blames a second child for another's feelings; it suggests that we do not own our emotions. In truth, no one *makes* us feel anything; we *allow* ourselves to feel the way we do. As much as I would like to be able to say that kids can make me crazy; it is I who allow and own my craziness. Simply changing the above phrases to: "How do you feel when Tanya hits you?" and "Tell Jackson how you felt when he took your pencil," gives back ownership. As long as any of us believes others control our feelings, we give up the power to change and the capacity to find emotional health. We are in charge of both our feelings and our actions. In order to hold our emotions in check and behave the way we choose rather than the way we are driven (a form of learned helplessness), we must first own our own feelings.

- **Notice children taking the Victim Path**   Never allow them to continue. Helplessness must always be addressed.

We must make sure we understand and see incidents of self-imposed helplessness when they occur. We must be aware and notice this style of operating. It is very easy to miss, to ignore, or to rescue. We must be careful to avoid these. Use these opportunities to teach; proactive language and problem solving are the most frequent lessons needed at these times. Please see the examples which follow.

- **Change reactive language to proactive language**

First, we must learn to recognize the early, innocuous signs of the Victim Path. One of the earliest and clearest signals of victimization is our language. This pattern has often been described as Reactive Language (used by victims) and Proactive Language (used by healthy individuals). Reactive language comes from a belief that others determine our behavior and emotional state. From this viewpoint, we have little or no control over our lives. On the other hand, proactive language stems from taking responsibility for our decisions and actions and for the resulting consequences and from a sense of ownership of self. Remember, *I am responsible for what I choose to do and for what happens to me and others as a result of these decisions and actions.* This belief is fundamental to maturity, self-discipline, responsibility, and any DISCIPLINE system.

Reactive Language	Proactive Language
I can't	I can
They won't let me	I am capable
I have to	I choose
If only	Let's change
They won't	I can influence others
She made me	I am responsible
It wasn't my fault	I did
He makes me so mad	I won't let him get to me, I control my feelings
I don't know why I did that	I am responsible for my choices
I would	I will
There's nothing we can do	We can figure out something
Others limit me	I limit myself and I set myself free
That's the way I am	I can change

Whenever you hear reactive language from a child, help him change to proactive.

Help change:
"I can't get up this morning."
To:
"I stayed up late last night, and now I don't want to get up. I wish I didn't have to, but I do."
Try saying to child:
"It's hard to get up when you're tired; it takes extra effort."

 Help change:
"Joshua makes me so mad."
To:
"I'm mad at Joshua!"   OR
"I don't like playing with Joshua; I think I'll play with Michael for awhile."
Try saying to child:
"You seem very mad!"

 Help change:
"If only the test hadn't been so hard, I could have gotten a better grade."
To:
"I chose to quit studying too soon, and I blew the test as a result. Maybe next time I should study longer."
Try saying to student:
"It sounds like you wish you had studied longer."

- **Teach problem-solving skills**
  If there is no wind, row. - Latin proverb

Children tend to have child-size problems, whereas adults have larger, adult-size problems. Of course, we hope adults also have greater skills. In order to develop these better problem-solving skills, we need opportunities to learn and practice small skills on small problems.

Every problem offers an opportunity for strengthening old abilities or learning and developing new problem-solving skills.

Work with children on their actual problems. These problems provide wonderful teaching opportunities. When a young child comes to me and says, "No one will play with me on the playground," a red flag for helplessness instantly rises. Here is an example of our conversation and an opportunity to teach.

"No one will play with me on the playground. They never let me."
"That must hurt very much."
"Yes, I hate it."
"It's difficult to be out there thinking no one wants to play."
"I want to be part of the group; I want them to let me play."
"Would you like to know some things other children have done to get children to
    play with them?"
"Yes!"

Notice that I did not say, "Here's what you should do." Advice says I am smart and can solve problems, and you are not and cannot. Nor is it generally helpful to say, "It's your problem, sweetheart." Abandonment says I don't care, and I will not help you. Nor, "I'll play with you." To have the solution given teaches "rescue, rescue, rescue"; look to someone else to rescue you; other people solve your problems. Too often we confuse nurturing, which means to further development or to educate, with rescuing and removing obstacles and problems as quickly as possible.

I now have this child in the palm of my hand - to teach. It is time to ask her what options she can think of and to offer several alternatives. The alternatives may depend to a certain extent on our knowledge of this particular child and her specific hurdles. Always make sure to give several choices; it is important that the child makes the final decision and selects the solution of her choice. Of course, one does have to know some alternatives. Our conversation continues.

"Some children let other children choose what game to play or let others go first."
"Sometimes it's easier to find someone who is playing by herself and ask her to
    play."
"Some children start a game or take a ball or jump rope or other toy and start
    playing with it."
"Sometimes children decide they want to play by themselves."
"Sometimes it's helpful to learn a way to ask to play that works."
"Which one would you like to try?" OR "What would you like to do?"

"I want to jump rope with that group."

"Let's practice these words so you can say them firmly. 'I want to play. Shall I twirl the jump rope or get in line to jump.'" *A statement rather than question, this involves a forced choice.*

When this child has practiced and feels ready, off she goes to try her new skill. Unfortunately, even a terrific line carries no guarantees. A group of children who has kept a child out is not very likely to include her just because she communicates more effectively. The leader may still say, "No, you can't play. Don't do either. Get away from here." So I increase the probability of success by walking behind the child; I will be close enough to hear and be noticed, far enough away to be unobtrusive. Have your ever noticed how children talk and behave differently when an adult is watching? (Eddie Haskell, where are you?) When the first child suggests that she wants to play, the child in command will look at her and start to say, "No!" but will then notice the adult present and immediately change to, "Well, go to the end of the line." We have a problem solved *by the child's actions.* Yes, I contributed, which is fine. We all like a little boost when we need it. Most importantly, the adult is neither the rescuer nor the one who selects the solution. We have effectively shared expertise and experience while still allowing the child the major role in solving her problem. We have reduced the risk of sabotage because the child owns the solution. We have taught a lesson in solving problems, we have helped a child increase her life skills, and we have sent excellent life messages. In *Celebrate Yourself*, Dorothy Briggs stated that past teaching can limit your options; her point is well taken. When children believe that they are not capable or that they regularly require rescue, their options become limited. However, the converse is also true, "past teaching can expand your options." When a child learns that she is capable and that she can solve problems with and without help, many options become available.

Let us look at another common problematic area, report cards.

"Here's my report card."
"Mmm. Tell me about it."   The prudent parent allows the child to talk first.
"I got an A in language. And I am happy with that. And with the two B's. And actually the C is ok, too; I worked real hard in math. I just don't get it. It's hard. But the B in science isn't good; I wanted an A. And my grade in citizenship is just fine."

"You're happy with the grade in language arts and two of the B's, unsure about the C in math, and unhappy with the science grade."

"Yea, I'd like a B in math but I don't have a chance."

"You want three grades to stay the same and two to change."

"Yea, I guess. I don't think I can get a B in math; it's too hard."

"Math seems awfully difficult."

"Yea."

"What do you think you can do to change the grade in science for the next grading period?"

"I need to make sure I turn in all of my homework. Mrs. Perry said I was late with four homework sheets and that's what pulled my grade down. I got A's on all of my tests."

"So, you are studying and know the stuff but sometimes fail to turn in finished homework on time."

"Yea. From now on I am going to make sure I get all of my homework in on time."

"Great. How will you pull that off? What kept you from turning it in on time last time?"

"Umm, let me think. I found one of them in my desk and one in my math folder. I didn't know I hadn't turned them in - they just kind of disappeared."

"How can you keep them from disappearing?"

"I know, we could get me a science only folder."

"Or perhaps a homework folder."

"No, just a science folder - that's what I need. Can we get one after dinner tonight?"

"Sure, I can take you. Now, what about that math."

"You mean impossible math."

"I mean really-difficult-but-not-quite-impossible math."

"Nice try."

"Thank you. Now, what is getting in the way of that math grade?"

"I just don't get it. And I do listen and study and do my homework. So don't be telling me to study harder."

"You've worked really hard and still have difficulty."

"Yea."

"Sometimes when I don't understand something, I get help from someone who knows."

"I could get Sarah to help me with my homework and explain things. She's really good in math."

"There's one idea. Do you have any others?"

"If I can't get it with Sarah, I can ask my teacher. And the school has a resource teacher if nothing else works. I really don't want to go there though; I have to miss other classes."

"So you plan to work with Sarah and see if your test grades go up. If not, you will get help from your teacher - after school?"

"No, before school is when she tutors."

"And your last resort is the resource room."

"Yea."

"Sounds like a plan."

"Yep."

"Your goal is to keep the A in language arts, keep the two B's, turn the B in science to an A, and the C in math to a B. Correct?"

"Yes. And I know, let's write it down so we can remember. And we can check when I get my first test back."

"Exactly."

Life Lessons

The key to emotional health is in taking *some* action not the right action.

Not taking responsibility for directing our lives is as much a choice as taking this responsibility; both are decisions.

Life Messages

I can think and do for myself; I am capable.

I can solve problems; I may need some help, but I know how to seek that, too.

It is of utmost importance that we teach all of our children that they have within themselves the capacity to solve problems. They may need help occasionally, but support and ideas are radically different from rescue. When they have a problem, all they need (for emotional health) is a plan of action they can and will take. No one needs to get overly excited or upset. It is not beneficial to seek fault or blame, rather it is important to look for helpful alternatives or solutions. They do not need ever to allow themselves to travel down the Victim Path.

No more self-made victims! No more helplessness!

Focus On What Is Right

Focus on what is right with them, not what is wrong.

Our roles as parents or teachers inherently include noticing what is wrong so that we can teach children how to change to what is correct, appropriate, or right. Children have so very much to learn; it is inevitable that they will come up with many wrongs. Too often and too quickly we pass over all that is right and point out the single thing that is wrong. A child arrives proud and smiling for breakfast on time, with shoes, matching socks, pants, and shirt. And we say, "Your shirt is on backwards." Goodbye smile and pride. This is classic discouragement. Almost all of us have heard our children complain, "You never see what's right, you just talk about what's wrong." They bring us a report card with A's in every subject but English. Too often, we ask, "Why did you get a C in English?" The alternative is to make sure we also address what has gone right along with what has gone wrong. The alternatives might sound like the following:

⌂ "You have your shoes and socks on; you even put your pants and shirt on, and you made it to the table before 7:15. You may want to turn your shirt around so that the tag is in the back and the neck doesn't ride so high." *Action started to remedy problem.*

⌂ As you back out of the garage, reply to the child who wails that he forgot his tennis shoes, "No, it seems you remembered them."

♟ To the young child who has spilled paint: "You washed all the red paint off the table; now all you need is a fresh paper towel to dry the table."

🍎 "Look at all those A's. You must have worked hard and turned in your homework on time and studied for your tests." *Pride and smile.* "What do you think happened in English?" *Pride and smile still intact. Thoughtfulness and problem solving begun.*

Self-pride and feeling good about accomplishments are developed and allowed to remain.

> **Life Lesson**
>
> One can view the glass as half empty or half full.

Show Value for Improvement or Effort

Celebrate small steps.

People seldom see the halting and painful steps by which the most insignificant success is achieved. - Anne Sullivan, *The Story of My Life*, by Helen Keller

There is no reason to wait for perfection; it may be a long time arriving, if it comes at all. Too often we wait for completion, excellence, or perfection before we acknowledge success. Success comes in steps, any of which can be recognized and noticed. Improvement also generally comes in increments rather than all at once. There is no reason to wait for the final product or final achievement. We sacrifice no affirmation, the final success can be recognized as well.

🏠 "You've already pruned three trees. Pruning takes time and effort. Just two more to go."

🏠 "When you're ready, you'll swim all the way across the pool. Let's try it to the second lane again."

🏠 "We've worked hard. Let's take a break before we finish. How does a glass of ice water sound?"

🧍 "Learning to tie shoes is hard. You seem to have the first part of the knot."

🍎 "You've been working on that book report for twenty minutes now."

> **Life Lesson**
> Success is a journey, not a destination. Each and every step can be celebrated if one notices them.

Encourage Each Child to Contribute

Allow and encourage each child to contribute to the family or class with ideas and action; help them strengthen their membership in the family, classroom, or group.

Contributing to a group provides two significant benefits. Contributing, whether with ideas (at home - where to go for a vacation, who does which chores, menu ideas and at school - rules, special projects, field trip locations, agenda, academic ideas) or actions (at home - cleaning, cooking, laundry, errands, baby-sitting and at school - cleaning up, moving chairs and tables, classroom tasks and responsibilities) increases self-esteem. Helping makes us feel better.

The second benefit is a strengthening of the bond with the group we assist and serve. We develop a sense of membership, of being not simply a part of a group, but an integral part. It is clear that more and more children and adolescents feel disconnected from and disenfranchised within their own homes and schools. They *belong* nowhere. A sense of belonging or of fitting in somewhere is vital to young children and becomes an even larger issue for adolescents. Society's failure to help children feel this has left many children lost and vulnerable. There are organizations which are snatching up these children and doing a superb job of making them feel and be a part of the group. What are these organizations? Gangs.

Gangs are an expanding threat to our children and to our nation. Gangs are excellent at recruiting and keeping members. National statistics are vague because it is difficult to determine accurate numbers concerning gang membership and crime. But if we look at a typical medium sized city and county, Fort Worth in Tarrant County, Texas, the statistics are chilling. According to the Texas Attorney General Gang report, there were 119 active gangs in Fort Worth and 1,657 identified gang members. The following year, the Texas Association for the Education of Young Children reported 215 gangs.

Sometimes when I am speaking to a group about creating a sense of belonging and membership and commitment, I feel as though I ought to have a gang leader helping me; they are frighteningly successful. Keep in mind that gang members routinely commit crimes *for the gang*; they are willing not just to wear "uniforms" and behave in a prescribed fashion, but also to steal, assault, and murder. Some children are unwilling to do dishes for the family, but will kill for their gang. Unfortunately, we have much to learn from gangs. And we are paying a huge price financially, socially, and often individually, in the meantime.

Consider also that, according to the Children's Defense Fund, nationwide 2,255 teenagers drop out of high school each day. The Department of Labor has estimated that in 1998 three out of four jobs will require not only a high school diploma, but training beyond the high school level. In Texas, each dropout is estimated to cost the state $203,488, and 93% of Texas prison inmates never completed high school.[22] Further it costs Texas taxpayers nearly $14,000 each year to incarcerate an inmate.[23] Not belonging at school costs all of us. Not just in taxes, but with fear of violence.

Where will our children find a place to belong, a place where they can become valuable and contributing members? It hurts not to belong; even a bad group is better than no group. Are our children made to feel they are genuinely an integral part of our families, our classrooms, our schools? Will business welcome them? Or will the gangs be the only group welcoming them? That choice is ours. We have them first.

Life Lessons

Belonging somewhere is important to emotional well-being.

Contributing helps one bond to the group. It is an essential part of membership.

Contributing feels good and builds self-esteem.

Focus on Capabilities

Help each child see himself as capable and essential.

They are able because they think they are able. - Virgil

Keep in mind that we, the important adults in a given child's life, are the mirrors from which she will determine largely who she is. Are we careful to reflect capable and essential, as well as valuable and likeable, or do we too often reflect to a child a sense of incompetence, uselessness, helplessness, dispensability? We must monitor both our words and our actions. We are sometimes unhelpful:

"Here, let me tie that for you."

"I'll do it, never mind; it's not worth arguing with you."

"All you ever do is watch TV; nobody ever helps."

"No, I'd rather do the laundry myself. It has to be done right."

"Did you remember to thank Mrs. Watson?"

"Did you play nicely?"

Do you redo a job you have given a child to complete?

Are your children little princes or contributors?

Do your children offer to help you with tasks?

Do your children believe that they can do a job well by your and their standards?

Do your children have increasing responsibilities and increasing freedom?

Do you pack your child's bag for overnight and small trips?

Can your children cook?

Can you send your children off to play or to school or to visit friends with a simple, "Goodbye, have a good time," and leave out all the extra baggage, "Be good, don't forget to say thank you, wear your jacket...."

By the time they are ready to leave home, will they have learned enough household management skills, money management skills, self-discipline skills - *life management skills* - to not just survive but to thrive on their own?

Your behavior will match your picture of yourself. - Alexander Dumas

The self-fulfilling prophecy has been recognized for generations. It is obvious that if we tell a child by our words or actions, "You are _ fill in description _" often enough, he will become more and more _ same description _. What we see and project to him is what he begins to resemble. In this way past teaching not only can but does limit options. We must be very careful about what color of glasses we put on to look through, for rosy and golden glasses see the potential good and grace in a child, and dark and gray glasses see only the potential problems and misery.

We can choose to deal with any time frame or verb tense - past, present, or future. Here are some examples of Historian (past), Reporter (present), and Prophet (future).

To the child struggling to learn to swim:

Historian: "I remember a child who was afraid to get his face wet."

Reporter: "I see a child who can swim all the way to the second lane."

Prophet: "When you're ready, you'll be able to swim to the other side by yourself." (I love this phrasing; did you ever meet a child who did anything before he was ready?)

To the young child who cannot get the straps on her overalls buttoned:

Historian: "I remember a girl who couldn't pull up her own slacks."

Reporter: "You can pull on slacks and shirts, and you know how to put on your shoes."

Prophet: "When you're ready, you will be able to handle overalls all by yourself."

To the student who is having difficulty with multiplication:

Historian: "In Kindergarten, you didn't know any addition facts; adding was hard then."

Reporter: "You seem to understand the process; it's just remembering all the different multiplication facts that's difficult right now."

Prophet: "Once you've mastered the multiplication facts, you'll have it!"

Life Lesson

Accomplishments frequently take time and effort.

Law of the Farm: Most things must be learned and accomplished by taking the correct steps in the correct order, in their own time. If you only water when you plant the seeds, nothing will come to fruition.

Children learn patience and the concept, ONE STEP AT A TIME.

> **Life Message**
>
> I have succeeded before, I will succeed again. I *am* capable.

Develop Character

Teach "Do the Right Thing - Make the Right Choice"

For years we've been shown numerous studies which proclaimed the correlation between high self-esteem and high academic achievement. Traditionally, we have believed that high self-esteem helps children learn, and there is truth in that. However, we may have overlooked that the formula works the other way as well, that getting good grades (choosing to work hard, to do homework, to study) helps children build and maintain high self-esteem. Self-esteem is a *result* of good work, not just a cause. We must teach children that choosing to do the right thing, generally the harder option, makes one feel better about oneself, feel right. Choosing any of the so-called virtues of honesty, generosity, justice, self-control, dependability, impartiality, kindness, diligence, to name only a few, builds self-esteem and self-regard. Giving in to temptations, or choosing the easy way, is often the less than honest or moral way and involves the so-called vices of pride, dishonesty, laziness, malice, greed, wrath, and gluttony. Generally, these make us feel good for only a moment, then inevitably make us feel worse about ourselves over the long run. Mary Pipher, in *The Shelter of Each Other: Rebuilding Our Families* defines character "as that within a person which governs moral choices ... it is teaching the young to make wise and kind choices." It is that simple. Pipher also states that when we lost track of character and focused on self-esteem, we made a mistake. I agree. She continues to say that

> ...true self-esteem comes from the belief that one is making the world a better place. It's a by-product of a life lived wisely. In fact self-esteem, like viewing Halley's comet, is best accomplished if not looked for directly.... When we focus on self-esteem instead of character and good works, we feed into narcissism. Self-esteem, if real, is self-regard and comes from ethical behavior.... People with self-regard can see others as real and interesting, not merely as vehicles to meet their needs.... Narcissism says, Look at me; self-regard says, I know who I am when I look at you.... In America we are encouraged to be narcissistic, to constantly examine ourselves for dissatisfaction and to evaluate

everything in terms of what's in it for us.... Many clients are more worried about their children's feelings than their behavior and they focus more on their self-esteem than their character. They want their children to be happy more than they want them to be good. It's understandable that parents feel this way, but it's misguided. Happiness ultimately comes from a sense that one is contributing to the well-being of the community. In reality, making wise moral choices is the most direct route to true happiness.

As one teacher noted, "Some parents send us a mixed message - build my child's self-respect but do not require anything of him."[24] This is as misguided as trying to teach my child responsibility while not holding him accountable for anything. Neither is possible.

It is clear then that we must teach our children to make "good" choices, those which are moral and prudent. We must ask them how they feel when they have chosen wisely, and also when they have chosen unwisely. Helping children see the difference between short-term "highs" and long-term real gain in self-regard is critical. Again, please note that this is consistent with my discussion earlier of delayed gratification and outcome choices, not just behavioral choices. (See Disciplinary Consequences.) Also consider how a "What's in it for me" attitude precludes and eclipses the possibility for developing these virtues. Recognizing what truly makes her feel right is a wonderful gift to a child. So are character and conscience. Virtues tend to have small beginnings and grow with practice. Let us look at how we can nurture them into full bloom.

Our most powerful teaching tool is, again, modeling, making good decisions and practicing the virtues we espouse. This is easier said than done, but nevertheless very important. We have again returned to our idea of integrity. The simple opportunities for discussion, as it arises and it will, especially at the family dinner table cannot be overrated. And if you don't sit down to dinner as a family at least four or five times a week, find a way. Give something up; whatever it is, it is most likely far less important.

Margaret Anderson discusses the four cardinal virtues: prudence, fortitude, justice and temperance, and some tips for teaching them to children.[25] These are a wonderful starting point for development of character. Starred tips are Mrs. Anderson's.

PRUDENCE is the ability to govern and discipline oneself by the use of reason. It must be taught by parents, and it requires maturity. Generally, it comes with age and practice, and allows us to choose actions which lead to real happiness.

1. Use discipline to teach children to choose correct/moral principles and actions. Do not shy away from the lessons.

2. Teach children to think through to outcomes when making decisions about how they will behave. Help them see that the outcome is far longer lasting than the behavior.

3. Work repeatedly with the child who makes impulsive decisions; continue to show her how heedless, undirected behavior frequently ends up being a poor decision.*

4. Teach clear thinking. Explain the reasoning behind some of your own decisions and actions. Ask children why they made certain decisions. Model stop and think.

5. I confess I am biased, but television tends to offer opportunities for discussion of imprudent decisions. Books generally portray wiser decisions.

FORTITUDE is courage and staying power. It is the strength of mind that enables one to bear adversity.

1. Practice patience during delays and grace during disappointments.* I witness grown-ups who have neither of these virtues; just ask any gate agent at the airport. I am also seeing more and more children who are given their way almost exclusively and have not learned that life will not always go their way and how to handle these times with maturity and grace.

2. Avoid overindulgence like the plague. Do not give in to a child's every whim and desire.*

3. Help children learn to persevere.* Chosen activities such as baseball, piano lessons, and dance are excellent vehicles. Persist, unless you chose the activity for them. Finishing tasks and chores also contributes to the development of fortitude or persistence.

4. Look for the good in others and in situations; even the worst situations and problems tend to teach very important lessons.

5. Guide children toward self-reliance. It is our job to help them grow away from us, physically, socially, and emotionally. Give them the skills to do so expertly. We must remember to balance this lesson with the equally important lesson of interdependence and connection.

JUSTICE is the ability to treat others fairly, and to look after the rights of others, even those absent. It means giving each his due.

1. Teach children to stand up against injustice to themselves and others.* When a child feels a teacher has treated her unfairly, help her write a respectfully descriptive note to help the teacher understand her perspective. Role-play the discussion and then let your child handle the discussion with the teacher. Teach children to address injustice to others, especially those weaker.
2. Show respect to all, even during times of anger. Remember, use respectful language.
3. Teach and expect honesty. Be honest; never ask a child to lie for you. ("Tell him I'm not here.")
4. Make and keep promises.*
5. Deal with stealing, cheating, lying, and manipulation as they occur. Name them.
6. Teach impartiality. Handle your children impartially - no favoritism. Deal with others impartially without regard to race, religion, social status, or gender.*
7. Teach them to judge themselves rather than others.
8. Teach generosity, but intelligent generosity*; overindulgence is not intelligent generosity. Give others their due and then some.*
9. Teach "please" and "thank you" and other courtesies not so common these days. Demonstrate, practice, and then expect, friendliness and kindness; these are due everyone.
10. Practice problem-solving and negotiation skills - over and over and over.

TEMPERANCE is moderation or self-control, the ability to limit or check oneself.

1. Help children learn to handle emotions. Time-out is most helpful. Also, never allow tears, outbursts, or tantrums to get a child what he wants. Replace these uncivilized behaviors with more civilized actions, such as removing oneself to a quiet place, counting to 10, taking a deep breath, learning respectful language, especially descriptive language.
2. Know and enforce true limits. Drinking may be alright, as is driving, but both are age-dependent. Drinking and driving together are never alright. Hurting others with words or fists is not alright.
3. Build self-esteem, but also teach humility, "the virtue that makes it possible for a man to know the truth about himself."[26]
4. Making things *right* is fine; getting even is not.

5. Learn to recognize your own warning bells. Listen to them and act on them.
6. Seek balance in life. Limit television. (A television, video game or computer with Internet capability does not belong in a child's room, but in a general, supervised area of the house so you know what they are seeing and doing. Otherwise, children isolate themselves. Limit outside activities to ensure family time.)
7. Teach that more is not necessarily better.

Character, excellent moral fiber, long-lasting happiness, and high self-regard - what more do we want for our children? For our future?

> **Life Lesson**
>
> It is knowing that we chose to do the right things, not being recognized for them, that is most important.
>
> Good choices make for healthy self-regard.

Sadly, those virtues so tough to come by are also so beneficial.

"...the struggle for moral perfection ends only at the grave." -- M. Anderson

Integrity, the ability to practice what we believe in, is key to self-esteem.

Trait: Confidence

The trait that accompanies self-esteem built in this area of Accomplishment is Confidence. Children who have tried at anything and have been effective, productive, or triumphant begin to build confidence, a firm belief that they have tried and succeeded before and will again. We know that success succeeds and that getting things right, mastering something, being productive, *accomplishing anything, large or small,* feels good and builds our self-confidence and our self-esteem. So does choosing to be the master of our destinies, our emotions, and our actions. Nothing builds confidence like knowing we have the skills to practice our principles - even in the most difficult situations. (Like being a parent.)

Please keep in mind, success or accomplishments are much like baseball. They are meant to be fun, not life-threatening.

16:
Mistakes

LIFE MESSAGE: I Can Solve Problems - I Can Get It Right - I *Am* Capable
TRAIT: Courage

Misfortune comes to all men. - Chinese proverb

This category of self-esteem has so much potential, and yet it is the area where we regularly diminish self-esteem rather than enhance it. We both waste and corrupt opportunities to build self-esteem. As pointed out previously, this area offers the quickest and most dramatic boost in self-esteem. The two most important factors determining whether we boost or shatter self-esteem are our true attitude toward mistakes and our skill with criticism - are we hurtful or helpful, encouraging or discouraging. First, let us address our attitude toward mistakes.

Opportunities for Learning

Is it alright for your children or students to make mistakes? How many times? Do you handle the third episode with the same grace as the first? Do you handle behavioral mistakes - mis(taken)behavior with the same attitude as academic or social mistakes? Is it acceptable for you to make a mistake? Are you sure? Perhaps it would be helpful to check your genuine attitude.

The last time you could not locate your car keys, what did you say to yourself? When I present this concept in a live seminar, I always ask if we should do a "sharing time" with the messages we send to ourselves. No group ever wants to do this. I rarely can find a participant who said anything remotely positive to himself. If this is true for you, I respectfully suggest that your integrity on this issue may be out of kilter. What we say we believe or want to believe and what we practice are at odds. What our heads believe differs from what our hearts believe. Our attitude is not so clean as we want and as we need it to be.

Do we believe and practice that mistakes are the last step or the first step of a process? When a mistake is the last step of a process, we end up with a failed person. This is not beneficial to self-esteem. When, alternatively, we view a mistake as the first step of a process, a problem-solving or learning process, we end up with a failed situation - *which can be changed*. No problem to self-esteem.

There was a time in my life when I had a toddler, just toilet trained, and an infant, breast-fed. We lived in Canada, and it was still quite cold outside, still snowsuit weather. If you have never stuffed a toddler into a snow suit, you have not experienced parenthood in its fullness. We had just driven home, so I know I had just had my keys in my possession. As we got to the door of our house, I had a screaming, hungry baby and a toddler in his snow suit doing the newly-trained-I-really-have-to-go-peepee-now dance. I could hear my keys in my purse, but I could not find them. It was on this day that I began to truly change my attitude toward mistakes. For in this turmoil, after berating myself and doggedly trying to keep from crying, I became determined never to let my keys get the better of me again. I was never going to get caught like this again. *This situation* was stupid, but *I* was not. I could beat it. The next outing, I found a purse with a key ring that snapped into the top of the purse; I bought it. I still have it (and several like it), and I still use the snap. And my keys do not beat me anymore. I handled it. This is clearly a small victory over an inanimate foe; it still feels wonderful.

Mistakes are opportunities for learning; they tell us clearly what we need to learn or teach.

To lose is to learn. - unknown

Without this heartfelt belief about mistakes, we are destined to model and reveal our less helpful attitude that mistakes tell us how stupid we are, that mistakes are bad, and that smart or good or capable people should not and do not make them. Is it any wonder then that many children will lie, cheat, hide, or run away from their mistakes? Most vulnerable are those children whose self-esteem is tied up in Accomplishment.

As noted previously, "whenever personal worth is dependent upon performance, personal value is subject to cancellation with every misstep."

Almost anything is better than feeling you have no value, including lying to yourself and others or cheating or disclaiming any ownership and responsibility for the mistake. At all costs, the true outcome - you are not the best or you did not succeed - must be avoided. It is easy to see how hurtful and scary genuinely owning a mistake can be for children in this situation; this is why self-esteem must first come from Existence and why the correct attitude toward mistakes is impossible without self-esteem firmly established in this primary area. Everyone makes mistakes; what we need to do is own them and then learn from them.

Parents have disparate attitudes toward mistakes, and consequently have different ways of coaching children. Some styles are more helpful than others. Here are examples of two very dissimilar parents. This time we play basketball.

Basketball is a complex game of strategy and skill. When played by young children, it is a most amazing game; it does not much resemble college or even high school basketball. The year my younger son, Tim, was eleven his team happened to be quite good. They had several strong players. They had managed to easily beat every team they played - until the last game. That last game they came up against a team who was better. For the first time that season, they found themselves behind. One parent could not handle this and caused great distress.

On Tim's team there happened to be a boy, we will call him Bob, who was under tremendous pressure by his parents to do well, to quite literally be the star - in everything, not just sports. Bob was good at being the star. He handled the ball more than anyone else; he shot and scored more than anyone else. He would finally pass the ball when he found himself trapped, but then would immediately call to have it passed back. It is easy to guess that Bob was not much of a team player. He could not afford to pass the ball to an open man; they might score, or worse still, outscore Bob. He was neither a playmaker nor a team leader; he was too absorbed in himself. He had to be the star. Anything less was unacceptable to his father. Throughout every game, Bob's father exhorted him to shoot, get the ball, score: "Come on, Bob, shoot! It's up to *you* to score! *You* have to win this game!" During the course of the season, Bob's father had managed to alienate all of the other parents; there were, after all, other children on the team and on the court.

During that last game, as the other team pulled farther and farther ahead, Bob's father became increasingly insistent and loud. He was unrelenting in his yelling to Bob. "Bob, *you're* behind. *You* have to shoot! Shoot, Bob, shoot! Get the ball, Bob!" Mr. Bob was directing Bob virtually every moment. The change in Bob as the game progressed was dramatic. At the beginning of the game, Bob would only shoot when he had a clear, close shot, and only from inside the foul line. Soon, in desperation, he was shooting from center court. Bob was a small eleven year old. He did not have the proverbial snowball's chance to hit the backboard from there, let alone score. Still Bob's father exhorted him. It was inconceivable and intolerable that Bob could *let* this team lose. Late in the fourth quarter, Bob came down the court with the ball, shot it wildly, and missed the backboard. His father hollered, "Bob, *you* can't afford to miss like that!" Bob froze. Then he turned to his father, and in a clear voice said, "F--k off, Dad!" Despite the profanity and disrespect, many of us in the stands silently cheered his remark. Bob's father's coaching style clearly hindered Bob's performance. It also sabotaged self-esteem, violated their bond, and was unhealthy. I am concerned whenever a parent needs to build his own self-esteem through the successes of his child. The team lost the game; Bob and his father lost something greater.

The next season my son returned to the basketball court with a differently configured, intramural team - new teammates and new coach, his own father. For those of you who have not witnessed youth intramural basketball, it is important to understand that the early games of the season are frequently enlivened by moments of Bozo basketball. Anything can happen. Plays are disorganized, and skills are not honed yet. Early in the first game of the season, Tim managed to steal the ball while one of his teammates still remained back in their own end of the court. Having this open man near his own basket, Tim seized the opportunity and threw the ball to him as hard as he could. Unfortunately, Tim had overlooked the fact that he had grown two inches and gained ten pounds since the previous basketball season. Fortunately, the ball sailed harmlessly past his teammate and smashed into the wall at the opposite end of the court. Big mistake, a missed opportunity for an undefended, easy lay-up, quick two points. Tim immediately looked over to his dad-coach. It is not unusual at times like this to see coaches frown and shake their heads, pull the player, or ask why he did that - as if the player knew or meant to do it. Tim's dad chose another path. He smiled and laughed and shook his head to acknowledge Bozo ball. It had been funny to see the look of surprise on Tim's face when he realized he had actually thrown the basketball that far. Freed from guilt and discouragement, Tim laughed too, and raised his hands palms upward to acknowledge that he had had no idea he could throw like that either. The rest of his game was not flawless; it was still that first game. But he played better and better, and his value and confidence were still intact. One simply needs to learn from one's mistakes. And sometimes, mistakes are pretty harmless and awfully funny. It is a gift to be able to laugh at yourself. I cannot remember whether they won that game; I do know that Tim and his dad won.

Jeff Salzman, co-founder of CareerTrack®, in his audio tape program, How to Get Results With People™ describes CareerTrack's handling of mistakes. Whenever an employee makes a mistake, he fills out a mistake form. The form includes three sections.

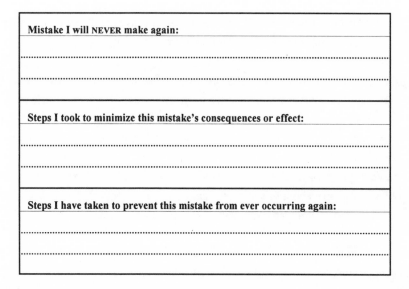

Mistake I will never make again. This speaks to ownership of the mistake. When someone denies or avoids ownership by lying or covering up the mistake, responsibility is bypassed, learning from the mistake is much less likely to occur, and the mistake's consequences may grow. (Spilled milk sours, the bathtub continues to overflow, a student gets further and further behind.)

Our house, like many others in neighborhoods with children, has had a window broken, not by the proverbial baseball but by a golf ball. The actual breaking of the window did not anger me; I expected that sooner or later this would happen. What did irritate me was the fact that no one claimed ownership and told us about it. We had to discover it ourselves. It happened in the dining room, a room we are not in every day. Had it rained before we discovered it, drapes, carpet, and windowsill would have been damaged. It is not the mistake that I begrudge; it is the failure to own it.

Steps I have taken to minimize the effects or consequences of this mistake. This looks after damage control. Isn't that what is most important after the mistake has occurred? If you have spilled the milk, all I really expect is that you clean it up so that I do not have to, so that it does not smell, and so that I do not sit down on a sticky, dirty chair. When you break something, all I expect is that you fix or replace it. This is Damage Control.

As adults in the work world, we recognize mistakes will happen. Owners, employers, managers, administrators seek minimized effects.

Steps I have taken to prevent this mistake from occurring again. This last declaration points out that when we learn from a mistake, we are more able to avoid it in the future. It is someone's repeated mistakes that make us crazy. It is at the third or fourth time a child spills milk in one meal when we lose our calm and our grace.

As your parent or teacher or even as your co-worker, I want to be assured that I do not have to worry about this mistake again; I need to know that you have learned from this mistake, that it was not in vain.

Interestingly, Mr. Salzman reports that at CareerTrack, a very fast-growing, leading edge company, each staff member fills out a form for every mistake and then brings these forms to his annual review. At CareerTrack, if you have *too few* Mistake forms, you are asked to leave and seek employment with a more conservative company because *clearly you have not taken enough risks, demonstrated enough courage, and learned enough* to work with a fast-paced, thriving company. This is a novel concept.

This form is a wonderful addition to detention where students generally waste time or do homework. Filling out this Mistake form pertaining to the deed which brought a student to detention ensures she knows exactly why she is here, promotes ownership and responsibility for the deed, fosters ideas for minimizing effects, teaches damage control as an important aspect of making mistakes, and clears the path to preventing this deed's repeated occurrence. In short, it promotes learning from mistakes.

Life Lessons

Everyone makes mistakes.

Mistakes create opportunities for learning.

Mistakes require damage control and amends.

In the end, when I solve my problem, remedy or make amends for my mistake, or learn something the hard way, my self-esteem grows.

The Fallacy of Separate the Deed from the Doer
Or Do We Own Our Actions?

With self-esteem intact in all three areas, we no longer have to be afraid of mistakes and the damage they could do to our sense of self-worth. It was this fear coupled with the knowledge that telling a child we do not like him is detrimental to the child and to our bond or relationship, that led us to the "Separate the Deed from the Doer" concept. For years, we have been taught never to tell a child we do not like him; rather, we are to tell him that we do not like what he has done. This constitutes separating the deed from the doer. It is past time to shatter this concept; it is untruthful, harmful, and dangerous. Again, like so many dealing with people and communication skills, we started with a concept which helped us take a more helpful direction; yet like technological inventions, we need to make improvements. Early models always seem to have bugs in them. Two major pitfalls are inherent in the concept "I like you, but I don't like your behavior."

First, it simply is not true. In the real world, we do not separate deed and doer. In live sessions, I ask participants the following series of questions to prove this point.

When you meet someone, how do you determine if you like that person? How do you decide whether or not you might be friends? The universal answer I receive is by what they do, by their actions. Could we not call this their behavior? We decide whom we like by whether or not we like their behavior. In truth, we do not separate deed and doer. Let us go one step farther. Do you like murderers? No? Then let us talk about serial killers, the worst of the murderers. Even serial killers spend less than one percent of their lives killing people. The rest of the time, many of them are model citizens with excellent behavior; this is what makes them so very difficult to catch. So, are you willing to invite these serial killers to dinner at your house for one behavior which occupies less than one percent of their time? No, absolutely not. I rest my case. We do not separate deed and doer.

Secondly, it is harmful to separate deed from doer because this undermines discipline. Fundamental to discipline is this concept, *You are responsible for what you choose to do and for what happens to you and others as a result of your decisions and actions.* Owning your behavior, owning all of your behavior is the foundation of discipline that leads to self-discipline and to responsibility. We corrupt our own discipline with this separate deed and doer. We have also sent two mixed messages to our youth. First, with discipline, we tell them they must own their behavior. With "I like you, but not your behavior" we tell them they are separate from their behavior, they do not have to own it after all. Then consider what we have done with praise. For years, we have told children that we like this behavior or that behavior and hoped they would own it and feel better about themselves because they had done something right or good. Thus, we have told them that when your behavior is acceptable, you own it. When it is unacceptable, you do not. No wonder children are confused. And no wonder "don't blame me" and accountability are problems currently facing the nation.

Certainly, earlier path finders were partly right. It is harmful to children to tell them we do not like them. The bind came into play because we did not know how to tell a child that something he has done or failed at (behavior, academics, mistake) is not good enough. We did not know how to criticize without being discouraging and hurtful, rather than encouraging and helpful. Yet children need to be told, and as parents or teachers, telling them is a major component of our job description. We are all aware that we need to be encouraging not discouraging and that the times we cause the most discouragement are when the child has made a mistake. The question, then, is how can we get ourselves out of this bind? How can we tell a child that he is off the mark and still encourage rather than discourage? The answer is DESCRIPTIVE CRITICISM.

Life Lesson

I own *everything* I do. My behavior tells me and others *who I am.* I am not separate from my behavior, good or bad.

Descriptive Criticism

Criticism that encourages rather than discourages.

I have yet to find the man - however exalted his station - who did not do better work and put forth greater effort under a spirit of approval than under a spirit of criticism. - Charles Schwab

Mr. Schwab was absolutely correct. Classic criticism hurts and discourages. It passes judgment or evaluates. It leaves the recipient feeling less capable and disheartened, and she is less likely to learn from the mistake and repair it. Criticism that encourages leaves the recipient feeling intact, capable, and more able to remedy and learn.

Helpful criticism is future oriented and empowering. It focuses not on what is wrong, but on what changes need to be made. It teaches by describing actions needed; it does not evaluate or attack character.

Two jobs which seem to require criticizing children are teacher and coach. Parents also criticize. In order to teach children life lessons, life skills, academics or athletics, we must at times point out to them mistakes, failures or deficiencies. Too often the end result is discouragement rather than encouragement. Coaches can be either a nightmare or a dream come true. They are the difference between a long season and a short season; sometimes they are the difference between a child loving or abandoning a sport.

When we moved to Texas, my elder son reentered baseball after one season of Tee-Ball (where the batters hit a ball off a large tee) and one season entirely missed due to a broken arm. Needless to say, his batting skills were minimal. I arrived at the end of one practice and watched as one of his two coaches struggled to help him learn to hit the ball. The coach would throw the ball; my son would swing and miss. The coach watched and then told him, "Don't bail out." Coach pitches, Kris swings and misses. "Swing, son, don't bail out," reminded the coach. As I watched, each became increasingly frustrated. Then I could almost see the light come on in the coach's head. A smile came across his face. This time before he pitched the ball, he said, "Kris, when I throw the ball, I want you to take your front foot, your right foot (Kris is left-handed) and step forward - move it towards me when you swing." Kris steps forward with his right foot and miraculously hits the ball. What worked? Telling him what *to do* rather than telling him what *not to do*. His other coach worked with him on bunting as well; bunting forces a batter to watch the ball. Did he become a fantastic hitter overnight? No, but he began his journey to better hitting which two years later found him as the lead off batter and bunter par excellence. Not bad coaching!

At times, it is helpful to include what not to do, generally only when what not to do is preventing the successful completion of what to do. However, telling what not to do is more often not necessary, and *telling what not to do by itself is never enough.* Far more helpful is describing what needs to be changed or done to correct the mistake, improve the deficit, or remedy the oversight.

By the nature of our work with children, we must criticize. It is our job to point out when they are off the mark and need to do better. There is a synonym or alternative word for criticize - one with which we will all be comfortable. For none of us is truly comfortable with criticism; it has become a word with a very negative connotation. I am frequently asked how to make bad news sound good. Each of us has been in a situation where we have been discouraged by criticism. So, too, have we been in a situation where seemingly magically, someone has helped us see our mistake or misstep and improve. We ended up encouraged and feeling better about ourselves. How was this done? It is helpful to compare classic criticism with descriptive criticism. In the process, we will discover the synonym which can forever and always replace the term criticize. You will never need to criticize again; still you will be able to communicate to a child or adult, "This is not good enough; you can get it right." First let's look at classic, common, discouraging criticism.

Early in first grade, my son arrived home from school, threw a paper down on the kitchen table, and pronounced, "My teacher says I can't write." If we pause right here, how would you guess he will write tomorrow? Worse or not at all. He is definitely discouraged. I picked up his paper and immediately saw two things. First, across the top of his paper were written the words, "Very poor handwriting." This is classic criticism which evaluates performance negatively. Second, I noticed that this was truly some of the worst printing I had ever seen. Indeed, the teacher's point was accurate; my son needed to do better. I looked at my son and remarked, "I know what teachers call good writing."

My son looked at me and said, "I'm hungry." Never try to work with a child who is tired or hungry. He snacked; he played outside. Later he returned and warily asked,

"So, what do teachers think is good writing?" He has just demonstrated remarkable courage simply by bringing up the subject again. He has already been hurt pretty badly by this incident.

Now it is time for helpful, encouraging, descriptive criticism. He has opened himself up to me, and he is vulnerable. He can be quickly discouraged; he has already been burned once on this issue. Still, he has given to me a wonderful opportunity to help him *get it right*. "Well," I answer, "they like the letters to rest on the lines, like this one and this one."

"I can do that," he responded as he printed several letters on the blank lines at the bottom of the sheet of paper. "What else do they want?"

"They like to have small, even spaces between the letters in a word, about like the spaces between those two," I said as I pointed to two good examples.

"Anyone can do that," he said more confidently as he again showed me he could. "What else do they want?" he repeated.

"They like to have bigger spaces between the words so they can tell which letters go with which words."

Again, as he showed me the desired improvement, "That's easy; I can do that! See my teacher doesn't know anything; I can too write."

Pause here and forecast how he will write the next day in his class. I bet he will show her just what he can do! Encouraged? Yes. Who wins? He does - he can now write more legibly. His teacher does - she will have what she was after - improved writing from him. I do - I helped facilitate this outcome.

Now, the synonym for criticize. What did I do that so magically and quickly encouraged? Pause for a moment; think about this. Rarely do entire groups come up with the answer. What I did and what you would easily have recognized, if I had not placed this story in the realm of criticism and merely described my telling him about letter placement and spacing, is called *TEACHING*. Albeit, more accurately, it was re-teaching; I am quite certain that his first grade teacher had mentioned placing letters on the lines before. Imagine, a child, a bright child, who did not tune into or act upon his first teaching! Know any adults who require re-teaching? Have you ever required a second lesson? A third lesson? We need never criticize again. No more evaluation; no more blame; only teaching is needed.

Teaching or if you prefer *Descriptive Criticism* simply describes what needs to be done for improvement or change. When mistakes are made or improvement is needed, *teaching* is the tool of choice. *Teaching* nets results, encouragement, and high self-esteem. Classic criticism is never needed.

When we do not seem to be able to get through to another and we are frustrated by continued, repeated mistakes, deficiency, or lack of improvement, it is time for us to reevaluate. Is there a better way or method to teach this lesson to this particular child? Is this child developmentally ready for the required task or skills, or should we wait? What mistake are we making? What is getting in the way of this child's learning?

As adults, this format continues to be helpful and productive. Most of us have been evaluated at a job. Sometimes we leave the evaluation with only numbers (evaluation) and discouragement. But every once in awhile, a gifted evaluator appears. The outcome of this session can be very different - helpful, encouraging, and productive.

One group subjected to periodic evaluations is teachers. Some evaluators leave us with a number-ranked evaluation and comments which are best described as classic criticism. "Well, Mrs. Smith, you smile quite a bit, but too often your students are not paying attention so I had to lower your mark in this area. Your lessons seem to be adequate; you just don't seem to be able to pull them back to you when their attention wanders. They are not learning what you are teaching."

How does one feel after such an encounter? Terrible, embarrassed, angry, saddened, discouraged? Thoughts may include, "I thought I was *meant* to be a teacher, but maybe I'm in over my head. Maybe I should leave education, maybe I'm just not cut out to be a teacher." Classic discouragement contributes directly to burnout, a problem in many fields, including education. This was not the evaluator's goal or purpose, but it was the net result.

What if the evaluator used the evaluation form and time to teach? What if only master teachers could be evaluators? What if she said, "Mrs. Smith, thank you for including me in your classroom. I have included strong ratings on many items which you can peruse at your leisure; I will not spend our valuable time on those now. My job is to help strengthen weaker areas. I noticed that you struggled with maintaining individual student attention at times. It happens in every class. Students, especially some types of students, fade in and out despite interesting lessons, and I found your lessons well-paced, engaging, and thought-provoking. Would it be helpful to discuss some of the strategies other teachers have used to bring back individual fading students?" After a brief discussion of tips such as moving around the room while teaching, standing beside students, including students in discussion, this teacher is able to leave the evaluation with these thoughts: "I did a number of things well, but I need to get better at noticing students when they are not paying attention. I *can* do that. And I *can* help them. I *can* walk around the room more during discussions and lectures. *I can do better. I can do this. I can handle this!* I'm not the perfect teacher, but I'm on my way." Genuinely encouraged? Yes. Burned out? No, fired up.

To the child who has folded the towels into wads:
  "First, lay the towel flat, then bring these two corners together with the other two
  corners. Smooth. Then bring corners together again and smooth."
  Instead of:
  "Not like that!"

To the young child who has spilled juice:
  "Do you know where the sponges are? You will need one." OR
  "Putting the cup near the center of the table keeps it from being knocked off."
  Instead of:
  "Don't knock it with your hand. Be careful." (How does one "be careful"?)

To the student who has failed a punctuation assignment:
  "Every sentence needs an end mark, such as a period or a question mark. Periods
  go at the end of the sentences that tell us something. Let's look for sentences that
  tell or give us information."
  Instead of:
  "Poor work."

Teaching is the remedy to mistakes and the alternative to criticism. Teaching is the key to encouragement.

We are all aware of how important it is to be encouraging rather than discouraging. Now you know how to accomplish this.

Life Lesson

Mistakes signal the need for teaching, not criticizing. Teaching can entirely replace criticism.

Life Message

I can get it right. I can solve my problems. I can learn.

Immunize Against Discouragement

Included here is a note on the damage done by others; for classic criticism is going to continue to exist. Others will criticize our children; others will belittle them; others will cause discouragement. We must include two important lessons for our children to strengthen their resistance and immunity to these negative influences. Eleanor Roosevelt stated the first lesson concisely and beautifully:

"No one can make you feel inferior without your permission."

Or as phrased by a child, "It is not what they think, it's what I know."[27] We are the ultimate judges of who we are and how much value we have. We determine this within ourselves. And we must not give this capacity and power away. We must help children to recognize that what they believe and know about themselves is more significant and generally more accurate than what others believe. We can help them become less vulnerable to criticism and belittling by others. I frequently find myself in a situation where a child comes to me saying someone has called her a name; I recognize this as an opportunity to teach this concept. The conversation invariably follows these lines:

"Jimmy called me stupid."

"Well, do you think you're stupid?"

Thoughtful pause. "No, I know lots of things."

"So, then, you believe Jimmy is mistaken?"

Short pause again. "Yes, I'm pretty smart."

"There you are! It's not what he thinks; it's what you know!"

"Yes, it's what *I* know!" Accompanied by a smile.

The heart of the second lesson is simply conceding the passage of time. That was then; this is now.

Have you ever considered the amount of freedom granted by this statement? Being able to wipe the slate clean and start over is important in any relationship and for all of us; it is particularly important for children who develop and change daily. The younger the child, the more vast is the difference between any *then* and *now*; they learn so rapidly, they sleep and forget, they simply forget, and they rarely hold grudges. For relationships to be healthy and to thrive, *forgive and forget* must be included and repeated. Without these, all of the ever present minor digressions and irritations begin to add up and accumulate. *That was then, this is now* fortifies healthy relationships.

There are a few experiences which may be forgiven, which allows the forgiver to get on with her life, but the lessons learned need never to be forgotten. The holocaust is one. Sexual abuse is another. The other side of the coin is that we need to beware of holding onto mistakes (especially within families and close friendships) and virtually keeping a tally of them. All families, all relationships have positive and negative experiences involved. Again, we can choose which type to focus on and remember.

Life Lessons

Our evaluation of ourselves is the most important. Other opinions must be considered, but ours is the final determination

That was then; this is now. We can choose to dwell on the past or we can choose to move forward from here. Courage is the ability to try and fail and to try again.

Take Time to Teach

Use mistakes and misbehavior as the opportunities for teaching that they are. But this means *taking time to teach*. It generally takes longer to teach a child than to ignore, punish, or manipulate around inappropriate behavior. It also takes longer and requires less effort and thought in the short term to teach rather than to do something right or remedy a mistake yourself. The latter also fall into the "spend, spend, spend" category - saving time only when viewed in the immediate short term, but devouring substantially more time in the long run. Teaching requires an *investment* of time now, yet over the long term, teaching consumes considerably less time. Again, the import of seeing and playing to the long term cannot be emphasized enough.

Although patience and skill are indispensable components of teaching, I believe that in these fast-paced, harried, hurried times, that *time* is the component which most frequently impedes or prevents teaching. Dolores Curran, tells about an incisive article found in the October, 1979 *Harper's* and written by Louis T. Grant.[28] He entitled the article "Fast Folk" and dissects an earlier article published in *Woman's Day* which had praised the fast-paced lifestyle of one mother.

> Listen to this woman's life. She rushes from home to work in the morning, eating yogurt in the car for breakfast; has lunch at the spa where she works out; leaves child care to her husband, who also has a managerial position forty miles the other side of home; pilots a small plane in her leisure time for pleasure; teaches on the side a class at a local women's college; leaves the kids with Grandma; leaves the kids with sitters; leaves the kids....

Mr. Grant labeled these people "fast folk"; know anyone who falls into this category? He likened this lifestyle to keeping up with the gerbils. Hits home does it not? There is no time for other members of the family, for intimacy, for building communication, for teaching important Life Lessons. These, the author says, are for slowpokes. And, by the way, he also points out that children are slowpokes - bless their hearts. In the 1990's we are still prone to glorify this type of lifestyle. The beginning of the millennium will not be different. We still struggle with tangible signs of productivity, of accomplishment, of value. When did producing a healthy family, with emotionally healthy, happy, stable children stop being important, stop being a major accomplishment? Are we so hooked into immediate gratification that we must see tangible proof of production daily? That *only* concrete proof counts? That without proof we have no value? We have lost our grounding, our focus, and our center. Perhaps I am tired of hearing so many people espouse family values as they eschew their own family. I confess it is exceedingly easy to get lost in ourselves, our jobs, and our chores and to lose not just our balance but our own sense of values, our own principles. I continue to catch myself behaving at odds with my principles, with my integrity yet again disintegrating; I have told my own children to get a grip, stop quarreling, and leave me alone so that I can finish this book. (I know, nice touch!) But I also admit to putting the book on hold while I *chose* to take time to be with my family. I am not suggesting that we quit jobs, take neither leisure nor alone time, nor forget about household chores. I am suggesting that too many of us have lost our control over our lives, and we have become time-stressed beyond belief and beyond health.

If you do not make time to teach your child principles, such as responsibility for actions and respectful communication, and practices, such as how to fold clothes and a more efficient way to avoid spills, who will? And what will be the cost of these lost lessons to our children and to all of us?

As teachers, are we lost in the time-stress of teaching academics so that our students do well on standardized tests? Do we take time to teach individuals rather than teach material, subjects, or a class?

Life Lessons

Teaching (or learning) is an extremely worthwhile investment of time.

One of our most important gifts and legacies to our children is the time we spend with them.

I believe that the second most common component which impedes teaching is exasperation caused by the stress from outside events, unrelated sources, and the lack of understanding or knowledge about children in general. Each of these factors leads to unrealistic expectations. Too many people have not taken the time to learn at least a little about *children,* about their stages of development, about normal expectations. This information truly makes life and decision making much easier. It is important for every parent to learn about children in general and their own individual children specifically.

Beware of Negative Expectations

Do you expect that your child will do a poor job cleaning up the kitchen? Or will nastily push her brother around? Do you expect a student to do a mediocre job writing his book report? To not pay attention? We must always strive to be aware of our own negative expectations and of sending the message, "You can't get it right; you won't do better." The self-fulfilling prophecy is ever-present. Both our language (especially with regard to the disrespectful BARRIERS TO COOPERATION) and our actions (usually unconscious but not unnoticed) tell children who we think they are. In turn, the children tend to take these messages to heart. Be careful what messages you send: they will be received. Negative expectations yield negative results.

Life Lessons

The self-fulfilling prophecy can work for us or against us. This choice is ours.

Trait: Courage
Help them back up on the horse.

Take risks: if you win, you will be happy; if you lose, you will be wise. - unknown

The trait which accompanies self-esteem built in the Mistakes category is courage. Remember the old story that advocates putting a child right back on his horse after he has fallen. Otherwise, courage diminishes and fear grows. Once again, courage is trying and failing and *trying again.* We must all learn to re-climb the horse. We may need to ask for help, to learn new skills, to seek an alternative approach, but we need to revisit our mistake and try again.

One of my favorite definitions of courage (from the French word *coeur*, meaning heart) is that courage is the ability to try and to fail and to try again. It is reported that it took Thomas Edison more than a thousand trials to discover the successful format for the electric light bulb. This certainly represents courage, a trait all researchers and inventors must have. If we are going to find a cure for AIDS, continue to make gains against various cancers and other life-threatening diseases, invent better artificial limbs, communication devices, and ways to technologically improve our lives, know that these will all, most assuredly, be found by persons with this type of courage, with self-esteem built in all three areas, including Mistakes. When it was pointed out to Mr. Edison that he had *failed* over a thousand times, it is recounted that he replied that he had figured out over a thousand ways that a light bulb will not work. What a marvelous attitude!

It is the trying again, not the ultimate success, that is important.

Life Message

I have courage.

You may want to work through the practice exercises to check application of skills.

Affirming Practice
- Parents

What will you say and do? Be specific.

PRESCHOOLERS
1. Joey spills his milk, again.
2. Marcia arrives home looking happy and excited.
3. Kris has reversed three of five *S's*.
4. Tim brings you a picture he has just finished and asks you, "Do you like it? Is it good?"
5. Lee informs you that Jamal just took the beach ball from Robin.

SCHOOL AGE
6. Bobby's clothes are stuffed in his drawer, again.
7. Juanita arrives home cheerful and pleasant.
8. Martha brings you her homework paper and asks you, "Is it good enough?"
9. Your first baseman just missed an easy catch at first, caught two fly balls, failed to make an important throw to home, laid a bunt down the third base line which barely went foul, and stole second and third.

TEENS
10. Ismael's done a terrible job mowing the lawn, again.
11. Melissa arrives home cheerful and excited.
12. Martha brings you her history report and asks you, "Is this good enough?"
13. Your teen, left in charge of two younger sisters for three hours, let other children in to play (not allowed), kept the phone busy for thirty minutes, made and cleaned up lunch for all of them, and handled a minor cut.
14. Robin informs you that Eric just took the remote control and started watching his show.

Affirming Practice
- Early Childhood Educators

What will you say and do? Be specific.

1. Joey tears his picture with his eraser, again.

2. Melissa returns from playing outside looking happy and excited.

3. Kris has reversed three of five *S's*.

4. Tim brings you a picture he has just finished and asks you, "Do you like it? Is it good?"

5. Haley informs you that Eric just took the beach ball from Robin.

Affirming Practice
- Teachers

What will you say and do? Be specific.

ELEMENTARY SCHOOL

1. Joey tears his paper with his eraser, again.

2. Melissa arrives in class cheerful and excited.

3. Martha brings you her history paper and asks you, "Is this good enough?"

4. Robert's bibliography is not alphabetized, nor are the entries in any organized form.

5. Robin informs you that Eric just copied his paper.

MIDDLE AND HIGH SCHOOL

6. Joe's done a terrible job on his book report again.

7. Melissa arrives in class cheerful and excited.

8. Martha brings you her history report and asks you, "Is this good enough?"

9. Robert's project is poorly organized and does not follow the assigned format.

10. Robin informs you that Eric just cheated on his test.

17:
Self-Esteem Summary

What You See is What You Get

Years ago, comedian Flip Wilson portrayed a brash, sexy woman named Geraldine. One of Geraldine's favorite remarks, made to a man and made with swaying hips and shoulders was, "What you see is what you get." Geraldine's point differs from mine, but her words are right on target. If we see our children as problems, they will be. If we see our children as wonderful gifts with the potential for civilization, they will become so. Invariably, what we look for and perceive is what we uncover and find. This quick quote blends the concepts of self-fulfilling prophecy and focus on what is right with them. We select the color of lenses through which we peer. **Think** *before* **you see.**

> You never know when a moment and a few sincere words can have an impact on a life. - Zig Ziglar

Teachers have profoundly influenced children's lives. Many stories have been written about this. It is not the children with high self-esteem and healthy families who need you most. The major and minor figures in these children's lives are already taking care of business. But those other children, whose numbers are increasing, need you desperately. Teachers may not be their last hope, but they are their last easy hope. Therapy can be an arduous journey; jail has been known to turn a life around; gangs offer membership and belonging. I prefer to see a child touched and helped by a teacher. Never underestimate a teacher's impact. Realize it may take years to unfold.

Elizabeth Silance Ballard illustrates this beautifully in "Three Letters from Teddy":

I have not seen Teddy Stallard since he was in my fifth-grade class, fifteen years ago. It was early in my career, and I had only been teaching for two years.

From the first day he stepped into my classroom, I disliked Teddy.... He was dirty. Not just occasionally, but all the time.... He knew I didn't like him, but he didn't know why. Nor did I know - then or now - why I felt such an intense dislike for him. All I know is that he was a little boy no one cared about, and I made no effort in his behalf....

As the Christmas holidays approached, I knew that Teddy would never catch up in time to be promoted to the sixth-grade level. He would be a repeater.

To justify myself, I went to his cumulative folder from time to time. He had very low grades for the first four years, but no grade failure. How had he made it, I didn't know. I closed my mind to the personal remarks:

First grade: "Teddy shows promise by work and attitude, but has poor home situation.

Second grade: "Teddy could do better. Mother terminally ill. He receives little help at home."

Third grade: "Teddy is a pleasant boy. Helpful, but too serious. Slow learner. Mother passed away at the end of the year."

Fourth grade: "Very slow, but well behaved. Father shows no interest."

Well, they passed him four times, but he will certainly repeat fifth grade! Do him good! I said to myself....

Teachers always get several gifts at Christmas, but mine that year seemed bigger and more and more elaborate than ever.... His gift was the last one I picked up.... Its wrapping was a brown paper bag and he had colored Christmas trees and red balls all over it. It was stuck together with masking tape.

The group was completely silent and for the first time I felt conspicuous, embarrassed because they all stood watching me unwrap that gift.

As I removed the last bit of masking tape, two items fell to my desk. A gaudy rhinestone bracelet with several stones missing and a small bottle of dime-store cologne - half empty.

I could hear the snickers and whispers and I wasn't sure I could look at Teddy.

"Isn't this lovely?" I asked, placing the bracelet on my wrist. "Teddy, would you help me fasten it?"

He smiled shyly as he fixed the clasp and I held up my wrist for all of them to admire.

There were a few hesitant *ooh's* and *aah's* but as I dabbed the cologne behind my ears, all the girls lined up for a dab behind their ears....

We ate our refreshments and the bell rang.... When they had all left, he [Teddy] walked towards me....

"You smell just like Mom," he said softly. "Her bracelet looks real pretty on you, too. I'm glad you liked it."

He left quickly and I locked the door, sat down at my desk and wept, resolving to make up to Teddy what I had deliberately deprived him of - a teacher who cared.

Slowly but surely he caught up with the rest of the class. Gradually there was a definite upward curve in his grades.

He did not have to repeat fifth grade. In fact his final averages were among the highest in the class.

I did not hear from Teddy until seven years later, when his first letter appeared in my mailbox.

"Dear Miss Thompson,
I just wanted you to be the first to know. I will be graduating second in my class next month.
              Very truly yours, Teddy Stallard."

Four years later, Teddy's second letter came.

> "Dear Miss Thompson,
> I wanted you to be the first to know. I was just informed that I'll be graduating first in my class. The university has not been easy, but I liked it.
> > Very truly yours, Teddy Stallard"

And now - today - Teddy's third letter.

> "Dear Miss Thompson,
> I wanted you to be the first to know. As of today I am Theodore J. Stallard, MD. How about that!!??
>
> I'm going to be married in July, the twenty-seventh, to be exact. I wanted to ask you if you could come and sit where Mom would sit if she were here. I'll have no family there as Dad died last year.
> > Very truly yours, Ted Stallard"

I'm not sure what kind of gift one sends to a doctor on completion of medical school and state boards. Maybe I'll just wait and take a wedding gift, but my note can't wait.

> "Dear Ted,
> Congratulations! You made it and you did it yourself! In spite of those like me and not because of us, this day has come for you.
>
> God bless you. I'll be at the wedding with bells on!"

There are thousands of Teddy Stallards all over our nation - the children we have forgotten or given up on.

Each of us knows one. Each of us has at least one in our classroom every year. How many will we let slip through our fingers? How many will never become who and what they might have been? How many times will each of us miss our calling? For it is the Teddys in our classrooms who need our love and a truly positive difference made in their lives.

The Sunshine Effect

The Sunshine Effect is a concept I have grappled with for years. Early in my professional career, I worked as a school psychologist, first as an intern where each of us was moved around to numerous schools and school districts, probably to see how we would fare in various environments. In my first early years, I worked with both rural and urban schools in two countries; my work took me to elementary through secondary schools, Kindergarten through high school, and in both regular and special education programs. From this quick, broad education, and despite my youth, I quickly came to realize how very alike all schools are in some general ways and how extraordinarily unique they are in the rest of the components. I also learned that I (or anyone) can determine much about the principal of a school before meeting her by simply walking through her school. The same, it turns out, is true for directors of early childhood programs and for teachers in classrooms and for parents in homes. Each of these pivotal figures sets the tone for the entire school or classroom or home, a vital, discernible atmosphere. Each brings their own *presence* to the setting. There are many nuances to these personally set ambiances, and it is helpful to each of us to be aware that we set a tone around ourselves that affects other people and permeates the environment near us. It is helpful to be aware of what tone we exude.

The tone I'm speaking of here is best likened to sunshine and clouds. Some schools and classrooms, like some homes, are filled with sunshine and light; joy, contentment, and health abound. Still others seem covered by clouds and pervaded with darkness; fear, discontent, and gloom prevail. It seems that in our positions, dynamic positions as educators or parents, we do set the tone on a daily basis for those around us. Have you ever noticed that when you are tired, irritable, or stressful, the children have a terrible day? If it can go wrong, it does go wrong. By contrast, when you are loaded with energy and good will, and ready to handle anything, little happens.

We radiate who we are and what we feel every day. Sometimes I wish I could just once have an off day and not have everything and everyone else seem to fall apart with me. (As the children get older, this wish is coming true.) When we are dealing with young children, this is unlikely. Children pick up on the mood we are in and the tone we set. Over time, they begin to know what to expect, what the feeling usually is around us. How is your tone? Do you generally offer sunshine or clouds? It is this "generally" and "over time" which are important; isolated, infrequent tones are much less significant. What we too often overlook is that we, too, are caught up in the light or the darkness and taken up or down with it. It is difficult to override our own attitude, although this can be accomplished occasionally. Thus, the real question to ask ourselves is: are we most typically filled with sunshine or with darkness? For what we are will certainly show and become our reality. What we sow, we shall reap.

> Those who bring sunshine into the lives of others cannot keep it from themselves. - J.M. Barrie

You Cannot Give What You Do Not Have

It is true: you cannot give what you do not have. If you have no sunshine within, you will not be able to sustain a sunny atmosphere. More acutely, if you do not have self-esteem established in all three areas, Existence, Accomplishment, and Mistakes, everything previous will become technique only. Not only will these skills fall into disuse, but when used, they will have a false or feigned ring to them. In order to handle mistakes as an opportunity for learning, one must *believe* the concept is true. To be able to convince a child that she has incredible value because she exists, one must *believe* it - not just for the child but for one's own self.

It is absolutely critical that we find ways to build our own self-esteem and make sure that we keep a steady, high balance in our own emotional bank accounts. Faking it is categorically different from *being* it. Solid, high self-esteem is required to work with or to parent children. So is emotional health.

Create the Best Place to BE

The Best Place to *BE!* Please note first that the phrase is the best place to *BE* not *DO.* Inherent in this concept is that Existence, being not doing, is the foundation of self-esteem. Further, we need to determine whether the home, the family place that we have created, is a good place to be. When your children return home, do their shoulders relax or tense? Are they emotionally comfortable and safe here? Is this a place where they thrive or wither? Do they live in the comfortable knowledge that they are welcome and valued, or live in apprehension that anything may happen and that they really do not belong here? How about you? Do you breathe a sigh of relief when you finally get to the door or do you tense up waiting for the next unpleasant remark or incident? Is this the best place to be, a haven in the stormy seas of the real world? A place where you find solace and people who are glad to see you? If our children do not thrive and feel secure at home, where will they find their worth, their membership, their peace?

For you teachers, fortunately or unfortunately, school is the second most influential place. It is certainly preferable that school is number two; home has the stronger effect on our children. Presently, for increasing numbers of students, home is not a good place to be, let alone the best. Our job, then, is to create a similar type of family and safety within our classrooms; for many of our students, it will be the best place to be. Too often children reach adolescence never having had a good place to be, no emotional safety, no warm, welcome place of membership. These children are vulnerable to gangs and drugs. It is, therefore, critical that when you walk into your classroom each morning (well, nine days out of ten) that you are entering the (second) Best Place to *BE* for you - certainly the Best Place to Work.

One of my favorite teachers, perhaps the most affirming teacher either of my children had, inadvertently gave me the secret to being a genuinely affirming teacher, or person for that matter. For months I had asked her what the secret to her magic was, and she had given me various tips for building self-esteem. I kept thinking that each was a nice technique, but it was not what I wanted to know. What I wanted was the *key* to her magic. Then one year I had lunch with her at a teacher professional development program the day before school started. She was happy to be going back into the classroom and excited about meeting her new students and starting a brand new year. Most teachers are. But the sentences this teacher used gave away the secret: "I don't know what I would do if they didn't let me teach. I love teaching. I *am* a teacher." Teaching is not just what she does; *it is who she is*. Second only to her home, her classroom is the best place for her to be, and, consequently, a best place for her students to be. To work with children or to parent children, you have to be happy with who you are and where you are.

Navigating the Tunnels

Funerals are always difficult to attend; funerals where a suicide has occurred are even more so. Sadly, the last two funerals I have attended were for men who had taken their own lives. Earlier, we considered one of these incidents; now we will address one aspect of the second. Each of us has had to wrestle with discouragement in our lives. Perhaps it is more accurate to say we have been oppressed by it. We seem to lose the will to continue when we become discouraged. Not wanting to wrestle any longer, or becoming paralyzed, becomes the core problem. We need to understand and come to believe firmly in the lessons of Navigating the Tunnels. These lessons provide immunization against lasting discouragement and suicide.

Everyone's life will contain problems or, shall we say, tunnels. This is a given. The first lesson we encounter teaches: **Expect problems. Life is a journey filled with both open road and tunnels.** When we realize that problems befall everyone, we can avoid becoming terribly upset when they do occur.

Since our road will have some tunnels, we will require bright, functioning headlights. Or, in other words, we will need procedures or skills to help us maneuver through the tunnels, the times of darkness. The second lesson is that we will each need to develop beneficial and productive problem-solving skills to deal with our problems. As we develop these skills, we begin to learn the second lesson, which is: **Tunnels can be navigated; problems can be solved.**

The last lesson takes place within the tunnel: **There is light at the end of every tunnel. Don't give up hope.** Of course, I could be wrong, and we will never have proof, but I am quite certain that everyone who chooses suicide as a permanent answer to a temporary problem has lost this lesson. This last lesson clearly reflects the third Critical Life Message, "I can solve problems, any problem."

These tunnel lessons are some of the most crucial lessons we can ever teach and learn. One of the most important tasks we will ever undertake is to engender and fortify these three lessons in our children. These lessons ought to be required "immunization" for all.

Frogkissing

Whenever I present ideas on self-esteem to early childhood educators and teachers, I include a segment which speaks to one aspect of their job descriptions which is ofttimes overlooked. Mothers or fathers may also enjoy this approach. The next time you find yourself at a boring cocktail party, your spouse's office Christmas party, or anywhere where someone asks you what you do with that "justify your existence" twist to it, try telling them you are a *Frogkisser*. I concede this is assuredly taking the low road, but sometimes taking the low road is more fun. (And most of us do not have enough fun in our lives.) For in truth, kissing frogs, just like in the fairy tale, is exactly what you do.

In many ways it is largely frogs, with many lessons to learn, who come hopping through our doors each day. Yet within each one is hidden a prince (or princess). It is our job to kiss these froggies and help them turn into princes. The fable was right on two accounts; it misled us on one. First, we must never forget that children come to us essentially as uncivilized little bozos, and I mean this in the most affectionate and kindest way. They have so much to learn about themselves and the world (the uncivilized part), and they are carefree, free spirits (the bozo part). Both of these attributes are as they should and must be. This is why I so easily picture any child as a little frog with a prince hiding and waiting inside. We must be able to see not just what they are, but what they can and will be. Thus, the first truth in the fable is that within each frog-child is a prince awaiting awakening and freedom, and it takes a genuine frogkisser's special vision to "see" the prince inside. Trust me, lots and lots of people cannot see anything but frog.

The second point which the fable makes is that it takes a princess or prince, royalty not ordinary folk, or at least someone very gifted and with a very special touch, to release the prince inside the frog. Virtually anyone can make a chair. But it takes a *skilled and gifted* woodworker, who has a keen understanding of wood and chairs, to find and release an exquisite chair from the wood. Anyone can work with, care for, and teach frog-children. But it takes a *skilled and gifted and caring* teacher or parent, who understands children and grown-ups, to find and release the prince within a child. The difference between the woodworker and the parent or teacher is that we can afford to bungle the chair; we get another chunk of wood and try again. We cannot afford to bungle any child. *No child is replaceable.*

If you bungle raising your children, I don't think whatever else you do well matters very much. - Jacqueline Kennedy Onassis

We certainly do get to make mistakes along the way. It is not the inevitable mishandlings or miswordings from which a child cannot recover. It is a parent or teacher continually on the wrong path, with weak skills and vision, who in the end has bungled and hurt a child. It is one thing to make mistakes and follow up with damage control and learning. It is another thing entirely to continually remake the same type of mistake and to even escalate mistakes and hurt and warp a child.

It is critical that caregivers and teachers be well-trained and gifted *professionals*. As well, it is crucial that parents become well-trained and skilled parents. Anything less, places at risk our most precious gifts, our most significant assets, and our future. We owe it to our children to have a fair idea of what we are doing and where we are headed. Training manuals do not come with children, but training manuals are available for those who are interested and willing to take precious time to search them out. You will need one, for as Bette Davis said in All About Eve, "it *is* going to be a bumpy night." Rearing children is bumpy business.

There is no more difficult and meaningful job than bringing up children. Time, thought, and effort will be required.

The element of the Frog and Princess fable that is misleading comes near the end of the story. Here, the princess finally kisses the frog, and lo and behold, he instantly, straightaway turns into the prince. I don't think so. Not in real life. In reality, we must kiss each of our frogs thousands of times over months and years to free the whole prince. Countless affirming skills and interactions are needed. Start kissing. To be an affirming parent or teacher, one has to acquire a taste for frog and a gift for magic! What other position offers you an opportunity to perform magic?

These moments of frogkissing become touchstones throughout the child's life. In the past he was someone valuable and important to himself and to someone else. A child can, and will, return to these touchstones in times of doubt and discouragement (frogginess). In this way his value *cannot ever* be taken away.

PART VI - THE JOURNEY CONTINUES

18:
The Journey Continues

Process

Parenting, and working with children, is an ongoing process. We learn; we practice; we succeed; we fail; we try again. What is important is that we *strive* to be the best parent for our child(ren) that we can possibly be. Remember the monkey in the side car. We do not have to get it right moment by moment and in every instance; we just need to get it mostly right and get our children going in the right general direction. We just need to take action, based on thinking and planning and ever increasing vision and wisdom. There is no crime in making mistakes or we would all be in prison! The crimes, if you will, are in not learning from mistakes and not recognizing the far-reaching import of your assignment as parent. How you choose to discipline, how you choose to communicate, what principles and life lessons you choose to teach, what life messages you choose to send, these signify who *you* are.

Guilt

It is my mission to reduce guilt among parents, not increase it. As well, I strive to increase integrity and confidence. Vision (recognizing where you want to end up) and skills (finding ways to get there) increase confidence and permit integrity. Consequently guilt and anguish diminish. It is a myth that raising children is a dreadful, thankless task which goes from bad to worse when children reach adolescence. The greatest joys in my life have happened because of my children and husband. And I am not alone in this feeling. Having children has caused me to develop character and traits (mostly positive) which I would never have had without having been a parent. I would not trade the experience of being a mother to my sons for anything in the world. I wish I had known this truth when they were young and I was so lost; this knowledge would have been most comforting. If you invest in your skills and wisdom while your children are young, though it is never too late, then during your children's rocky teen years, you will reap what you have sown. For these years are indeed the toughest on the children. Would you go back to age thirteen? I wouldn't, not for a moment! One of my greatest sources of strength is a growing, quiet confidence I have about my children. They are becoming less frog and more prince every day!

Please do not let what you have learned here or in any book make you feel guilty about the past. Instead, when you catch yourself doing something you recognize as unhelpful, pat yourself on the back for knowing more today than yesterday. And offer yourself understanding - change takes time, is frustrating, and can be awfully stressful. If parenting were easy and natural, none of us would struggle. Trust me, everyone is challenged by being a parent. Everyone.

Tolerance

Tolerance is a virtue, and one seen less and less frequently. It is important to develop tolerance for other parents and other teachers. It is exceedingly important that you develop this for the other parent(s) of your children, birth and step. No one agrees entirely on an issue as complicated as parenting. I will turn to the Bible (John 8:7) for words of wisdom, "He that is without sin among you, let him first cast a stone...." No one has all the answers. Many answers work. Each of us finds answers in our own time. Teaching, not criticizing, hastens answers.

Tolerance for our children's differences from us (and there will be many - it is their job to separate from us) will also be important; with our teens, it is required. Your children are not you. Their job is to discover who they are. They must make their own mistakes. No one can live his life for or as someone else.

Gifts

There are only two lasting bequests we can hope to give our children. One of those is roots, the other, wings.   - Hodding Carter

Most of us invest so much time, effort, and thought into helping our children become grounded and rooted and secure, that when it comes time to soar, we adults hang on for dear life. Some of us are afraid that this soaring can lead to crashing to the ground. To be comfortable with themselves and secure in their own worth and identity, children need roots. But to be confident and courageous and free, to be *herself or himself,* every child will need wings. Please do not stop at roots. Freedom is essential and the fun part. It takes wings to enter adulthood. Isn't that where we were headed from the outset?

> You are the bows from which your children as living arrows are sent forth.
> - Kahlil Gibran, *The Prophet*

And lastly, I ask you to take this, as my husband would say, as seriously as a heart attack. Nothing is more important or meaningful than bringing up emotionally whole and healthy, happy children. My husband also understands the importance and wisdom of fun. It is not going to be worth it if you cannot manage to find the fun and enjoyment in family life. You will choose to leave your family or perhaps worse, resent and begrudge your time spent in it. Thus, I also implore you to recognize (almost constantly and even in the worst moments) that your children are the most precious gifts you will ever receive. Although it may seem entirely out of the realm of possibility, they do grow up and leave, probably much, much sooner than you would ever believe. And you will miss them. Will they want to return on occasion? That's entirely up to you. Thus, I entreat you to enjoy them simply as much, and as often, as you can. For truly, they are life's most precious gift.

NOTES, REFERENCES, & INDEX

Notes

1. Dodd testimony to U.S. Congressional Joint Session hearing on Keeping Every Child Safe, March 10, 1993.

2. Edelman testimony to U.S. Congressional Joint Session hearing on Keeping Every Child Safe, March 10, 1993.

3. "Day Care & Early Education," 1991.

4. Edelman, M. "The State of America's Children Yearbook 1997." Washington DC: Children's Defense Fund, 1997.

5. Anderson, Margaret. *Raising a Family is a Pleasure.* n.d., n.p., out of print. My thanks to Mike Anderson for sharing this book with me.

6. "The State of America's Children Yearbook 1997." Washington DC: Children's Defense Fund, 1997.

7. Clarke, J.I. *Time-In: When Time-Out Doesn't Work.* Seattle, WA: Parenting Press, 1999.

8. Anderson, Margaret. *Raising a Family is a Pleasure.* n.d., n.p., out of print.

9. For additional information concerning allowances and chores, you may find Barbara Coloroso's audio tape, "Winning at Parenting Without Beating Your Kids" helpful.

10. See text by Faber and Mazlish, *How to Talk So Kids Will Listen & Listen So Kids Will Talk.*. New York: Avon Books, 1980. I am indebted to these authors for their concept of barriers to cooperation and descriptive language.

11. Bailey, B. *There's Gotta Be A Better Way: Discipline That Works!* Oveido, FL: Loving Guidance, Inc., 1997.

12. Clarke, J.I. and Dawson, C. *Growing Up Again: Parenting Ourselves, Parenting Our Children.* New York: Harper & Row, 1989.

13. Based upon a poster designed by Mick Johnson.

14.   See text by Dreikurs and Grey, *A New Approach to Discipline: Logical Consequences*. New York: Hawthorn Books, Inc., 1968. I am indebted to these authors for their concept of logical consequences upon which Disciplinary Consequences is based.

15.   I an indebted to Barbara Coloroso for the technique of mutual permission.

16.   Clarke, J.I. *Time-In: When Time Out Doesn't Work.* Seattle, WA: Parenting Press, 1999.

17.   Bauer, K.L. and Sheerer, M.A. with Dettore Jr., E. "Creative Strategies in Ernie's Early Childhood Classroom." *Young Children.* 52.6, Sept. 1997: 47-52. For the three examples for clean up time which follow.

18.   See text by Thomas Gordon, *Teaching Children Self-Discipline*. New York: Random House, 1989. The title of this text was later changed to *Discipline That Works*. I am indebted to Dr. Gordon for this strategy as well as Determine What Child Needs and Limit the Environment and the transition phrases.

19.   Clarke, J.I. *Self-Esteem: A Family Affair*. San Francisco, CA: Harper & Rowe, 1981. I am indebted to Mrs. Clarke for the concepts of Being, Doing, and Can Do Better upon which the concepts Existence, Accomplishment, and Mistakes are based.

20.   The audio and video programs are available from Childright. Call 1-817-488-4664 or 1-800-422-4337 for additional information.

21.   Ginott, H.G. *Between Parent and Child.* New York: Avon Books, 1956.

22.   "Day Care & Early Education" 1991.

23.   TAEYC, 1993.

24.   Pipher, M. The Shelter of Each Other: Rebuilding Our Families. NY: G.P. Putnam's Sons, 1996.

25.   Tips indicated with * are excerpted from Margaret Anderson's book, *Raising A Family Is A Pleasure.*

26.   Anderson, Margaret. *Raising a Family is a Pleasure.* n.d., n.p., out of print.

27.   See text by Faber & Mazlish, *Liberated Parents Liberated Children.* New York: Avon Books, 1974, p.65.

28.   Grant, L.T. "Harper's" October 1979. I am indebted to Mrs. Curran for directing me to this particular article.

References

Andrews, R. *The Columbia Dictionary of Quotations.* New York: Columbia University Press.

Anderson, M. *Raising a Family is a Pleasure.* n.d., n.p., out of print.

Aspy and Roebuck. *Kids Don't Learn From People They Don't Like.* Amherst, MA: Human Resource Development Press, 1977.

Bailey, B. *There's Gotta Be A Better Way: Discipline That Works!* Oveido, FL: Loving Guidance, Inc., 1997.

Ballard, E.S. "Three Letters from Teddy" *Home Life,* March 1976. ©1976 The Sunday School Board of the Southern Baptist Convention. All rights reserved. Used by permission of the author.

Bartlett's Familiar Quotations. Boston, MA: Little, Brown and Company.

Bauer, K.L. and Sheerer, M.A. with Dettore Jr., E. "Creative Strategies in Ernie's Early Childhood Classroom." *Young Children.* 52.6, Sept. 1997.

Briggs, D.C. *Celebrate Yourself.* Garden City, NY: Doubleday & Company, Inc., 1977.

Briggs, D.C. *Your Child's Self-Esteem: The Key to Life.* Garden City, NY: Doubleday & Company, Inc., 1970.

Cansler, Martin, and Valand. *Working with Families.* Chapel Hill, NC: Kaplan Press, 1976.

"CDF Reports" February, 1994, Vol 15, No 3. Washington, DC: CDF, 1994.

"The State of America's Children Yearbook 1997." Washington, DC: Children's Defense Fund, 1997.

Clarke, J.I. *Self-Esteem: A Family Affair*. 2nd ed. Center City, MN: Hazelden, 1978, 1998.

Clarke, J.I. *Growing Up Again: Parenting Ourselves, Parenting Our Children*. rev. ed. Center City, MN: Hazelden, 1998.

Clarke, J.I. *Time-In: When Time Out Doesn't Work*. Seattle, WA: Parenting Press, 1999.

Coloroso, B. *Discipline: Winning at Teaching*. Boulder, CO: kids are worth it, inc., 1987.

Coopersmith, S. *The Antecedents of Self-Esteem*. San Francisco, CA: W.H. Freeman & Co., 1967.

Covey, S. *Principle-Centered Leadership*. New York: Summit Books, Simon & Schuster, 1990.

Covey, S. *The Seven Habits of Highly Effective People*. New York: Simon & Schuster, 1990.

Curran, D. *Traits of A Healthy Family*. New York: HarperCollins Publishers, 1983.

Curwin, R. and Mendler, A. *Discipline With Dignity*. Alexandria, VA: Association for Supervision and Curriculum Development, 1988.

Dreikurs and Grey. *A New Approach to Discipline: Logical Consequences*. New York: Hawthorn Books, Inc., 1968.

Faber, A. and Mazlish, E. *How To Talk So Kids Will Listen & Listen So Kids Will Talk*. New York: Avon Books, 1980.

Faber, A. and Mazlish, E. *Liberated Parents Liberated Children*. New York: Avon Books, 1974.

Fisher, R. and Ury, W. *Getting to Yes: Negotiating Agreement Without Giving In*. Boston: Houghton Mifflin Company, 1981. New York: Penguin Books, 1983.

Ginott, H.G., *Between Parent and Child.* New York: Avon Books, 1956.

Gordon, T. *P.E.T. Parent Effectiveness Training.* New York: Peter H. Wyden, Inc., 1970.

Gordon, T. *Teaching Children Self-Discipline.* New York: Random House, 1989. The title of this text was later changed to *Discipline That Works.*

Greven, P. *Spare the Child: The Religious Roots of Punishment and the Psychological Impact of Physical Abuse.* New York: Alfred A. Knopf, Inc., 1991. New York: Vintage Books, Inc., 1992.

Kohn, A. *No Contest: The Case Against Competition.* Boston: Houghton Mifflin Company, 1986.

Lombardi, D. and Corsini, R. *C4R: A New System of Schooling.* Holistic Education, 1988.

Pipher, M. *The Shelter of Each Other: Rebuilding Our Families.* NE: G.P. Putnam's Sons, 1996.

Popkin, M.H. *Active Parenting Handbook.* Atlanta: Active Parenting, Inc., 1983.

Satir, V., *Peoplemaking.* Palo Alto, CA: Science and Behavior Books, Inc., 1972.

The Rubicon Dictionary of Positive, Motivational, Life-Affirming and Inspirational Quotations. Newington, CT: Rubicon Press, 1994.

Webster's Seventh New Collegiate Dictionary. Springfield, MA: G.C. Merriam Company, 1983 ed.

Ziglar, Z. *Raising Positive Kids in a Negative World.* Nashville, TN: Oliver-Nelson Books, 1985.

Index